Published by:
The Indie Press
203 East Main Street
Boalsburg, PA 16827

Printed in the United States of America by Advanced Color Graphics,
2185 Sandy Dr., State College, PA 16803 **www.advancedcolorgraphics.com**

First Edition November 2007

ISBN 978-0-9795842-0-6

Cover design by Rose Ann Hoover
Inside layout design by Bryan Benner
Map design by Michael Hermann - Purple Lizard Maps

The author and publisher encourage all readers to visit and support
all the places listed in this book and recommend those who partake
of any alcoholic beverage to do so in moderation and travel with a
nondrinking driver.

TABLE OF CONTENTS

Preface 1

About This Book 5

How It Works 8

Rating? 10

I. Boalsburg, My Home 13

II. Happy Valley, My Neighbors 35

Chapter 1 81

Chapter 2 123

Chapter 3 137

Chapter 4 161

Chapter 5 175

Chapter 6 191

Chapter 7 201

Chapter 8 211

Chapter 9 237

Chapter 10 261

Chapter 11 271

Chapter 12 281

Conclusion 295

Index 296

DEDICATION

To Jesus, who hooked me up with God and generously gave me the opportunities and abilities to pursue a life of art. And what a sweet life it's been.

To my mom and dad, who believe in me and support me in all my crazy endeavors.

And thank you to my extended family, friends and all those whose help and encouragement made this book possible.

PREFACE

Since my days of traveling to arts festivals all
around the country and traveling the world to create
paintings for those festivals, I've made it a point
not to go to any of the chain places but rather to
ask locals where they eat, have a beer or coffee.
Almost without fail, these inquiries have taken me
to some of the best food and coolest places on the
planet! Before that, it's hard to remember the time
when my taste for good food came about, but maybe
it's when a girlfriend suggested escargots as an
appetizer at a State College restaurant.

At that stage of life, I would grimace just at the
thought of snails and made all those typical gagging
sounds associated with such a disgusting "food."
However this girl was extremely hot and I needed all
the points I could get. So, with a sheepish grin and
trembling voice I said, "Okay, why not?"

While we were waiting, I kept thinking of all of the
classic movie moments involving escargots. There's
that great scene from The Jerk where Steve Martin
(a.k.a. Navin Johnson) stood up in the middle of a
fancy French restaurant and loudly exclaimed that
they had put snails in his girlfriend's food. "What
kind of a place is this?" he asked, and they stormed
out. Or how about that scene from Pretty Woman when
the Julia Roberts character launches an escargot
shell through the air while just trying to grip it
with tongs (I can't believe I just referenced such
a chick flic).

Arriving at our table only moments later were six
little snails, all cozy in puff pastry and floating
in hot buttery garlic sauce. My date took the first
bite, closed her eyes, and made a yummy sound that
would melt steel as if it were a cheap candle. She
slowly opened her eyes, gracefully wiped the corner
of her mouth and said, "Go ahead. Try one." Nervously,

I plucked one of the little suckers out of its toasty
warm nest and drew it toward my mouth, the whole time
praying that I wouldn't spew it across the table.
I put it in my mouth, bit down, and...At this point,
I must make something clear. When I was a kid, I was
a neurotic little wuss. When my mom and dad would
take us kids on a road trip, and along the way we
might see a detour sign, I would make myself physi-
cally sick from worry. My folks would eventually
have to pull over for me to barf. Are ya gettin' the
portrait I'm trying to paint? Well for those less
astute, this appetizer was like a giant detour sign
with no place to pull over. However, I digress.

I bit down, and...WOW, it was really good! Kind of
rubbery, but damn good! I loved it!

Well, that girl and I eventually broke up, but my
love affair with escargots, as well as food exploration and appreciation, has continued hot and heavy
to this day.

When it comes to good beer, there are no maybes. My
discerning taste began with an encounter I'll never
forget. The place and situation rest in my mind like
the memories you get when you put on your favorite
sweater or pair of shoes - you remember exactly
where you got them and where they've taken you.

I was just 21 at the time, full of life and eager
to let fly my new rights to purchase alcohol. In
those days, my beer of choice was Stroh's. I kept
a can of it in my truck for years (the same can!)
as my "Emergency Beer" in case I was in a situation
where I really needed a beer and didn't have one.
One day though, I walked into a local historical
tavern just down the street from where I now live.

Duffy's Tavern had a six-pack cooler in the back,
and there I found my precious brew - Stroh's in
cans. I grabbed a six-pack and started toward the
bar to pay. As I walked, I heard a voice behind me

say, "Excuse me, are you going to buy that beer?" I stopped, ready to flash my ID and prove my manhood (at least my 21-hood), and saw a group of "older people," probably in their thirties, sitting there. The guy said again, "Are you sure you want to buy that beer?" A bit confused and put off, I said, "Yeah, why?" He then enlightened me about a new genre of craft-brewed beers, hand-made in small batches by brewers who were passionate about yielding a brew that would make the medieval monks salivate.

He then did something that will go down in the anals of history (I know it's "annals" but "anals" is just funnier). He said, "Let me buy you a six-pack of a new and really good beer, brewed in a tradition of purity and excellence." Well, what choice did I have? Here's a random guy, offering to buy me beer, and from his short dissertation, a damn good one too. He walked my Stroh's back to the cooler and returned with something called Samuel Adams which I had never heard of. But I thanked him, tucked it under my arm, and walked away. When I left I was thinking "What a nut!" and "What a nice guy!" at the same time. I jumped in my truck, grabbed an opener, took a swig and drove away. Kidding! Honestly, I don't remember drinking it at all, but what I do remember is throwing my good ol' Emergency Beer away shortly thereafter.

I hope that ending wasn't disappointing, but the gist of it was that it's not the taste I remember, but the act of a stranger who took the time to enlighten a young, naïve buck, and set in motion a love and appreciation for what passionate brewers and winemakers can create. He also helped me think twice and even refuse big-batch, small taste beer companies, wine and food makers, who think more about the bottom line than they do about what's in the bottom of their kettles.

Almost a week or so after that fateful encounter, I picked up our local paper to see the face of the guy who had bought me the beer. Turns out he was a local lawyer named Ben, who also wrote a beer column for the paper. "That's the guy!" I exclaimed and realized what a fortuitous encounter that had been.

Ben and the hot girl named Kristina probably have no recollection of these events or of the epiphanies they inspired. Only now, with the publishing of this book will they ever know.

I thank them both.

ABOUT THIS BOOK

This is more than a guidebook - it's a journal, travel log, memoir, fact, fiction and hopefully a good resource and read as well. In fact, I've written it more like a journal. It's about my experiences as I've traveled over this great state and even beyond in some examples, and the places I've discovered and folks I've met along the way.

Most of the time these journey's are with my favorite traveling companion and source of transportation, The Mighty Steed, my sweet 1994 Harley Davidson Sportster. Don't be surprised if I write as though I'm with another person sometimes, but when you've logged as many miles together as I have with The Steed, it's hard not to think of him as a friend. He's always ready to go on an adventure and never fails to give me all he has when I roll back on his throttle to get there. Not only do I humanize my bike in this book (and in real life), but I tend to do the same with roads. However, they are of the female persuasion. Especially the sweet, wild and dangerous ones! But I digress (as you will notice I do a lot).

My intention as we travel together on these adventures is to be an advocate not a critic, a scout and messenger rather than a reviewer. Also, just a lover of la vie (the life), whose experiences and discoveries will be like an adventure and discovery for you too. This book is not meant to honor one place more than another and is not a definitive work. I wanted to save some for another edition and I also wanted you to find some on your own - using your map, asking locals, and by just hitting the road to discover what's around the next curve.

I live in a cabin that I built with the help of some great local guys. The massive and beautiful logs came to me as the result of a wrong turn on a back road. However, there was nothing wrong about where that turn took me. This seeming error turned out to be one of the sweetest blessings in my life, which is exactly what I desire for you - to be blessed by what's down the road and around that next curve.

Please keep in mind though as you are reading, that I will ramble, digress (like above), go off on tangents, get on soap boxes, pretend I'm an historian, share experiences, spin tales, make stuff up and have a lot of fun! Also, I'm not really a writer. In fact, my elementary school teachers told my mom and dad that my English skills were dismal and not to expect much from me in that realm or any other. I was put in learning disability classes in junior high and my folks heard the same. So to be able to bring this book to you despite some spelling, grammar and punctuation struggles and a total lack of literary skill, I, as well as my mom and dad are quite thrilled.

My hope is that this book will inspire and encourage you to break away from the chain gang (chain restaurants) and fast food places, to experience for yourself the rich blessings of indie (independent) owned eating and drinking establishments that we have here in Central Pennsylvania. I fear that if we don't support our local businesses and the old school mom and pop places, they will fall by the wayside and be forgotten.

Other blessings here in the heart of our state are incredible natural resources, areas of pristine beauty, wonderful roads, sweet byways and little towns and villages that are like a kind of utopia for everyone - especially those from urban areas. One thing though, as I was writing this book and something I feel needs to be addressed is how to tell you about all these amazing places without ruining them at the same time? This is a major quandary for me that I will dig deep into with a real-life story later on. But I must admit I hope this book is as much about preserving these utopias as it is about opening their doors for you to enjoy them.

Along with that, this book is about a desire for you to enrich your life through the great experiences of food, drink and the places that serve up both. I want to encourage you to slow down and take time to share these experiences with your sweetie, friends, kids, folks, or even a stranger. And, to inspire you to have your own adventures and maybe write your own stories as well.

Above all, this book is about *going LOCAL!* and supporting the indie sole proprietors that were the foundation of our country. The megachains are a new thing within the past 40 years, and how in the world did people survive before them? I'll tell you how, by shopping at their local markets, stores, shops, pharmacies, other businesses and dining at their neighbor's restaurants, pubs or cafes. By supporting them they will in turn support you.

So there ya go - keep it local and keep it alive! That's what it's all about.

HOW IT WORKS

Since this is somewhat of a guide book, I've tried
to set it up in a way that's easy to follow. I've
also started each listing with a section called
"Just a Taste." Here you'll find the name of the
establishment, the address, contact information and
other stuff so you can plan your visit and know a
little about the place before you go. My friend Mike
Hermann of Purple Lizard Maps also created a cool
map for me that you'll find towards the back. It's
detachable if you prefer, and allows you to navigate
your way around and find the places I've listed.

The map starts with two small circles in the center.
From there, my area goes approximately 70 miles (as
the crow flies) out and 360 degrees around, to form
a larger circle of about 140 miles in diameter.
Then I thought of a way to divide that large circle
into twelve regions so that you could easily picture
them in your mind. It's like a combination clock
and dartboard.

I figure everyone can visualize the state of Pennsylvania, a center point, dartboard and clock. I also
think we all understand the concept of directions
according to the numbers of a clock. Here's an example: If I say something's at 12 o'clock, I mean
straight up. If it's at 6 o'clock, then it would be
straight down. And, if I said to look to 9 o'clock
then you should look directly to the left. The
dartboard part simply refers to the center circles
and lines that divide the area and create a pie shape
for each region. Within these regions will be towns,
next to them will be numbers which will correspond
to the pages where the places I've written about
can be found.

I'll begin the book with two regions which are the
circles in the center. The tiny circle (bull's eye)
is for a region titled "Boalsburg, My Home," and is

represented in the Table of Contents as Roman numeral
I. A small circle (representing about 10 miles)
around that will be called "Happy Valley, My Neighbors," and will be Roman numeral II. Then, the pie-
shaped region at 1 o'clock will be represented in
Chapter 1. Chapter 2 is the 2 o'clock pie-shaped
region and so on. At the head of each listing, there
will be a little PA state icon indicating the region
by a shaded piece of the pie.

Sound confusing? It's not, just dive in and start
reading, find a place you want to try or region you
would like to visit, unfold the map and have fun.
What are you waiting for?

Enjoy!

RATING?

Several years ago, I was showing my art in Syracuse, New York. As with all exhibitions, I include a "fun factor" as a way to gauge how I do. For example, if I sell a lot of artwork and make a lot of money, but don't have fun at an exhibition, I don't consider it a success. If I do poorly financially but have loads of fun, then it's not necessarily a disaster either. The ideal is great sales and great fun!

After this exhibition in Syracuse closed for the day, I asked a local for a recommendation on what to do and where to go. I was sent to a part of downtown called "The Armory," and the place was buzzing with activity and lots of great places to eat and drink. Young and old alike were sitting at outdoor cafés, restaurants and brew pubs as I walked up and down the sidewalks checking out possible pubs for a beer before finding a place for dinner.

I settled on one place and moseyed up to the bar. There before me was a lineup of taps that made my "fun factor" jump up a few notches. However, the downside of this was that there were so many choices, I couldn't decide. For me, and I will continue to try and convey in this book, it is not about consumption; it's about quality, enjoyment and a good experience.

So there I was, standing before a cornucopia of taps, all vying for my attention. There was an older guy at the bar and when I started chatting with him I found out he was a local and frequents this pub. I asked him for his opinion on what was good. "What do you think of this one?" I said as I pointed to a Pilsner. "Damn good" he replied very matter-of-factly. I was waiting for an explanation or at least a brief description of the beer, but none was given, just the words, "Damn good." I saw a Wheat Beer and said, "What about that one?" "Damn Good!" was the response again, but this time with a little more passion.

Now my curiosity was piqued. What would he say about the next one - I had to ask. I eyeballed my favorite style of beer among the line up, an India Pale Ale. I pointed at it, braced myself for his answer, and said, "What about that IPA?" This time didn't say, "Damn Good!" he said "DAMN GOOD!" Needless to say, I chose the IPA and let me tell you, it really was DAMN GOOD!

Note: This is why the American Indians didn't bother with a written language. Sometimes, written words just can't express passion and emotion in their fullest capacity.

So from that fateful day on, my buddy Mike and I say those two words whenever we taste a great brew! In part, because of that guy, but mostly because it's usually fitting! As I researched this book, those two words have been uttered countless times. Not only to describe the beer, but the food and place itself.

Like I said, this book is not a critique or review (I really don't know crap). But if a place is listed in this book, something about it is damn good. If it's not, it's not in here. Maybe they have some peculiarities or lack one thing or another, but in some way they're all Damn Good!

Note: Please keep in mind that the information I'm providing about all the listings is the most current I could gather prior to printing. In some cases, the establishments may have changed hands, been sold, or even closed. So if you're going to call to make sure, do it from home. Please don't call from your cell while you're driving. Those behind you will appreciate it and you'll be safer, too.

MAP

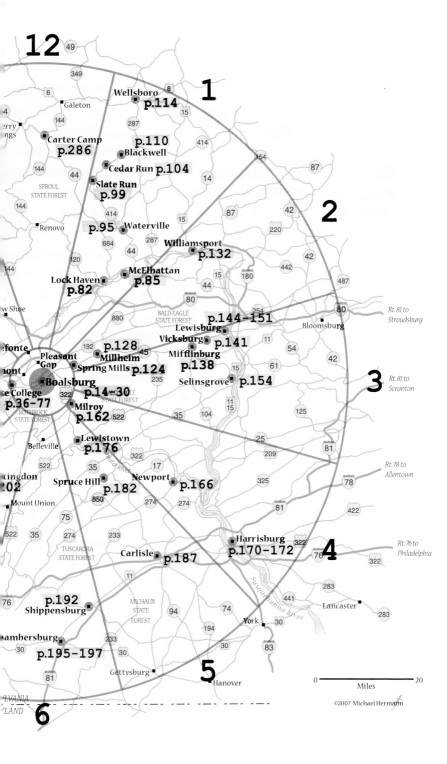

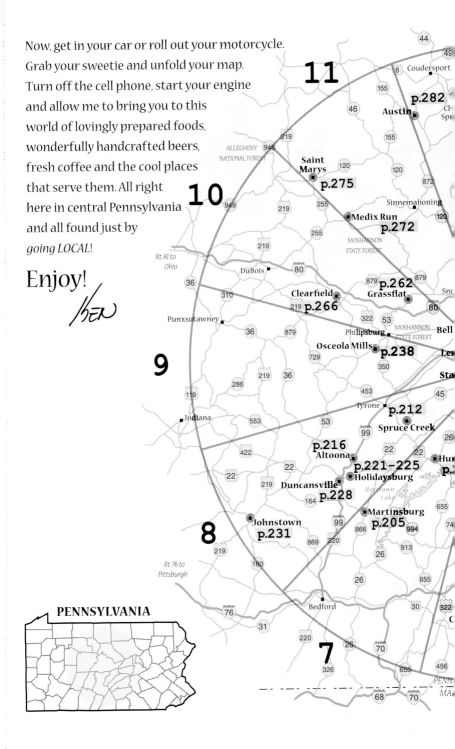

Now, get in your car or roll out your motorcycle.
Grab your sweetie and unfold your map.
Turn off the cell phone, start your engine
and allow me to bring you to this
world of lovingly prepared foods,
wonderfully handcrafted beers,
fresh coffee and the cool places
that serve them. All right
here in central Pennsylvania
and all found just by
going LOCAL!

Enjoy!

11

Coudersport

p.282
Austin

ALLEGHENY
NATIONAL FOREST

Saint
Marys
p.275

10

Sinnemahoning

Medix Run
p.272

MOSHANNON
STATE FOREST

*Rt. 81 to
Ohio*

DuBois

Clearfield
p.262
Grassflat

p.266

Punxsutawney

Philipsburg
MOSHANNON
STATE FOREST

Osceola Mills
p.238

9

Indiana

Tyrone **p.212**

Spruce Creek

p.216
Altoona
p.221-225
Holidaysburg

Duncansville
p.228

*Raystown
Lake*

Martinsburg
p.205

8

Johnstown
p.231

*Rt. 76 to
Pittsburgh*

PENNSYLVANIA

Bedford

7

I.
BOALSBURG,
MY HOME

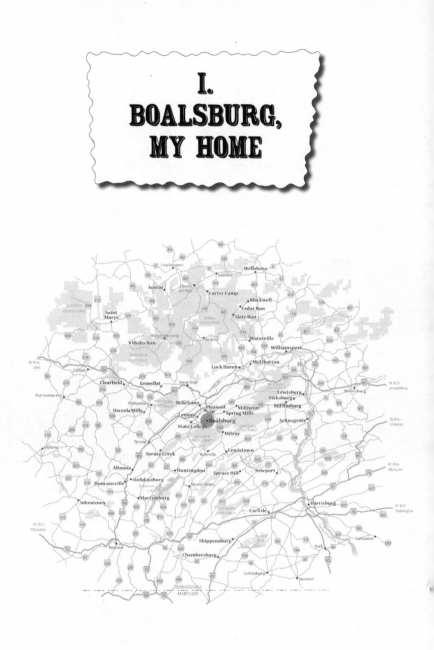

Since I consider my little village such a special place and have put it at the center of my map, it only seems right to begin there.

For those of you who are not yet acquainted with Boalsburg, let me tell you about my first experience there. About two years after I started my career as an artist, I found out about a little building that was being vacated by a local architect in this quaint historic village three miles from my parents' home in State College.

Fifteen years earlier, Robert Hoffman graduated from Penn State as an architect and needed a place to set up shop. He found an old brick building recently acquired by the Hacker family when they purchased the Duffy's Tavern property in 1969. Bob went to Carl Hacker and offered to restore the "little brick" in exchange for office and work space. Fortunately, Mr. Hacker agreed and Bob lovingly restored the tiny two-story building that was built with handmade bricks and used as the village armory in the year of its construction, 1820.

When I acquired it for my art studio in December of 1985, I quickly settled in and began some of my greatest works. On one particular evening, only days after moving in, I decided to drive down to the new studio and work for awhile despite a heavy snowfall. It had been snowing all day and about six inches had fallen when I pulled into the village. I parked my truck, got out and was immediately taken by that silence that seems to only exist with a snowfall at night. I looked around and stopped in my tracks – it was like I had walked into a Currier & Ives Christmas card.

There to my right was the tavern, a huge building built from local limestone with walls 20 inches thick. Its eaves were supporting curling waves of snow as it crept slowly over the edge. Every window was lit by candles and snow-laden bushes at its base formed a white mountain along the sidewalk. Looking further on and towards the square, were a mix of homes and shops built in colonial times. Their windows were candle lit too and the warm glow of fireplaces made the scene complete.

As I pondered this surreal moment, I faintly heard what sounded like a combination of cantering horse hooves and bells. I shook it off thinking that all this visual stimulation was making me hear things too but, it continued to grow louder and seemed to come nearer. I turned around in front of my studio and looked up East Main Street. Above me was an old style street light mounted high on a telephone pole. It was illuminating about a fifty foot area and as the snowflakes fell within its light, they were all illuminated like thousands of tiny pieces of cotton.

The sound I was hearing was coming closer for sure, and seemed to be up the street beyond the reach of the light. Louder and louder it came and by this time, I was sure of my initial guess. Then, out of the winter darkness and into the glow of the street-light came the quintessential element of this living Christmas card that I was in.

A horse drawn sleigh with a family of four was coming down Main Street and cutting through the virgin snow beneath. Around the horse's neck was a collar of sleigh bells, ringing a sound that was both chilling and beautiful at the same time. His hooves kept a syncopated rhythm while his nostrils burst puffs of steam like that of a locomotive in full stride. The sleigh, simple and sweet, held up by runners of wood and steel, carried its passengers along who were all snuggled together in a deep sea of blankets.

The family waved at me as they passed and called out, "Merry Christmas!" Honestly, I'm not sure if I even waved back. I just stood there, drop-jawed and oblivious to the biting cold and to the snow that was forming on my shoulders. I watched them as they

glided past Duffy's, then through the square and out
of sight. Did that just happen? Was that for real?
Yes, of course it was – this is Boalsburg. And as I
turned back and unlocked the door to my new studio,
I said to myself, "I love this place. This is where
I need to be," and I've been there ever since.

Over the years, Boalsburg has changed. Not for the
bad by any means, but as a lover of food and libations, a change for the good. Maybe "change" isn't
the right word here, maybe "grown" would be better.
Duffy's Tavern, the patriarch of the village, has
now been joined by several other places all creating
a culinary renaissance to a town that already embraced history, culture, art and community. Not only is
it the birthplace of Memorial Day, but for me, the
birthplace of an art career and now a book about
cool places to eat and drink.

**So with that, let's get started, and what better
place to start than Boalsburg, My Home.**

Enjoy!

16

Duffy's Boalsburg Tavern

This is a place where people have been meeting, eating, drinking and having a good time for almost 200 years.

Built in 1819 by Col. James Johnston and his wife Hannah Bethesda, the Boalsburg Tavern originally catered to town folk and travelers not just as a pub, but as an inn as well. Back in the day, the dirt street out front was hazardous and challenging, so when the pilgrim explorers saw the warm glow of the tavern through its many windows, they likely felt a sigh of relief.

Those weary travelers journeying by stagecoach or horseback would be welcomed with a bounty of food, drink and soft beds. Legend has it, there was nightly fan dancing by local girls for "entertainment" which undoubtedly made even the coach driver glad to be there too! His quarters and the blacksmith's shop was just down the street (near where my house is now) and I can only imagine him stumbling back at night, full and satisfied after an evening of festivities.

In 1934 the building was decimated by fire but was purchased three years later by Mrs. Billy Hill Windsor,

JUST A TASTE

Name of establishment :
Duffy's Tavern

Owned by :
Carl & Joanne Hacker

Contact Info :
113 East Main Street
Boalsburg, PA 16827
814-466-6241
Duffy16827@lycos.com
Duffystavern.com

Hours:
11:30am – 1:30am

Price range:
$5 to $35

Cuisine / Specialty:
American Cuisine

Offers vegetarian, heart healthy or organic selections:
Yes

Support local farmers:
No

Locally owned accommodations:
Springfield House B&B
126 East Main Street
Boalsburg, PA 16827
888-STAY-N-PA (782-9672)
innkeeper@springfieldhouse
bb.com

Local attractions:
Historic Boalsburg Village
Heritage Museum
28th Division Shrine
Mt. Nittany
Memorial Day Celabration

who completely restored it. In 1946, Harry Duffy bought it and renamed it Duffy's Tavern. Harry died in 1961 but in 1971, a young engineer named Carl Hacker bought the Tavern and moved in.

He, his wife Joanne and three kids lived on the third floor while setting about the task of running a full scale restaurant and bar. Carl and his son Chuck still run the place to this day and changed the name again to honor the old and new. Now, Duffy's Boalsburg Tavern is as much about food and great experiences as it is about history.

One of my most memorable experiences might have been when a buddy and I went there for a beer last summer. We took a seat up in the loft of the Brick Room which is by far my favorite spot in the tavern (In fact, I've done a lot of drawings there over the years as well as writings for this book). A wicker floor lamp and old wall sconces fitted with amber bulbs gently light the space, likely reminiscent of the gas lights that once did years ago. A classic winder staircase leads up from below, but you need to watch your head! The rafters dip low as you ascend and you might be stunned (literally) by the ambiance.

My buddy Jeff and I got a table right near the edge of the loft opening where you can watch the goings-on of the Brick Room and even call down to your server for a refill (if you are quick enough).That night, we ordered a pitcher of Tröegs. A young woman with the combined talents of a gymnast and mountain climber came up the narrow stairs, sat our pitcher down with two glasses, and then off she went to tend to her other guests.

That same night there was an auction going on below founded by Jo, the daytime bartender to benefit our local volunteer fire company – the Boalsburg Bull-dogs. Many locals including me donate everything from merchandise to art for this annual event, but this year's highest bid item turned out to be a "service." A local woman paid $80.00 to have the chance to shave the beard off some guy named Elbow (Don't ask)! After this "lucky" lady made the winning bid, the shaving cream and razor came out. Elbow sat down at the bar and locals as well as loyal volunteers watched as one of their comrades was shaved clean.

So there we were on a Friday night, the place was packed and every table in the house was full. As I was waving my hands around telling Jeff a funny story, my hand hit our full pitcher of beer and the whole thing flew right off the table and over the edge of the loft. Completely debilitated with shock, we watched as our 64 ounces of Tröegs, along with its container, plummeted through the smoky atmosphere like a doomsday asteroid on a death mission to earth.

It landed on a table below and the whole place (and I mean the entire tavern) went dead silent. With fear and trembling, I slowly peered over the edge. Below me were eight, wet and shocked firefighters looking up at me. Just before their faces went from shocked to red, one member in the group said..."It's Kenny Hull! What in the hell are you doin' boy! Do you know how lucky you are? You better get your wallet out because you're buying beer and lots of it! Oh yeah, and thanks for the donation tonight!" (I feel our Bulldogs are the best volunteers in the county AND the nicest bunch you'll ever meet! However, if a "non local" were to have pulled this stunt as I did, I think a major scrap might have occurred!)

It turned out that at the table below was a group of guys I've known for years and once they all realized it was just me and I agreed to their terms of free rounds of beer for the night, they all laughed and so did the rest of the tavern. It ended up being a very fun evening and our Bulldogs made out pretty well between the auction revenue and free beer. But the next time I order a pitcher of beer up in the loft, I'll be sitting on my hands!

Duffy's Tavern offers dining experiences from casual to elegant. In the tavern side where I like to go, they serve up pub-grub all the time and great lunch specials at the bar on weekdays. Monday night is half price burger night but get there early or go late because it's always packed at dinner time. Here, friendly bartenders, great old time atmosphere, local color and characters all combine to create the same feeling the stagecoach passengers must have felt years ago. But sadly there is no more fan dancing. Bummer.

Duffy's is also known for its fine dining and well appointed rooms full of antiques as well. On that side they offer appetizers ranging from Phyllo Wrapped Brie to Crab Stuffed Mushrooms to soups and salads. The entrée menu features dishes like pasta, Tavern Chicken or Salmon, Veal Purnell and Filet Mignon.

So pull up a chair, have a glass of wine or beer, chat with friends and eat well! The past meets present here and you'll be hard pressed to find such history, architecture, atmosphere, good food, fun times and great experiences anywhere else! And no matter how hard they try, the chain restaurants will never match it. I love Duffy's, I've been made to feel just like a part of the family and you will too as well.

Enjoy!

Eddie Agostinelli's Italian Market & Deli

This is a very cool little place! A once plain, non-descript building that housed everything from a pizza shop to a Laundromat now cradles a classic Italian-style market. Around you meats hang from the ceiling and cheeses cool in the deli case. Pastas, sauces, and olive oils fill the shelves along with specialty items to help make your homemade dinner a success. But if you want something prepared to eat in or take out, just pick up a menu and head to the counter.

You can choose from a modest but complete menu, mostly sandwiches but other good stuff too. One thing (among many) that's cool about Eddie's place is that there is also a full service bottle shop right next door which means that you can bring your friends, buy a six pack of Troegs, Straub or your favorite craft brew. There are of course other beverages available in the cooler and lots of chips and stuff to enjoy with the best that Eddie can offer from the cucina!

JUST A TASTE

Name of establishment:
Eddie Agostinelli's Market & Deli

Contact Info:
306 E Boal Ave,
Boalsburg PA 16827
814) 466-3444
website agostinellis.com

Owned by:
Eddie Agostinelli, Jr.
and Charles McCaffrey

Hours:
M-F 11:00-7:00
Saturday 11:00-2:00

Price range:
$4.50 - $18.00

Cuisine / Specialty:
Italian

Offers vegetarian, heart healthy or organic selections:
Yes

Support local farmers:
Yes

Locally owned accommodations:
Aikens Cabins at Bear Meadows
400 Bear Meadows Road
Boalsburg, PA 16827
Website: www.aikenscabins.com
E-Mail: maikens@aikenscabin.com

Local attractions:
Historic Boalsburg Village
Military Museum
Tussey Mountain Resort
Mt. Nittany Winery
Grange Fair

Owner, Eddie Agostinelli looks like he either just walked off the set of The Soprano's or just got off the boat from Italy. He is 100% Italian, handsome, friendly, very personable and funny! It would be hard to walk out of his place and not have a smile on your face. His personality is contagious and customers often join in with banter and joking. However, when it comes to food, with Eddie, it is no joking matter. Here are a couple of examples:

For months he took his delicious hot sausage sandwich off the menu because he couldn't find a sausage to suit his high standards. Or this one. One day I called him to place an order for lunch and asked Eddie what he recommended. Without hesitation, he told me about his signature Gorgonzola cheese steak sandwich. This didn't go over well because my friend Mike and I refer to any cheese from the Blue family as tasting like...!

Well, I expressed my great aversion to this so-called "gourmet" cheese and Eddie just wouldn't accept it. No matter what gagging sounds I made or words I used, he refused to budge and kept telling me how much I would like it if only I would just try it. He then uttered that most prized word when it comes to food (or just about anything for that matter)- Free! Yes, Eddie said that if I try this Gorgonzola Cheese Steak and didn't like it, it would be free!

Ok guys, remember the snail story? Well, that "detour" sign was rearing its ugly head once again. However, the sign flashing FREE was even bigger! So I reluctantly agreed and placed my order for one. I walked down the street to get it and was wondering the whole time if I was making a mistake.

I picked up my sandwich and was ready to carry it out when Eddie asked a curious question. "Ken, do you have tissues at your place?" I twisted my face and said, "Yeah, why?" "Good, you will need 'em, that sandwich is so good it'll make you cry." Some other folks were there at the time waiting to order and they really got a kick out of that. I think they thought the whole scene was staged to lure them into getting cheese steaks also. They did, and he made them the same offer! I just laughed and walked out.

After I sat down at home and unwrapped my (soon-to-be-free) cheese steak, I grabbed a roll of paper towels and kept them close. I bit into the monstrous molten mess of fresh made bread, meat and "cheese" just waiting for the gag reflex to kick in. I stiffened up and reached for the paper towels, but nothing! No gagging, no coughing, not even a dry heave.

Without hesitation though and totally involuntary, I heard myself make a deep convincing yummy sound. What just happened? Something big just happened. I LOVED IT! I took another bite and it was just as good. Then another and that one was good, too. It was all good - damn good! And it was all gone in a matter of minutes.

Then it happened. As I wiped the corners of my mouth, I felt something in my eyes. A tiny bead of salty liquid came forth and fell softly across my cheek. Eddie was right! From that day on, I always carry a few tissues when eating at Agostinelli's. Don't forget to bring yours.

Enjoy!

Brewer's Café

Here's a nice little place, or perhaps a hidden treasure, one might say. It's an official contender for the world's smallest coffee and  sandwich shop, tucked neatly between Keene's Barbershop and a cozy Cape Cod home. It's Boalsburg's newest old neighbor - Brewer's Café. Why new/old? Because Brewers has been serving up coffee, drinks and great sandwiches for several years, but now has a new home. Actually, it's in the renovated garage of the Cape Cod next door

Jen Bishop, a young woman who was fed up with the high rent and restrictions of her former location and also renting an apartment to live in at the same time, decided to buy herself a place to both live in and work out of. In a rare moment, a sweet place came up for sale along Church Street and was just what she needed to try and keep her business and life going without losing all of her profits to rent. She did something that they do a lot in Europe, where people convert a street-side room of their home or a space next door into a little shop - a pastry shop, bakery shop, tobacco shop or something.

JUST A TASTE

Name of establishment:
Brewer's Cafe

Contact Info:
Address: 209 N. Church St.
Phone: (814) 466-2086
email: j.bishop223@excite.com

Owned by:
Jennifer Bishop

Hours:
Monday - Saturday 9:00 a.m.
to 4:00 p.m.

Price range:
$2.99 - $5.69

Cuisine / Specialty:
Sandwiches,Wraps,Fresh
Salads,Soups, Espresso Drinks,

**Offers vegetarian, heart healthy
or organic selections:**
Yes

Support local farmers:
Yes

Locally owned accommodations:
Pabo's Bed and Breakfast
223 East Main St.
Boalsburg, PA 16827
814-883-3680
www.pabosofboalsburg.com

Local attractions:
Bear Meadows Natural Area
Tussey Ski
Blue Spring Park,
Penn Roosevelt Park
Penns Cave

Here's how she was able to pull that off: Back in the day, the founding fathers of the Boalsburg Village Zoning Office put into local law a cottage industry clause. This allows those in the village district who own a home, to turn a living room or dining room into a retail shop. And a lot of people over the years have done just that.

I wish more local governments would follow our example. Instead of towns dying a slow death at the hands of chain stores, municipalities should be doing all they can do to keep themselves alive and bring back that great downtown spirit. They should be the kind of town that lets someone open a coffee shop in their garage, or lets a retired couple have an antique or bookstore in their never-used formal living room.

Now maybe you can find an old house in a cool downtown or neighborhood district that needs some TLC and bring new life into it and open up that café that you've always dreamed about. Be proactive! Meet with your local government to see how you might do this and revitalize your town. Maybe then you can be like Jen who just took a chance and now owns her own shop next to her own home. Two dreams in one have now come true.

I encourage you to come to Boalsburg some day and stop in at the shops here and ask the owner/operators about their efforts. Sure, they will probably joke about being crazy to do what they do, but I bet none of them would want anything else. There's a spirit here, but it's the same spirit that's in every little town all over the world. It's an

indie spirit, a spirit of passion, pride, service and love that these owner/operators have.

Jen must love what she does or she would have given up, but she didn't. Her dream, hard work and a desire to provide a special little niche in the community are working both for her and for you. She offers a variety of sandwiches and wraps both hot and cold, soups, salads, sides, drinks and of course coffee. All at very affordable prices and all made to order. Go check it out, but like I said at the beginning, it's a tiny place. Take a big appetite but just a few friends - otherwise some will be standing outside.

Enjoy!

Pump Station Café

AN ODE TO KEN'S TEXACO

Here's a wonderful transformation.
In 1946, Ken Tennis opened a classic
full service filling station along Rt.
322 at the intersection of Church
Street. Ken's Texaco was "the" place
for gas, lube and general maintenance but also a hub for locals –
mostly older dudes who would gather
there every morning. On any given day, as many
as eight gentlemen would sit around, drink coffee
and spin tales. They all had their own personal
mugs and no one else was allowed to use them.

If Ken didn't have enough to do at the station, he
also helped his wife Margaret, who owned a lamp shop
in their home next door. Her lamp shop was quite
famous and folks from as far away as Philadelphia,
Pittsburgh and beyond would come for antique lamp
restoration and parts.

After forty-six years though, Ken's Texaco closed its
grease stained doors on November 30th 1992. The gas
pumps and holding tanks were removed and the place

JUST A TASTE

Name of establishment:
Pump Station Cafe

Contact Info:
103 Boal Avenue
Boalsburg, PA 16827
814-466-6202
Fax 814-466-1006

Owned by:
Craig Avedesian, Sam Malizia
and Mark Shelow

Hours:
6:00 am to 9:00pm

Price range:
$1.55 to $6.35

Cuisine / Specialty:
Coffee and Sandwiches

**Offers vegetarian, heart healthy
or organic selections:**
No

Support local farmers:
Yes

Locally owned accommodations:
Autoport
1405 S. Atherton St.
State College, PA 16801
Toll-Free: 800-932-7678
Phone: 814-237-7666
Fax: 814-237-7456
Website: www.theautoport.com
E-Mail: email@theautoport.com

Local attractions:
Boal Barn
Military Museum
Boal Mansion
Tussey Mountain

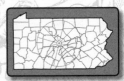

sat silent. Gone were the
daily powwows and the buzz
of activity at the old
corner, and gone was an
indie gas station that served the community so well.
Years after that Ken Tennis
himself passed away.

Margaret is still going strong though at 79, but
has closed the lamp shop. She's still very active in
the Boalsburg community and has the lead role in the
planning of our annual Memorial Day celebration. We
considered Ken as the honorary mayor of Boalsburg,
now Margaret is our honorary ambassador. But their
old gas station remained closed until our township
government and a couple of local business men had
the vision to give it a new life and a new purpose.

The Pump Station Café has the old corner buzzing
again. There are tables inside and some outside for
those who take their coffee with a little sunshine.
The view from outside is beautiful – huge red umbrellas with flowers all around you provided by
Blackhawk Mountain nursery, provide a little "oasis"
effect. Right and across the street is our wonderful
Pennsylvania 28th Division Military Museum and
Memorial Shrine, where you have four to six acres of
grass, stream, trees, walking paths, museum and the
original veterans' wall. This is a hand-built limestone wall commemorating vets from WW I and WW II.

Across 322 is the old Zion Lutheran Church and graveyard where the first Memorial Day began in 1864.
As I was writing this, the bell tower rang out 12
times for noon and serenaded the village and the
Pump Station with a classic hymn, just like a little
village in Europe! Within the graveyard is a sculpture by my artist friend Lorann Jacobs. It portrays
the three women who first decorated the grave of a
fallen Civil War Colonel and set in motion a national
holiday that continues today.

Believe me, Ken Tennis would be right at home at the Pump Station and hopefully beaming with pride about how his beloved Harris Township and some clever businessmen not only preserved his little filling station, but secured its future. It's still a place for full service, good conversation, and fuel for life. Now friends, neighbors, the community and travelers alike can once again say "Fill'er Up!"

Enjoy!

Note: As I was writing this piece under the umbrella and soaking in a perfect summer day, a local historian and friend of mine Ann Harpster walked in for her daily coffee and asked what I was up to. I told her about this book and the story I was writing. She asked if I knew about the coffee guys that came to Tennis' everyday. I smiled and read her an excerpt. She loved it and then told me something I never knew. (This folks is why I can't stress enough to talk to people, especially locals when you're out - you can keep to yourself at home. Turn off your cell, open up, talk to the person at the next table and you may hear a story like this)

On that fateful day when the last gallon of gas was pumped and the last engine lovingly tuned, the "Old Dudes Coffee Club" walked out into the garage where the grease pit was and where Ken spent most of his life. The men gathered around, and with some words of wisdom, sentiment (and jokes of course), threw back their last gulp of coffee. Then in an act that will go down in history, they threw the mugs into the bowels of the grease pit, smashing them like lovers do with their empty Champagne glasses. I guess the old guys must have thought that it just couldn't get any better. I wish they could be sitting here with me now.

Kelly's Steak & Seafood

This book focuses more on unique places – mostly small, maybe with some history or just different in some way. My general rule is not to include any chains, "big-time" operations or really upscale restaurants, unless they possess some uniqueness,

creativity, oddities, or happens to be here in my town and owned by my good friends.

That said, here's the first exception to my "rule."

Kelly's Steak and Seafood is a little big and a bit upscale, but it's also cozy, casual, has a good atmosphere and great high quality food. They welcome the areas "rich and famous," as well as bikers and folks just like me with the same generous greeting and great service. It was created from the ruins of a former restaurant and bar at the same location called The Boalsburg Steak House (which we "loving-ly" referred to in years past as "The Snake Pit"). Thank goodness a wonderful local family bought it and turned it into one of the best places around!

JUST A TASTE

Name of establishment:
Kelly's Steak & Seafood

Contact Info:
316 Boal Ave.
Boalsburg, PA 16827
814-466-6251
www.kellys-steak.com

Owned by:
Sean, Tien, John Kelly

Hours:
Mon–Sat: 11:00am-2:00am
Sun: 10:00 (brunch till 2:00)
till 2:00am

Price range:
$7.00-$38.00

Cuisine / Specialty:
Pacific Northwest

Offers vegetarian, heart healthy or organic selections:
Yes

Support local farmers:
Yes

Locally owned accommodations:
Earlystown Manor B&B
2024 Earlystown Road
RT 45, Centre Hall, PA
Toll Free: 877-466-6481
Phone: 814-466-6481
Fax: 814-466-6118

Local attractions:
Shopping
Museums
Galleries
Farmers market
People's Choice Festival

Dr. John Kelly and his wife Carol set about the task of basically gutting, stripping and replacing every square inch of the former Steak House both inside and out. They recruited a top executive chef from Seattle – their son Sean and his wife Tien who is also a chef, along with their two baby boys. John and Carol's youngest son, Brian also join in and the five worked like crazy for months. Dr. John even kept his pediatric dentistry practice going and travelled to third world countries as a volunteer doc during this time.

Chef's Sean and Tien took this opportunity of a "fresh canvas" to create a masterpiece of food, drink, décor and dining excellence! They're both passionate about what they do and you can see it. Better yet, you can taste it! And don't think you'll see either one of them out schmoozing customers (that's for John and Carol). No, they're in the kitchen bustin' hump to give you all they can so that when you're enjoying your meal you'll most likely say "Holy Cow!" Or instead, at Kelly's, it's more like Holy Bull! You see, it's not just the awesome food, presentation, or the great décor that makes Kelly's an exception to my rule. Nor is it on the inside or the outside of the building, it's actually on top!

Towering above the restaurant and standing guard like one of those guys outside Buckingham Palace, is the biggest statue of a bull I've ever seen. This sucker is Huge! He's held down by guild wires and is a landmark for hungry carnivores traveling along Routes 45 and 322. And if it's not fun enough to have a giant mutant bull looming over your neighborhood, just wait until a day like we had here last winter.

Some friends and I were standing in the parking lot of Kelly's chatting and waiting for some others to arrive when I looked up at the bull. The previous night we had a freezing rain and it coated everything in the village like a candied apple, and the bull was no exception. Not only that, but the melting ice had formed about a three foot long icicle hanging

from a very compromising location near the bull's
"soft underbelly." I pointed this out to my compa-
nions and we laughed like hyenas - I think my friend
Serena even peed in her pants. After we composed
ourselves (and Serena went back to my place to
change), we walked into Kelly's pub room. All that
laughing had left us parched and hungry, so we
bellied-up to the bar, ordered a round of Otto's
Double D, some burgers and fries and continued to
laugh the day away. Serena still talks about the
bull's "icicle" to this day. Actually she talks
about it too much!

We love the bull though which you can use as a landmark. How cool is it to be able to say to someone
"Yeah, go a couple of miles till you see the giant
bull." But it's not just the bull on top that makes
Kelly's a great choice, it's the inside too. The
dining room is big, open and smoke free. The bar/
lounge room is big too, and huge ventilators keep
the smoke at bay so you don't leave smelling like
a stinky ashtray.

They even have pool tables, dartboards and great
local musicians like Dominic Swensky, Andy Tollins
and Richard Sleigh (who happens to be a world renowned
harmonica player - and my friend) who play there
every week. One Thursday night, I stopped in and
Andy and Richard were there laying down the Blues
like nobody's business! I could hardly believe I
was just in central PA - it could have easily been
Austin, New York or even Paris. Sean supports a
lot of great local music and folks from all around
support his effort by turning out in droves.

For summer months and mild days, Kelly's also has
great outdoor seating with a Tiki Bar. "Tiki Tuesday"
is a fantastic deal with the coolest drinks served
in huge ceramic mugs shaped like South Pacific totem
poles. Kelly's also supports our local brewery, Otto's,
and offers their beers on tap at all times. They

don't look at Otto's as competition but rather as a complement and a way to support another local business. Way to go Kelly's!

Their menu rivals any big city restaurant as does the quality. Sean offers an unbelievable variety at reasonable prices. And like I said, it's so laid-back that all feel welcome and appreciated whether in a business suit or a leather jacket. The sign of the bull has beckoned bikers for years and on any given Saturday or Sunday, the parking lot is packed. Kissell Motorsport, a local bike dealer, even puts a new bike in the foyer that makes me drool every time I walk in. It would be cool if Kelly's had a Bike Night during summer (hint, hint) because it could be a bit more "civilized" for us less hardcore bikers, but just as fun.

Sean, Tien, John, Carol, General Manager Jean Harrison (another local!) and a great staff (including my pal Josh Meyers) will do their best to make you feel good, treat you right and tantalize your taste buds with cuisine that will truly please. Everything here is first class with a hometown feel. And everything from the mascot on the roof, to the owner/operators, will bring you back time and time again. Trust me, I would never "steer" you wrong, and that's no Bull! Uh, I guess it is, but you know what I mean.

Enjoy!

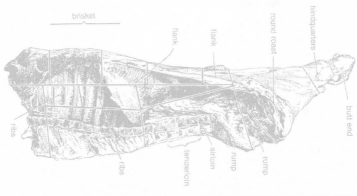

II.
HAPPY VALLEY,
MY NEIGHBORS

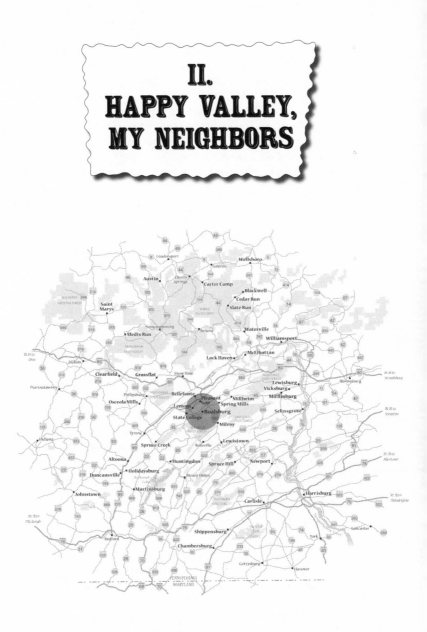

I'm not really sure how Happy Valley got its name but however it came to be, it's appropriate. The valley is basically a ten mile area stretching out from State College and is more formally known as The Centre Region. Towns like Bellefonte, Lemont, Linden Hall, Pleasant Gap, Potters Mills and others are among those that make up this region in the very heart of the state. Beauty, culture, diversity, education, recreation, pride, fun and of course great food, awesome beer and excellent coffee are just a few things that makes the nearly 100,000 locals and PSU students so happy!

I was born in Lemont at the base of Mt. Nittany just east of State College. Actually, I represent the fifth generation of my family to be born there. My mother's family settled there in the early 1700s' and when I built my cabin in Boalsburg I laid a rock into my foundation that was taken from the original homestead up on that mountainside. And if you walk though some woods due west of that original site, you will come to a clearing which looks west, out over the valley.

There, shaded by a huge oak is the family cemetery where my ancestors and those of the Dale Family are buried. Two Hundred and fifty year old tombstones worn almost blank by the weather stand as a testimony to my family who worked the land for sustenance and food. In those days, hopping in the car to go out to a cool brewpub in town was not even a dream. First - no cars or motorcycles. Second - no brewpubs. But more than that, my family had no money or time for such "foolery."

When my mom was a little girl growing up on the mountain, you never went "out" to eat unless it was literally outside when you were bad. Even as a young woman and after my grandparents moved down off the mountain to the village of Lemont, my mom was still busy cooking meals because both parents worked (No wonder she's the most awesome cook of all time! Her apple pie is like a slice of heaven!). Going out to eat just wasn't practical. Plus, why would you, when every night your dinner was fresh, lovingly prepared and home cooked.

Nowadays we live in a world where going out is not only practical but almost essential, especially if you're me and writing this book! I'm sure when my mom was a young woman she would never have imagined the amount of choices and quality of restaurants now in the area. However not all choices are good ones.

State College is being overrun by the chain gang save a handful of passionate, dedicated and hard working folks. It's them that keep alive the practice of fresh, lovingly prepared, home cooked meals. I love them all but selected only a few for my book. The following pages will give you "a taste" of why we call The Centre Region "Happy Valley."

Enjoy!

Mount Nittany Winery

LINDEN HALL, CENTRE COUNTY

And an ode to Dr. George Whitfield

Thirty some years ago I was invited over to this old dude's house to ride motorcycles up and around the side of Mt. Nittany. Well, Dr. George Whitfield may have been an old dude but only in years. He was amazing and could ride a trail bike like nobodies business. George was also a retired professor of physics at Penn State, but his colleagues had little knowledge of this "other life" he lived.

He owned a huge property on the southeast slope of the mountain and loved to ride all through the woods above his beautiful house that he built. He rode a classic 1970 Ossa 250 like he was riding a Brahma Bull. No finesse, little balance, but a lot of skill and always with a gnarly stub of a cigar clamped firmly between his teeth at the corner of his mouth. Most of us were trying to get up the side of the mountain without touching our feet to the ground but not George – he paddled his way up with both feet flailing like a hamster in an exercise wheel!

JUST A TASTE

Name of establishment:
Mount Nittany Vineyard & Winery

Contact Info:
Phone 814-466-6373
Fax 814-466-3066
Email: sales@mtnittanywinery.com
Website: mtnittanywinery.com

Owned by:
Joe & Betty Carroll

Hours:
Tues – Fri 1:30-5pm
Sat – 10am-5pm
Sun – 12:30-4pm, closed Mondays

Price range:
No charge to taste wine
Wine $8.99 to $18.99 per bottle

Cuisine:
Wine and locally produced cheese and other local food products.

Offers vegetarian, heart healthy or organic selections:
No

Support local farmers:
Yes

Locally owned accommodations:
The Bed & Breakfast at Rock Garden
176 Brush Valley Road
Boalsburg, PA 16827-1025
Phone: 814-466-6100
Toll Free: 888-620-7625
info@therockgardenbandb.com

The Springfield House: 814-466-6290
The Keller House: 814-364-2225

Local attractions:
This winery
Penn's Cave
Penn State University

With his cigar clamped tight, smoke all around his head, no helmet (of course) and cursing the whole way, he would make it up the mountain and his old Ossa would never miss a beat. And while most of us were looking up and trying to find his path through the trees, George was already off the bike and re-lighting his stogie. He would laugh and yell down "What's taking you boys so long? Hell, I'm an old man and so is my bike!"

Once we finally got to the top we would ride to a nearby spring for a drink. Us boys would be trying to slurp-up water like dogs but George just reached into his pocket, pulled out an old crushed-up Dixie Cup, un-crush it and scooped up a cool cup of spring water. He just smiled as we, with our wet faces, continued to grope for refreshment. Then we'd sit around and BS for hours and just enjoy life – those were great days! Sadly George Whitfield passed away, and the days of riding up the side of Mt. Nittany are gone forever I'm afraid. Gone also are the cigar clouded trails and BS sessions by the spring.

In 1983 another PSU Professor became the keeper of the mountain. He and his wife fell in love with the property and retired there on the beautiful sunlit slopes. Their purchase of Doc's sixty-five acre property was followed in 1984 by the first planting of grape vines. In July of 1990 Mount Nittany Winery was opened for business by Joe and Betty Carroll, who had been amateur winemakers for 20 years during Joe's tenure as a professor in the College of Business Administration at Penn State.

The entire winemaking operation was initially contained in the original chalet-style building which now houses a state of the art bottling line. A spiral staircase leads upstairs to the tasting room witch provide views of the adjacent pond, mountain range and the five acre vineyard which surrounds you

like a warm ocean of peace and tranquility.
During the fall harvest, the grapes are processed on
a covered cement loading dock with a modern, stainless steel crusher/destemer and bladder press.
Several additions to the winery have increased tank
and barrel storage capacity to over 10,000 gallons.
The latest addition in 1998, provided needed bottle
storage and a second-floor banquet room for winery
events, conferences, and catered events.

One reason behind the success of the winery is a
well-suited microclimate. The open exposure and
excellent air drainage off the southern slope of Mt.
Nittany protects against early and late frost damage
and creates a favorable environment for growing
European wine grapes. The five acre vineyard has
seven varieties, including Cayuga, Seyval Blanc,
Riesling, Chardonnay, Vidal Blanc, de Chaunac, and
Cabernet Sauvignon. All this science and nature
brings home medal after medal from some of the most
recognized wine festivals and competitions in Pennsylvania.

Recently the Carroll's brought on another couple to
"plant" them into the vineyard and hopefully grow
and blossom a new generation of winemakers. Jinx and
Natalie Proch are friends of mine and even own my
artwork. Their passion is right up there with Joe
and Betty and with their hard working and talented
crew, Mount Nittany will be here for a long time and
the medals will just keep coming in.

One of the things I like most about this place is
that on any given day when the weather is right, I
like to head up to the winery for a Euro style
picnic. Me and a friend or two and sometimes more,
pack a pile of yummy foods, breads and desserts, buy
a couple bottles of wine at the chalet and then walk
over to the pond. There, a huge old willow spreads
out like a giant green beach umbrella and a picnic
table nearby provides a nice place to sit and eat if
you like, but I prefer spreading out a big blanket.

With friends alongside I open the wine, pour some
into our glasses and we raise them in thanks to God
for such blessings. Then, drawing in the bouquet
through our noses, we sense the vision and hard
work of Joe and Betty. After that and with a gentle
sip, we drink in their passion and dedication, the
sun, time and the fruit of the vine. And as the
wine rolls across our tongue, spilling into our
spirits, we acknowledge these sweet times and such
wonderful places.

For me, it all started with a cigar smoking, wild
motorcycle riding professor of physics. Now it's
about passion and a wine making legacy, and I hope
it never ends.

Enjoy!

Meyer Dairy
STATE COLLEGE, CENTRE COUNTY

This is a big stretch I know, but there are just some exceptions in this world that have to be considered. When brothers Don and Joe Meyer decided to open a dairy store along Route 322, I am sure they had no idea what an icon they were creating. But, I can guarantee that the two dairy farmers were hoping to at least supplement their meager living off the land. Don and Joe are from an era when hard work, honesty, quality, value, good service and customer satisfaction were the foundations on which every business was built.

Their story is similar to that of my dad, a local businessman who's been installing quality floor coverings since the 1950s. His reputation is unmatched because of the craftsmanship and customer service. He teamed up with my mom in 1975 because he needed a good salesperson, bookkeeper, manager, secretary, organizer, shipper, receiver and most of all a good partner. They've been at it ever since, and are still at the store every morning at 7:30 a.m.

JUST A TASTE

Name of establishment:
Meyer Dairy

Contact Info:
2390 S. Atherton Street
State College, PA 16801
814.237.1849

Owned by:
Joe Meyer

Hours:
Summer 8 -11, 7 days
Winter, Sun – Thurs close at 10

Price range:
$1.65 - $3.55

Cuisine / Specialty:
Milk (hormone-free), ice cream, sandwiches, homemade soup

Offers vegetarian, heart healthy or organic selections:
No

Support local farmers:
Yes, Joe is the farmer.

Locally owned accommodations:
The Autoport
1405 S. Atherton St.
State College, PA 16801
Toll-Free: 800-932-7678
Phone: 814-237-7666

Fax: 814-237-7456
Website: www.theautoport.com
E-Mail: email@theautoport.com

Local attractions:
Grange Fair
Boalsburg Village

42

My dad is out on the job and mom runs the retail shop. He's 77, she's 75 (2007), and they didn't get where they are by cutting corners or being hell-bent on the bottom line. No, they work for a living and love it! My dad sings on the job and my mom always beams when a customer walks in.

I can only imagine that this was how Don and Joe went about their daily routine when they first opened Myer Dairy in 1970. Sadly though, Don was killed in a plane crash in 1982, but Joe, now 83 years old, is still at the dairy store every day. Just the other day I stopped in at nearly 11 p.m. to grab a half gallon of milk and Joe was still sitting behind the cash register (this is a man who not only runs the store but owns, operates and manages at least two other farms besides the one directly behind the dairy). As he handed me my change he asked how my parents were doing and how my art was coming along. What a guy!

So, why am I talking about an old farmer, a carpet-laying dad and bygone eras in a book about unique eats, cool pubs and cozy cafés? Well, it's one of the things this book is about - people that are defined by what they represent and strive for - quality, commitment, customer satisfaction, a strong work ethic and an honest profit. That stated, let's visit one of the last and sweetest locally-owned dairy stores in the region.

Perched on a hill overlooking State College is a single-story, wood-framed Mecca for connoisseurs of milk, ice cream and chili dogs (yes, chili dogs). Let's start with the milk though because at Myer's it's so fresh, I swear I hear mooing in the basement. Actually, it is all local milk and Joe owns over 200 head of Holsteins himself. However, the popularity of the product is so great that he needs to buy milk from other local farmers just to meet the demand.

His milk incidentally, is BST free (some sort of hormone). Something else that makes his milk unique is that it's bottled.

That's right, cool retro-looking, half-gallon glass bottles. And by "retro," I don't mean to imply that he buys bottles made to look like they're from the 70s, these bottles actually are from the 70s. Most of them are probably the same ones that Joe and Don first purchased for the bottling plant. When you buy your milk you pay a one-time deposit on the bottle. Then when the bottle is empty, you bring it back and exchange it for a clean, fresh and full one – recycling in its truest form! The deposit amount is then subtracted from your new milk purchase. What I like to do (and think is really fun) is to save up enough bottles so that my deposit discount is more than my milk purchase – free milk (in my mind)!

Then there's the ice cream. Don and Joe were making handmade ice cream and selling it to a cult following before Ben and Jerry were in underpants. Meyer Dairy ice cream rocks! It's creamy, tasty and the masses agree. If you don't believe me, stop by the dairy store on any summer evening. If you can even get in the parking lot, you will immediately be daunted by the line of customers, which is always out the door.

My friends and I have studied this phenomenon for years and have come up with a clever plan to beat the crowd and get our precious ice cream without much of a wait. We noticed that, for some reason, there is a lull in patronage from about 7:45 to 8:15 in the evening. So then we slip in, order, and by the time we have a half-dozen licks in, the masses descend again. (Obviously, my friends and I have way too much time on our hands and spend way too much time at Meyer Dairy)

Now for the chili dogs, Meyer's offers many menu items, but the chili dogs are what most people want at lunch time. Local lore has it that Joe got the recipe from "Pop" of the now-legendary Pop's Mexi-Hots while Pop was on his deathbed. I can only imagine a scene like the one from "Citizen Kane" when the Orson Welles character uses his last dying breath to faintly murmur "Rosebud." Only, in this case, the murmuring was a detailed monologue about the ingredients and preparation of the chili dog that has been served in the State College area since the 1940s.

From milk to eggs, butter to bread, ice cream to chili dogs, Myer Dairy has it all and does it right. When you go, and I know you will, you might see Joe hovering around or even working the cash register. In any event, give him a smile and a "hello." Keep in mind that he represents the quintessential era of customer service and satisfaction, but also the pure essence of going local.

Enjoy!

East – West Crossings

LEMONT, CENTRE COUNTY

One afternoon on my
way home from a trip
to Bellefonte, I took a
slightly different route
than usual. As I merged
on to the Mt. Nittany Expressway, I noticed a bright
sign with just three simple words Books, Teas, Arts
out of the corner of my eye. If I wasn't up to speed
and entering a busy expressway, I would have slowed
down to see exactly what this was all about. But
since it was only a few miles from home I knew I
would be able to stop back and check it out.

On the following Saturday morning, I drove the three
miles to the other side of Lemont and to the old
barn that houses the place I saw from the expressway.
The first thing you notice is a wonderful trellis,
hand-built using old tree limbs for the framework.
Beautiful, almost sculptural vines work and weave
their way through, under and over the limbs. Through
out the growing season, the trellis is green with
leaves and blooming with flowers, creating a live welcome sign to the century old structure.

JUST A TASTE

Name of establishment:
East-West Crossings

Contact Info:
201 Elmwood Street
State College, PA 16801
Phone: 814-234-8810
Fax: 814-234-8840
E-mail: info@eastwestcrossings.com
Website: www.eastwestcrossings.com

Owned by:
Joy and Ranadhir Mitra

Hours:
Monday-Saturday: 11 AM to 7 PM
Friday Live Music to 8 PM
Sunday: Closed except for
Special Events

Price range:

Cuisine / Specialty:
Tea's

**Offers vegetarian, heart healthy
or organic selections:**
Yes

Support local farmers:
Yes

Locally owned accommodations:
The Stevens Motel
1275 N. Atherton St.
State College, PA 16803

Phone: 814-238-2438
Fax: 814-238-7548
Website: thestevensmotel.com

Local attractions:
Historic Boalsburg

I passed by the trellis and around to the backside of the barn where I saw the big sign. On the door of the lower level was a little sign reading "East – West Crossings" and beside it, that one wonderful word "Open." I walked through the door and I realized that yet again serendipity was with this project. The vibe was sweet from the moment I stepped in – a clean simple décor blended traditional with contemporary perhaps like the fine blends of teas offered. Cherry-stained bookshelves lined the old barn foundation walls and free standing shelves also created a sectioning of sorts in the large, open space.

Books were placed so that most covers were facing you instead of the traditional spine view display (a great touch considering so many books have artistic covers but are hidden from sight). The book covers were in good company with lovely East Indian art pieces on the walls, and everything was gently lit by tiny halogen lights hanging from the underside of the old wooden floor above.

Throughout the room, massive hand-hewn beams, joists and support posts remain exposed and provided a natural feel that somehow gave a sense of security. New Maple tables and chairs, a love seat and stuffed seating provide comfort for patrons looking to read, work, talk or just chill. Soft music played and the wonderful smell of freshly brewed teas filled the air. The gentle combination of sight, sound and smell hug you, as though old world and new world just met and fell in love.

Life beyond the senses was there as well, as two women sat in the cushy love seats and sipped tea and talked about life. A man with a soft and pleasant voice was helping someone pick out a book about yoga and a young woman sat at the far end, fresh Chai in hand and doing school work. Within a few seconds of my entrance, the man who was helping his customers excused himself for a moment to greet and welcome me.

He told me that he and his wife, Joy, had just opened in January 2007 but had not yet been able to set up for serving teas as part of the business. He told me however that he had teas available for free tastings at a little self serve table. He encouraged me to try them and take a look around. I walked over to the table to find two green teas offered. One was Chinese and the other French. Some glass tea cups were available, so I poured a small amount of the Chinese and walked around the store.

Their books at EWC were of a nice variety with many leaning towards an eastern Buddhist influence. A couple that stood out were about the Dali Lama, but others included books on yoga, cooking, travel and gardening as well as a few kid's books. After the owner finished with his customer, he came to me with his hand out and introduced himself as Ran (pro-nounced Ron). In his soft and gentle Indian accent, he asked me how I liked the tea and if he could be of help.

I love this about small locally owned businesses – so much pride and personal attention from the owners gives you an assurance that you matter and that they really appreciate your business. After a few tea samples and some writing there, I asked Ran if he knew of a word like serendipity in his native langu-age. He said "Ghatonachakrey," which is Bengali for "By way of the wheel of events." In other words, as one travels around life, one experiences events that lead to unexpected discoveries. Awesome! I took a different road home, saw a three word sign and found the coolest place this side of the Taj Mahal.

Now months later East - West Crossings is a full service tea house, book store and mini art gallery. The teas are amazing and the way they serve them is so nice. Each selection is loose leaf and put into a perforated basket set into the top of a little ceramic teapot which also comes with a hand-made Indian cozy. That, along with a ceramic cup and

butter cookie, is placed on a bamboo tray. A timer
is clipped to the side of the tray and gently beeps
when the tea has steeped for the proper amount of time.

Warm weather affords you the opportunity to sit outside either on the huge wooden deck or out along Slap
Cabin Creek and under a canopy of willows. This place
is so nice and peaceful, so gentle and welcoming
that I'm sure the Dali Lama himself would hang out
here if he were in town.

So come and experience 'Ghatonachakrey' for yourself.
Even if you can't pronounce it (I can't) don't worry,
because you will certainly feel and understand it
as you discover for yourself what happens when East
meets West.

Enjoy!

Herwig's Austrian Bistro
STATE COLLEGE, CENTRE COUNTY

I first met Herwig Brandstatter in 1982. He and his
wife Gundi had just pur-
chased a house and settled
here in State College while passing through on their
way to Australia. They had come from a beautiful
mountain village in the south of Austria where "Brandy,"
as his friends call him, owned and operated a grand
chalet/hotel with a five star restaurant inside.
European dignitaries, as well as U.S. and other world
figures frequented his place.

So while on holiday, he and his family decided to
visit a friend here in State College. When they
arrived, they fell in love with the area and the opportunities it provided. Shortly after their decision
to settle here, he and Gundi decided to bring the
tastes of Austria along with them and their talents
for running a first class restaurant as well. And in
1982 they opened Herwig's Edelweiss at the Lodge at
Tussey Mountain Ski resort, formerly Skimount. It
was there at the first Herwig's, at the dawn of my
new career, that I first exhibited my work as a professional artist.

JUST A TASTE

Name of establishment:
Herwig's Austrian Bistro

Contact Info:
132 W. College Ave.
State College, PA 16801
Phone: 814 238-0200
E-mail: unitrav@aol.com
Web: herwigsaustrianbistro.com

Owned by:
Herwig, Gundi and Bernd
Brandstatter

Hours:
Mon–Wed: 11:45 am until last
seating at 8pm; Thu–Sat: 11:45 am
until last seating at 9pm. Closed
Sundays and Holidays.

Price range:
$7.50 - 17.95

Cuisine / Specialty:
Original and Authentic
Austrian Cuisine

**Offers vegetarian, heart healthy
or organic selections:**
Yes

Support local farmers:
Yes

Locally owned accommodations:
Chatelaine Bed & Breakfast
347 W. Pine Grove Rd.
Box 326
Pine Grove Mills, PA 16868

Toll-Free: 800-251-2028
Phone: 814-238-2028
Fax: 814-238-1699
E-Mail: kkeeper0@comcast.net
Web: http://www.chatelainebandb.com

Local attractions:
PSU
Central PA Festival of the Arts
Shopping
State Theater
Otto's

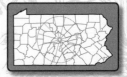

That night was great! Brandy served wonderful home-cooked appetizers and he totally captivated my patrons with his great personality as if the art was his own. He had just met me only weeks before but on that night, you would have thought we had been friends for years (that's just the kind of guy he is). He didn't even charge me for the space. I only sold one drawing that night and who do you think bought it? Brandy and Gundi Brandstatter. And even now, over twenty years later, they continue to support my work and remain my good friends. But I can't possibly talk about my association with Brandy without telling one of the funniest stories of my life involving him.

When Brandy first arrived in Happy Valley, along with his culinary traditions, he also brought with him another tradition. You see, back home, men (and maybe women - yikes) would inhale snuff (tobacco). This isn't the crap we have here in little round flat cans and whose names are painted on race cars, this is of a much higher grade and finer ground. Brandy kept his in a little antique silver container that he always had in his pocket.

Every hour or so he would take this container from his pocket, tap it a few times gently against his palm and then turn it within itself to expose a tiny hole from which the powered tobacco would come out. He then carefully tapped out a very tiny amount on that muscled part of the side of his hand between the base of his index finger and the base of his thumb. He would then raise his hand carefully to his nose, and with a short, very quick sniff, would inhale the tobacco into his nostrils. As a young man this really impressed me. I had no desire to smoke. Smoking wasn't for me, but this was cool! Damn Cool!

Wanting to be as cool as Brandy, I convinced some friends of mine to go with me to the local mall where there was a little privately owned tobacco shop. I asked the guy if he carried tobacco in little cans from Europe and amazingly he had some. My friends and I went directly out to the parking lot to give it a try.

I took the can and tapped it against my palm - just like Brandy. I twisted it to expose the opening - just like Brandy. I pointed it at that little spot on the side of my hand and gently bumped the container - just like Brandy. However, unlike Brandy, nothing came out. I closed it and tapped again - nothing!

Here I am with my friends trying to flaunt my new European sophistication and basically looked like a dork. I wasn't about to toss it out, so I thought if maybe I just sniffed directly from the can, something will come out (you can imagine where this is going). So I tapped it again, spun it open, tilted my head back and put the hole to my nose. With the same sucking power of an Oreck vacuum, I inhaled as hard as I could. Unbeknownst to me, there had been a ball of tobacco forming inside the container and growing larger and larger with each tapping of the can.

Like a Trident missile topped with a fifty-megaton nuclear warhead, this immense ball of pure tobacco finally broke loose and launched itself into my brain! The look on my friend's faces was only eclipsed by the explosion of terror and seizing pain that was being expressed on mine! I jumped, spun and flailed myself across the parking lot as my so-called "friends" were laughing their butts off!

Needless to say, none of them wanted to try it, and as soon as I regained consciousness and the blood receded from my head, I walked over to a nearby dumpster and tossed my "European sophistication" away and never touched it again. True story!

Herwig's Edelweiss at Skimount eventually closed because I honestly think Brandy was way ahead of his time and folks around here just didn't get it. Well, with time, all things change and in this case for

the good. Brandy, Gundi, and now with their very
talented and "entertaining" son Bernd, have revived
their passion and desire to bring the taste of their
home country to Central Pennsylvania once again. But
instead of being out of town and on the side of a
mountain, Herwig's Austrian Bistro sits proudly on
the main drag of downtown State College and directly
across from the Penn State Campus.

Today they are packed every lunch and dinner and
cook for a generation that not only gets it, but
loves and supports it. Students, non-students, young
and old come to Herwig's (heck, even my mom and dad
love it). The food here is awesome, lovingly prepared, hot, and in large supply! Unlike the chain
gang which has everything shipped in frozen from a
commissary kitchen sometimes hundreds of miles away,
everything at Herwig's is prepared in the morning
for that day and evening (Brandy even makes every
bratwurst from scratch, using meat from a local
butcher shop). So, if they run out of food, they
close. Don't believe me? Go on a busy weekend night
and if the door is locked before the posted closing
time and the place is still packed, they've run out.
Maybe it's due to their portions, because they're so
generous, but generosity is what they're all about.

At Herwigs Austrian Bistro you will find a near endless amount of brats as well as many other home cooked Austrian delights. Some other offerings include: Viennese Beef Gulyas - a thick and spicy beef stew; Tyrolean Gröstl - assorted meats sautéed with potatoes and onions and Leberkäse - beef and pork Bavarian style sausage loaf, and on occasion, peg legs - mmm mmm! Oh, if you haven't figured this out, this is not a place for someone on a diet. Their motto at Herwig's is "Where bacon is an herb." So for the lighter appetite types, there's a cereal place next door.

Some of you may say "I don't like German food" or "I don't understand the German language so how will I know what to order?" Well first off, it's not German - it's Austrian. Second, as far as ordering, they have English subtitles. Bernd or Brandy or one of the crew will be happy to explain everything they make. But, if Bernd is behind the counter and you say any of those things I mentioned before, you will find yourself suddenly lapsed into that episode of Seinfeld and "The Soup Nazi." I'm not kidding. Don't worry though, all the shenanigans are in good fun and hysterical if you have any sense of humor. Even Eric, their right-hand-man who has been with them since they opened the new place gets in on the fun.

So, from a grand chalet in the Austrian Alps, to a hillside restaurant on Tussey Mountain and now a street side bistro in State College, the Brandstatter family has proven their worth in the world of great cuisine. Herwig's Austrian Bistro offers amazing food at very fare prices and they're BYOB too! So what are you waiting for? Pack up your favorite wine or beer (hopefully Otto's), dress in your lederhosen if you like, but be sure and take a sense of humor. Otherwise you might hear "No knoodle for you! NEXT!!!"

Enjoy!

The Cheese Shoppe
STATE COLLEGE, CENTRE COUNTY

The neon sign in the window reads "cheese" but if you are on Calder Alley in downtown State College on any given morning, the smell in the air is definitely COFFEE!

Below street level and only detected by the strong scent of roasting coffee beans and that cool neon sign is a tiny place where the bean is king, and the wide selection of cheese, gourmet delights, fresh breads and loyal patrons are its court. Bill Clarke, the shop's proprietor is very serious about his craft. He barely has time to talk, let alone run the cash register while he's roasting.

With a stopwatch around his neck, a keen eye for color and the nose of a bloodhound, Bill hovers around a beautiful Probat roaster like a mother around her newborn baby. And in this case, the roaster is the only baby in town. Nowhere else in the State College does anyone roast their own coffee beans, but here at The Cheese Shoppe, it is the only way. Those in the know come here when they want it fresh.

JUST A TASTE

Name of establishment:
The Cheese Shoppe

Contact Info:
234 East Calder Way
State College, PA 16801
(814) 234-4244
www.wcclarke.com

Owned by:
William C. Clarke

Hours:
Mon –Sat 7 AM – 6 PM

Price range:
From forty cents (for a piece of chocolate) to $23.99/lb. for fancy cheese

Cuisine / Specialty:
Cheese, gourmet foods, fine coffees (roasted in house)

Offers vegetarian, heart healthy or organic selections:
Yes, organic coffees

Support local farmers:
Yes

Locally owned accommodations:
The Stevens Motel
1275 N. Atherton St.
State College, PA 16803
Phone: 814-238-2438
Fax: 814-238-7548
Web: www.thestevensmotel.com

The Garman Inn
116 E. High St.
Bellefonte, PA 16823
Phone: 814-353-8803
Fax: 814-353-8813
Web: www.garmanoperahouse.com
E-Mail: questions@garmanopera-house.com

Local attractions:
Farmer's markets (downtown State College, Boalsburg, Belle-fonte, etc.)

So it's not the cushy sofas, not the clever décor, not the "flare" of uniformed employees, and it's certainly not the millions of locations and fancy coffee drink names that put The Cheese Shoppe on my map. No, it's the commitment, passion, hard work, love and plain desire of

Bill, his select staff and patrons who all share the same vision. Those who know and appreciate quality over kitsch come here to TCS. You'll find business people, students, professors, construction guys, locals and even the occasional out-of-towner who is drawn in by the magic carpet of caffeine laden smoke floating through the early morning air.

Once inside, and unless you sit on top of a bag full of coffee beans, you really can't sit down at all. Most customers stand around and sip their brew while discussing everything from politics to academics, to what's on Bravo that week or how long it will take the borough to raise the street parking to $1 per minute (jerks). TCS is a lot like the coffee bars I've been to in Italy. Italians stand and talk, a few sit down and many sit outside on a terrace in good weather. Bill's place has a little terrace as well but most of Bill's customers just get their coffee to go. And here's a classic example of what sets this place apart from the others and one of the reasons that I like it so much.

Remember what I said about Bill nursing and cuddling his coffee roaster and not having time for the register? Well, when he's in the groove, he's in the groove! If you stand there waiting for him to get you your coffee or take your money, you'll be standing there for a while. The seasoned Cheese Shoppe patrons help themselves. They come in, grab a cup, select their grade, and pump away at the air pots. But here's the best part, they just throw down some money and walk out. Seriously. Go down there any morning and you will find a pile of one dollar bills and a ton of change heaped up on the counter. After the morning rush and his precious beans are roasted to perfection, he sorts it all out, sets the tax man's share aside, pours himself a cup and sits down on a bean bag to engage in his unique style of banter.

Bill is also known for his amazing selection of domestic and imported cheese - hence the name The Cheese Shoppe. Legend has it that Bill drives to New York City, scours the stalls of cheese makers and returns to State College with a bounty that would make any true Frenchman beam with delight. This cheese is the real thing and it's Damn Good! He also has fresh breads from Tony Sapia and other gourmet treats along with his awesome coffees. You can get his fresh roasted coffee in whole bean form or ground to your liking.

However you get your coffee, cheese or bread, it will all be fresh and full of flavor. Try and get there in the morning when the smoke of the roaster fills the streets, patrons fill the shop and happy faces abound. Bill will be in his element and the coffee will be unforgettable.

Enjoy!

Webster's Bookstore & Café

STATE COLLEGE, CENTRE COUNTY

I wasn't around during the early 1950's to hang out in one of those coffee shops in New York City where the "Beat Generation" was born and nurtured great minds and talents like that of Jack Kerouac, but if there's a place here in the mountains of central Pennsylvania that comes close, it's Webster's.

I can totally see Kerouac, Ginsburg, Burroughs, and other writers, thinkers, and dreamers, along with those of the "underground" movement gathered there. They would be sitting outside along Allen Street or inside amongst the thousands of lovingly used books. They would smell the earthy scent of coffee along with the comforting smell of toasted bagels that weave together in the air, along with the murmur of conversation and melodic groove of a young guitarist playing in the corner. They would connect and appreciate the atmosphere, which is unhurried and laid-back, yet tense with the buzz of a generation looking to break away from the establishment and leave their own mark. And, like these "beatniks" of an era gone by, the patrons of Webster's today are creating an

JUST A TASTE

Name of establishment:
Webster's Bookstore & Café

Owned by:
Elaine C. Meder-Wilgus

Contact Information:
128 S. Allen St.
State College, PA 16801
814-234-9712
Elaine@webstersbookstorecafe.com
www.webstersbookstorecafe.com

Hours:
M-F 7am – 10 pm
Saturday 8am-8pm
Sunday 8am-8pm

Price range:
2.50-5.95

Cuisine / Specialty:
Coffee, Tea & Café foods

Offers vegetarian, heart healthy or organic selections:
Yes – exclusively

Support local farmers:
Yes

Locally owned accommodations:
The Stevens Motel
1275 N. Atherton St.
State College, PA 16803
Phone: 814-238-2438
Fax: 814-238-7548
Web: www.thestevensmotel.com

The Chatelaine Bed & Breakfast
47 W. Pine Grove Rd.
Box 326
Pine Grove Mills, PA 16868
Toll-Free: 800-251-2028
Phone: 814-238-2028
Fax: 814-238-1699
Web: www.chatelainebandb.com
E-Mail: kkeeper0@comcast.net

Local attractions:
Historic Boalsburg
PSU Campus
State Theater
Hiking, Biking and Fishing

underground vibe and groove in place that not only supports them but joins with them as well.

Webster's Bookstore & Café seems to attract and encourage a funky mix of both young and old. My friend and neighbor Ben, a twenty one year old student at Penn State, says "it's the clientele that sets Webster's totally apart from your average coffee shop and one of the biggest things that makes it what it is." For me, it's a place where you can be yourself - no one thinks any differently toward the eccentric old dude, grad student, high school kid or the mom buying cool books about everything from cooking and parenting to women's place in a global society.

Then there's the wave of undergrads that ebb and flow discussing local, state, national, world, and university affairs. Yeah, they probably watch Lost, but I bet they'd rather be helping the community or marching in a walk against the atrocities of governments gone awry. Most are a hands-on and a well-informed group that probably thinks more about the earth and peace rather then shock and awe - more about the needs and welfare of fellow humans than world domination and oil profits. All in all it is a nice gentle group. You will always feel like you've stepped into a room of friends and you never know when one of them will pull a random act of kindness on you.

I was there one day to have a coffee and a bagel. There was a queue at the counter and the young woman ahead of me placed a complicated order for her and some girlfriends who were catching up on some much needed downtime. Several times, she turned to me and the others behind me and apologized for holding us up. We all let her know that all was cool and that we didn't mind. I think she also felt bad for the barista who was buzzing behind the bar all by herself.

The young, dreadlocked coffee creator smiled and even joked around with us as she tried to work as fast as she could. After pulling four double shots, steaming a pint of milk, preparing two French presses of green tea and toasting six multigrain bagels, she then got out all the plates and accoutrements to make the morning pow-wow complete for the weary students. The sweet young woman who ordered all this bounty quickly whipped out a crinkled ball of cash and whispered something to the Rasta barista – I figured she was just apologizing again.

She got her change, stuffed the tip jar with more crinkled cash and went off to chill with the girls. I ordered my simple coffee, a multigrain with cream cheese and got out my cash to pay. The young woman behind the counter just smiled and said "That girl paid for you – you're free to go! Just pay it forward someday."

I'm convinced Elaine Meder-Wilgus, the owner/operator, somehow transmits this type of behavior which is received by others who just can't help themselves but to do good. She is bright, kind, generous, passionate, committed, down-to-earth, very friendly and helpful. Sometimes you will find her working behind the coffee and tea bar as well as in the bookstore. I think she knows where every single book is and always seems to have time for her customers and will exhaust every resource to find whatever they are looking for.

She is a great mix of business woman, barista, librarian, hippy and artist. Her husband, Bill, is a gifted guitar player and singer, so the two of them are an excellent mix. Elaine also supports local, organic and sustainable agriculture. Her coffees are Fair Trade and shade grown. She uses Meyer Dairy milk, her baked goods are all local and her tea selection is huge. She also now offers a simple lunch and dinner menu, as well. Her book selection is bountiful and diverse with some hard to find titles that the chains would never carry because they're not the market "status quo."

In this indie owned store there are no worker bees running around with price scanners, no cattle shoots at the register, no clever marketing ploy to get you to buy one book over another, no uniformed McCoffee slingers and certainly no freeloaders hanging around all day taking up space for actual customers. Oh wait. Uh, strike that last one (smile). But hey, it's a new beat generation! The Bohemian lifestyle that's encouraged at Webster's also creates an atmosphere that melds the poets of the past with an enlightened and world-embracing future generation.

Now, if we could only get one of these peaceful humanitarians and brilliant young thinkers to run for president some day!

Enjoy!

Note: Webster's now has a second location on the north end of town, and is one of the sweetest little cafés I've ever been in. Elaine and her hubby Bill along with a very talented architect took a plain space in a mini-plaza and turned it into something far from plain! Bill's choices of colors on the walls are of a deep, warm Mediter-ranean hue.

The layout is very thought out and totally set up. What I mean is, the coffee bar and small kitchen is equipped with all the latest professional grade stuff and arranged for efficiency. The customer area is brightly lit, with comfortable tables and chairs and outlets everywhere to plug in your laptop and local artists are represented on the walls. Then they have a very nice deck outside and again, very comfortable and it even has outlets too! They thought of everything.

My friends Morgan Hummel and Gretchen Smith run the place and are both State College High School alums. It's all about local at Webster's. In fact, "This is what local looks like."

Otto's Pub & Brewery
STATE COLLEGE, CENTRE COUNTY

Here's a place that is as close to my heart as you can get. What you're about to read is more like a love story than my typical prose. And it's not just a story from my heart but from the owner himself. It's also a story of dreams, passion, hard work, creativity, community, patrons and overcoming disappointment to provide a great place for folks to enjoy.

As I reflect on that pervious paragraph, I realize how many other places I could have written that same introduction for. There's just something about indie owned restaurants, pubs and cafés that bring out the very best in everyone. But for some reason it's the independent breweries and brew pub owners that take the prize.

Maybe it's simply that they make beer. Think about it, have you ever met a monk that brews beer that wasn't jolly and full of good cheer? And if it wasn't for the indie brewer and his or her fermented drink,

one of America's founding fathers and international ambassador Benjamin Franklin would not have said "Beer is proof that God loves us and wants us to be happy." Or take the famed Greek philosopher Plato, who said "He was a wise man who invented beer." Well Charlie Schnable, Brewmaster and co-owner of Otto's, didn't invent beer but his contribution to the art of brewing here in central PA is most worthy of such high praise to his craft.

Charlie's awesome. Not just because he brews the sweetest beer this side of Straub, Bullfrog, Selin's Grove, Tröegs, Market Cross, Marzoni's and Johnstown, but I also consider him a friend and fellow artist. Seriously, he is an artist. No one can do what he does without being creatively gifted. I also call him the Einstein of the beer world because legend has it that he showed signs of a "baby genius" early on.

One time his mother found him in the kitchen after she heard an explosion and ran in finding her little boy flat-out on the floor. Around him were a jumble of copper kettles, some rubber hose, a jug of old cider and various spices. In the mix was the family dog that was furiously licking up the liquid concoction and his cat that seemed to be only slightly amused sat perched above it all. The cat's name? Otto.

Since that first attempt, Charlie's skill and mastery at the science of brewing has become one of true genius like his predecessor Albert Einstein. Unlike Al however, who only played with numbers, Charlie's ability to calculate the right combination of ingredients adds up to create his own special theory. And when he sets water, barley, malts, hops and yeast in motion, it creates an energy that's equal to the mass of flavors across the tongue, which is then realized as a beer of relative greatness! Yes, he's a great brewing scientist, but in some ways he's like a mad scientist. You hardly ever see him out around the pub because he hides himself in the bowels of the brewery, shuffling around his cherished fermentation tanks checking SG's, ABV's and crap like that.

Keeping with the science theme, I think it's fun to envision Charlie in a lab coat, crazed hair (Einstein?) and wearing goggles (those round ones that old school welders wear and the kid standing in line to see Santa in the movie *A Christmas Story*). With Bunsen burners all around him, and those ball things that shoot out lightening bolts, Charlie stands hunched over a beaker of bubbling mash and fresh hops rubbing his finger tips together and murmuring "excellent, excellent." Really though, he's not mad at all, he's a great guy. He's soft spoken, humble and very generous. I had an opportunity to sit down with him one day and found out his story, the "back story" of how our beloved Otto's Pub & Brewery came to be.

It all started in the small town of Hughsville PA. Actually, it started in a college dorm room but that's another story. Charlie and his pal Steve Koch had a dream to open a brewery (not a brew pub) and thought Hughsville would be ideal. The town needed the commerce, they could walk to work and real estate was cheap. Being the good neighbor though, Charlie and Steve approached all the businesses around to let them know of their plans to open a brewery. All were supportive except for one - the church across the street - Charlie's own church (apparently those folks never heard of Ben Franklin or Plato). They protested the boy's application for a brewing license and succeeded. Hurt, discouraged and disappointed, but not crushed, they set their sights to Williamsport and the community was behind them.

The two began the hard work to renovate an old Pennsylvania Railroad office building to not only brew, but now include a pub and restaurant too. Knowing Charlie the way I do, I doubt he was into the restaurant scene, but this was an opportunity to be successful in multiple layers and the boys needed as much success as possible. In August 1996, Bullfrog Brewery was opened to a town that embraced and supported them (way to go Williamsport!). Charlie honed his skills as a Master Brewer at Bullfrog, but the young prodigy eventually wanted to go it alone. Like most gifted artists, he wanted to express himself un-tethered and free to create without boundaries. Steve, his friend and talented restaurateur stayed on and continued to build a very successful brew pub. Bullfrog remains to this day a favorite of mine as well as many other beer and food afficionados. But Charlie needed a fresh, blank canvas to paint, new lab equipment to produce his amazing brews and a new audience to taste and appreciate his genius.

Hmm, what's close to home, the fastest growing town around and is well on its way to being the third largest city in PA (Not to mention a well educated customer base whose tastes are discriminating and primed for a renaissance of beer)? Until Charlie's arrival, State College was ruled by big batch, small taste beers. We had some micros available, but no one could imagine what locally made beer from the hands of a master would taste like but that was all about to change.

Unfortunately, and once again, members of the "cloth" would rear their heads and try to stop something that has "Made glad the hearts of men" for millennium (silly members). According to the Bible and sensible souls, love conquers all, and Charlie Schnable's love for his craft, his passion to create and share his art with others, conquered the naysayers and the entire region.

In 2002, Otto's Pub & Brewery was born. Named after Charlie's little cat, this brew pub and restaurant opened its doors and the beer poured out. The towns-folk poured in and now we have a place where young and old can enjoy the fruits of a labor of love. And a region known as Happy Valley became a whole lot happier!

Charlie now offers eight standard brews, rotates 3 to 4 seasonal ones, has two on cask and still manages to tap a fresh Firkin keg every Friday. Here is a taste of what he offers.

Hellas Lager: A light refreshing lager that has a malty smooth character and low hop bitterness. ABV 4.8%

Apricot Wheat: An American wheat ale with the delicate aroma and flavor of apricot. ABV 4.7%

Hefeweizen: A south German style wheat ale. This beer is served traditionally cloudy due to the suspended yeast. Banana and clove esters are characteristics of this wonderful yeast strain from Weinstephan Germany. ABV 5.0%

Red Mo Ale: An American red ale brewed with Palisade hops for the bittering and Liberty in the hopback. Very malty and crisp, this ale has all the fun without a high alcohol content. ABV 5.0%

Mt. Nittany Pale Ale: An American pale ale brewed with Centennial hops and hopbacked with Cascade, it's refreshing and has a spicy, citrus aroma with a slightly nutty malt flavor. ABV 5.0%

Double D IPA: Forget the frilly mumbo-jumbo - I'll give you just two words - Damn Good! ABV 8.2% (And that's on a bad day my friends, expect higher. Oh that Charlie!)

Black Mo Stout: A dry Irish-style stout served via nitrogen. Black Mo is very smooth and creamy with a pleasant roasted malt character. A lot like Guinness (some say better). ABV 4.6%

Jolly Roger Imperial Stout: Named for Charlie's new business partner and dad-in-law, this Big stout is not for the kids. It's hand drawn from the cask, served in a Brandy snifter type of glass and packs as big a punch as it's packed with flavor. ABV 216.9% Kidding!

Thirsty?

I started this whole dissertation writing about love - Charlie's love for what he does and the story of what his love has brought forth. Hurdles he's overcome and the wonderful beers and pub he created. But this love story cannot be complete without mentioning the staff and patrons of Otto's. Roger Garthwaite, partner/honcho/dad-in-law/retiree of Penn State, is now the "face" of Otto's. He's taken over the business and schmoozing end so Einstein can stay in the "lab" and focus on his bubbling beakers of brew. Roger's schmoozing is genuine and sincere because he really enjoys talking with the customers. Not only to see how they like what they're eating and drinking, but to also add that owner presence that is what sets small business apart from the corporate monsters. Roger is proud of his son-in-law's creation and it shows.

It's not just Roger though that keeps Otto's running - it's a great management, bartending, kitchen and serving team! And the patrons? They're kinda like family and a lot like best friends. Two of my favorites (who also happen to be fellow Boalsburgers) are Bruce and Jenni. These two are the best. The funny thing is they're like yin and yang - Bruce usually sits or stands at the bar and friends come to him - Jenni floats around like a little social butterfly from friend to friend - Bruce is an American - Jenni is from Melbourne Australia - Jenni talks to everyone and her laugh is infectious - Bruce is the quieter type. But what these two do have in common is super kind and generous hearts, tons of friends, a love for craft brewed beer and a sweet love for each other.

So you see my friends, this is as much about a love story as it is about awesome beer. Now go, order a lunch or dinner and a brew that suits you and fall in love yourself. And if any church folks ask, tell them Ben was right, especially when it comes to Otto's.

Enjoy!

Red Horse Tavern

PLEASANT GAP, CENTRE COUNTY

This is a place I have known about since I was a kid. Back then I thought it was a Wild West saloons where bar fights were a nightly thing. Keep in mind, I had never been inside this place (I was a little kid, after all) but back in the day, the Red Horse Tavern had a huge sign out front with a 20 foot-high painting of a charging red horse coming right at me! It burned an image into my young brain like a red hot branding iron and scared the crap out of me! But, it also set in motion an imagination that is still fertile to this day.

In my overactive mind, this great red horse was a charging messenger of a time that I only knew about from John Wayne movies and Sunday afternoon television shows like Rawhide while curled up on the floor with my dad. But this wasn't Texas or Oklahoma, this was Pleasant Gap, PA, and the only cowboys around there were Amish guys who got up at 4 a.m. to milk the cows.

JUST A TASTE

Name of establishment:
Red Horse Tavern

Contact Info:
104 North Main Street
Pleasant Gap, PA 16823
rsherman2@msn.com

Owned by:
Randall & Paula Sherman

Hours:
Mon.-Thurs. 11:00 a.m.-11:00 p.m.,
Fri & Sat. 11:00 a.m.-12:00 a.m.
and Sun 12:00 p.m.-9:00 p.m.

Price range:
3.99 - $24.99

Cuisine / Specialty:
Comfort food

Offers vegetarian, heart healthy or organic selections:
Yes

Support local farmers:
Yes

Locally owned accommodations:
The Queen – Bellefonte
The Reynolds Mansion – Bellefonte
The Garman - Bellefonte

Local attractions:
Penn State of course, for all there sports and Bryce Jordan Concerts, The State Theatre, The State College Spikes, Arts & Crafts fairs and festivals, The Bellefonte Cruise

So what was going on inside that place? Were there poker games, loose women and bottles of whiskey being chugged and then smashed over the head of some unsuspecting cowpoke? Could Doc Holliday be in there, sitting at a table, one hand on his cards while the other gripped his .44? Was Billy the Kid standing at the bar waiting for someone to give him the stink eye so he could "fill him full o' lead?" Or was a lady in a fancy dress sitting on top of a piano while her colleagues danced with dust-covered men wearing chaps and spurs? If I could only get inside...

Well, its 40 years later and I'm well aware that this isn't the Wild West and that dance hall girls weren't just for dancing. Still, I decided to check the place out. I had heard that it had recently changed hands and the once scary, seedy western bar had become quite genteel. I walked through the door and as it happens in most local watering holes, every head turned and every eye looked my way. I gazed across the length of the bar and saw not a cowboy hat in sight. There were plenty of baseball caps, but no Stetsons. One dude was even texting with his cell phone and Cold Play was on the juke box. There were women too, but instead of big ornate dresses, these girls wore low-riding jeans and tight NASCAR t-shirts.

Beyond the bar was a spacious dining room with beautiful wood floors and wall paneling. Tiny lights entwined with ivy were draped over door openings and wrapped around support posts. Every table was filled with friends and families enjoying homemade dinners and libations from the bar. Laughter and conversation from the dining room was eclipsed by the din of the barroom. I took a seat at the far end of the bar so I could soak in the vibe. At first, it was hard to shake the Wild West memories, but when Aerosmith blasted from the jukebox and I saw that they had Guinness on tap, I knew I wasn't in Kansas anymore.

I must admit that the tap selection was a bit weak, but I ordered the Guinness and looked over the menu. As I did, I kept an eye on the young woman behind the bar as she drew my stout. I wasn't expecting a good pour from this cutie, but she did a great job. She poured the glass half-full, let it sit and settle, then like a barkeep from County Cork, she drew the rest, straight down, and brought the creamy blonde head right to the brim. Just then, her husband walked in with a beautiful bouquet of flowers for her. Darn it! It was just my luck - a beautiful woman who could pour a proper Guinness. But she was already spoken for so I just turned my attention back to the menu.

The selection was mostly sandwiches and burgers, but they had some really nice entrée specials including prime rib and crab cakes. I was told that everything on the menu was homemade except for the beer battered fish sandwich, and that was exactly what I was hungry for. The bartender brought me my Guinness and I asked about the fish sandwich. She took her hands, spread them apart to about 12 inches, and said that was how big the piece of fish was.

Well, mama didn't raise no fool, and I come from a long line of "fish liars," so I anticipated eight inches, tops. But when the sandwich arrived at my table, I was happily wrong. I have never seen a piece of cooked fish that big! It was at least a foot long, garnished with lettuce and tomatoes, and was served on a hoagie roll that would make Dr. Atkins spin in his grave! Fresh-cut French fries nearly overflowed from what little space was left on the plate.

So there I was, Kenny the Kid, sitting in his boyhood Wild West saloon, drinking Guinness and chowing down on a beautifully prepared fish sandwich and fries! No bar fights, no gun shots fired into the ceiling, no dusty cowpokes crawl-fishing (cheating) on a poker hand and getting blasted in the belly for it. And no perfumed petticoat-clad women escorting men to the "dance floor." Sigh.

After dinner I met the owners and found out that they were locals who met and fell in love while they were both working at another local eatery. He was a cook and she was a waitress. They got married and moved to Boston where he attended culinary school. After that, they started a family and returned to central PA.

Randy and Paula Sherman are like the poster kids for this book - supportive of local farmers and passionate about their business. They promote a smoke-free bar and dining area, encourage friendly interaction and greet you not just as a customer, but as a friend and neighbor. They love what they do and they love that they can do it here - in their hometown.

Sadly, the infamous sign of the charging red horse is no longer there, but the inspiration that it brought to an aspiring young cowboy is alive and well today in a still-youthful, metro-sexual, foodie/beer geek. What once frightened me now delights me, and the Red Horse has become a gathering place for locals as well as the occasional "drifter." Gone is the cheap whiskey and saloon grub of my imagination, but what is real is the haute but humble cuisine of a passionate and dedicated husband and wife team. YE-HA!

Enjoy!

La Bella Trattoria
BELLEFONTE, CENTRE COUNTY

This charming little eatery lies under The Garman Opera House which was built in 1890. It was a venue for live performances and was a stop on the vaudeville circuit with visits by such notables as Harry Houdini, George Burns and Gracie Allen, The Flora Dora Girls and Tom Mix, who all performed there onstage. With the arrival of motion pictures, the Garman closed its doors as a performance place and became a movie house in 1931 and continued to show feature films until 1961.

Due in part to the demise of small town theaters by the corporate monsters, the Garman served as a furniture warehouse for 29 years, just to stay alive. In 1990, the theater part was completely renovated and once again became a live performance venue until 1999 when sadly, it closed its doors once again.

Thanks to a local family who had the vision and dream to restore and revive this entertainment and cultural icon, it was purchased and saved through a Sheriff's Sale in July 2000, and the grand old building was

JUST A TASTE

Name of establishment:
LA BELLA TRATTORIA

Contact Info:
116 E. High St. Bellefonte, PA
814-353-8808
questions@garmanoperahouse.com
www.garmanoperahouse.com

Owned by:
Allison, RJ & Kathryn Iadarola

Hours:
Tues-Thurs. 5:00pm-8:00pm
Fri.Sat. 5:00pm-9:00

Price range:
$10.00-$23.99

Cuisine / Specialty:
Italian & Nouveau

Offers vegetarian, heart healthy or organic selections:
Yes

Support local farmers:
Yes

Locally owned accommodations:
Garman Inn
116 E. High St.
Bellefonte, PA 16823
Phone: 814-353-8803
Fax: 814-353-8813
questions@garmanoperahouse.com
www.garmanoperahouse.com

Local attractions:
Garman Opera House Theatre

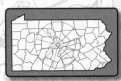

again reopened as a movie theater. Feature films, classic, art and foreign films play daily on the huge screen, and digital surround sound and reclining seats are some of the amenities in this 335-seat movie house.

The Iadarola clan – Ron, Kathryn, their son RJ and daughter Allison, poured not only their life savings into the Garman, but their hearts as well. They dreamed of an old time movie theatre with a working balcony, decorated cathedral ceilings and a proper screen (not like the chain gang with screens just slightly bigger than a TV). Well, no dreams of such grandeur come easy and this was no exception. Think about it, an 1890 Opera House, that means old wiring, pipes, old brick and plaster walls and ceilings, hidden rooms, aged balconies, flyways, lighting, seating, and…well, you get it. That doesn't even include bringing everything in the entire structure up to modern safety and fire prevention standards.

Well, walk into The Garman Opera House today and you will be transported into the grand age of the Motion Picture era! Most days Kathryn will greet you from behind the glass of one of those cool booths where they sell the tickets, which by the way, cost less than the mega-plexes and is another great reason to *go local* – you're saving money and helping to support your neighbors and community (Right on)! But the family didn't stop at the theater with their dreams - the floors above are now hotel rooms!

One afternoon I stopped by the restaurant to say hi and Ron and Kathryn were there. I asked how things were going with the hotel and Ron sprang up from his lunch to give me a tour. He was like a little kid showing me his new fort or tree house he had built in the backyard and beamed with pride as he took me through the whole place, step by step and room by room.

We took the stairs, but you can take an elevator up to the outside of the old building to be delivered to two floors of rooms that look and feel like what the old time hotels back in the day must have been like. Along with the 14 regular rooms, there's even a bridal suite and a conference room. One particular room is more than a room - it has two floors and sleeps up to 10 people! It seemed more like a Fifth Avenue apartment, with huge arch windows of old glass and a full kitchen.

Speaking of kitchen - tucked sweet and cozy under the old opera house and below street level is the gem of the whole project, La Bella Trattoria. Allison and RJ run a sweet place that you've got to check out! The cuisine is modern Italian and there's lots of it. It's presented exquisitely and fairly priced. And the décor would make those experts on HGTV cringe, because you would never want to improve it or give it a "make-over."

Interior walls of stone, wood tables, soft lighting and little hidden booths all make for the true romantic dinner out. The low ceilings and dark wood give a sense of coziness rather than closeness and the vibe here is great - somewhere between old world Europe and turn of the century America. Toward the back of the building there are more booths up against the old stones with a wooden framework around them that holds velvety curtains that can be pulled closed to provide a feeling like the old speakeasy days.

Usually Allison will greet you at the door as her brother and chef RJ prepares the evening selections. Every meal here (and I've had a lot of them) has been nothing short of superb! Between that and the comfortable setting and very affordable prices, why would you go to a chain restaurant? They offer a full service bar at La Bella and they're smoke-free!

So here's your itinerary as I see it: Go to La Bella early, have a great meal and take your time. Then walk up and see a movie the way the filmmakers and directors meant for you to see their work. And then, don't go home. Check into the hotel for the night even if you're a local. Why not! Live a little! Get out of the house! Send the kids to grandmas and enjoy a complete night out in one totally awesome place (very romantic - your sweetie will love you for it)! Heck, all inclusive is all the rage anyway, and by doing it there you will be supporting a family run enterprise that's committed and passionate about what they do and why they're doing it.

Enjoy!

Café on the Park

BELLEFONTE, CENTRE COUNTY

What a charming addition to an already charming town.

Bellefonte is not only the most architecturally beautiful town in Centre County but the history, culture, natural amenities, street layout, topography and now a place of renaissance – make it a favorite destination for me and my friends. Two of my closest friends are Topher and Anne Yorks. When I told them about my book they were quick to give me one of their very favorite places and wouldn't you know it, it was Café on the Park. I sat down with them and got their story on this great little eatery in historic Bellefonte.

Anne said that one thing they love to do is go there with a deck of cards, order dinner and just hang out together. They would also pack a bottle of their favorite wine because Café on the Park is BYOB! Topher is somewhat of a fellow foodie and his take on the cooking at CP is "very good." He told me that they also love to go there for breakfast and lunch too and that the French toast is his favorite. "They

---

JUST A TASTE

Name of establishment:
Café on the Park

Contact Info:
325 West High Street
Bellefonte, PA 16823
kim@cafeonthepark.net
phone: 814-357-8442
fax: 814-357-8440
web: www.cafeonthepark.net

Owned by:
Kim Kowalczyk

Hours:
Monday, closed; Tuesday-Saturday, 7:00 am-3:00 pm; Sunday, 9:00 am-3:00 pm..

Price range:
$1-$20

Cuisine/Specialty:
American Homestyle

Offers vegetarian, heart healthy or organic selections:
Yes

Support local farmers:
Yes

Locally owned accommodations:
Garman Inn
116 E. High St.
Bellefonte, PA 16823

Phone: 814-353-8803
Fax: 814-353-8813
www.garmanoperahouse.com
questions@garmanoperahouse.com

Local attractions:
Historical sites
Fisherman's Paradise
Bellefonte Museum
Centre County Historical Library
American Philatelic

use good bread, thick and fresh. It's got a great taste and almost melts in your mouth." He also talked about sitting outside and how much it reminded him of a café in Europe. However one other thing he said about CP that was rather profound was, "they're aware of where they are." I asked what he meant and he had a great explanation.

You see, there's a reason it's called Café on the Park. Talleyrand Park is right across the street and is a wonderful place to take your lunch or dinner. Toph said that CP makes some really nice Wraps that are perfect to eat while you stroll through the park. He said that having "portable" menu offerings which can be enjoyed while walking says that CP thought that through so that you can enjoy their food and enjoy the park at the same time.

Talleyrand is along the famous Spring Creek and is a spot for concerts in the warmer months. It also has plenty of grass space and benches for picnicking with nice walking paths and a suspension bridge over the stream. But what I think is really special about this park is that it's the home base for the Bellefonte Historic Railroad. The old station built in the mid 19th century still stands and has been lovingly restored as the station house, museum and chamber of commerce. The train still runs for tourists and offers many different themed excursions including a dinner cruise.

The small building that houses Café on the Park was originally Boscano's Store which served the town for over 100 years. Kim Kowalczyk the owner and operator of CP bought the building and transformed it but left cool key elements still in tact. The soda fountain bar, bar stools and beautiful hardwood floors are just as they were when town's people would drop in everyday for their newspaper, staples, ice cream, coffee, and sundries. Now in the 21st century, it's all about good eats and a dream come true.

Kim had a very good position with the American Philatelic Society but always dreamed of having a little restaurant. When she had the opportunity to retire early, she couldn't wait to start cooking. She talked her husband into joining her and now the two of them are living her dream. They have created a sweet café and are committed to the reality of life as restaurateurs. Her cozy space, great food, historic setting, pleasant surroundings and gracious welcome are all evidence of Kim's true calling. Thank goodness for retirement!

My friends and I love Bellefonte. We love the beautiful buildings, old world charm, the hills and back streets, parks, stream, and now a host of eateries – not the least of which is Café on the Park. Whether you're like the Toph and Anne and go for a dinner and a game of cards, lunch and a stroll in the park or just a relaxed wake-up breakfast, you'll find a place that's welcoming, comfortable and serves good food at an affordable price – a dream come true for all of us.

Enjoy!

1 O'CLOCK
CHAPTER 1

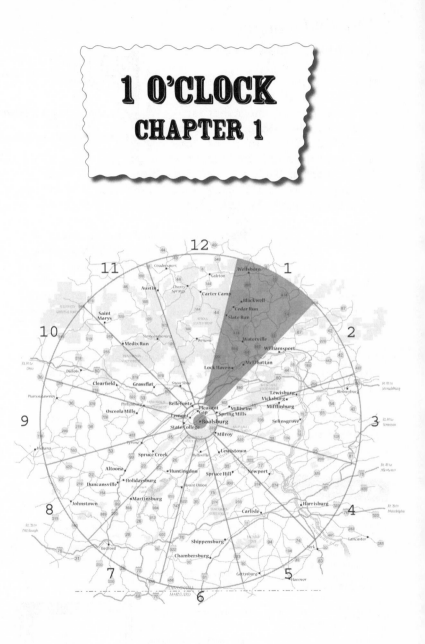

The Old Corner

LOCK HEAVEN, CLINTON COUNTY

This is my pick for the smallest pub in central Pennsylvania, but it's one of the sweetest ones too. The Old Corner which is tucked neatly into the former Beck's Hotel, reminds me of a pub that one might find in Boston back in the early days of that city's history. There, small pubs were tucked into the corner of old buildings in just about every neighborhood.

According to local historian and Old Corner bartender Jennifer Charney, "The Beck's Hotel offered accommodations and the staff served food and provided fine wines and beer in the lounge area, which is recognized presently as the bar." She also wrote the following history for a school paper and graciously allowed me to use it here. Thanks Jennifer!

"The hotel was built in 1877 and ownership has passed through many hands for a price anyone could afford. The original owner, Michael Beck, sold the building to his brother-in-law, James Martin, for $1. Beck offered this affordable price in hopes of solidifying family ties to the hotel business. Martin accepted

JUST A TASTE

Name of establishment:
The Old Corner Grill

Contact Info:
205 N. Grove St.
Lock Haven, PA 17745
570-748-4124
donnie@theoldcorner.com
www.theoldcorner.com

Owned by:
Don M. Powers (Donnie)

Hours:
11am to 2am, 7 days per week.
Kitchen until midnight

Price range:
Inexpensive

Cuisine / Specialty:
American pub style

Offers vegetarian, heart healthy or organic selections:
Yes

Support local farmers
Yes

Locally owned accommodations:
Carriage House B&B
570-748-5799

Local attractions:
Rails-to-Trails
Foliage season
Lock Haven Historic
The Heisey Museum

the deal without hesitation, but didn't have much success. He decided to sell the hotel for the same price that he paid. This time, Philip Vanucci took over, but it wasn't until 1961 when Joseph and Angeline Leone purchased the building from Vanucci that things began to look up.

Tim Leone, son of Joseph and Angeline, inherited the bar in 1986. From 1971-1994, there was only one section to the building still in operation – the bar area. In 1994 renovations were completed on the additional section that included a bottle shop unit connected to the bar. In 1996, Don "Donnie" Powers purchased The Old Corner on October 1 from Tim Leone. As a former employee during his college days, Powers came back to claim a part of his past, and he made it better than he ever could have imagined."

From the moment I first walked up to East Main Street and North Grove Street in Lock Haven, The Old Corner just seemed right to me. Being a 129 year old building, it's hard not to have a cool façade, and the architecture back then was as much about art as function. Some enter from the back door on Grove Street, but I prefer the main corner entrance. Like I said, this is a classic. Old handcrafted woodwork, antique etched glass and a vintage pub door (that I would pay dearly to have) combine to set the mood for what's inside.

Upon entering, the beautifully crafted bar embraces you – literally! Remember, this is a small pub. I met a young woman recently who said that The Old Corner was like having a pub in her hallway. And like most neighborhood pubs, those seated at the bar turn and look at you as you walk in. Not to be nosy, but to see if a friend has arrived. The Old Corner has also been compared by many to that now famous TV bar where "everybody knows your name."

High tables and a narrow wall counter provide a place for people to sit, and I'm sure on any given weekend night it's packed. Cool memorabilia adorns the walls, but that's about it, except for the bottle shop adjacent to the pub. No dining room, no deck, no froo froo lounge - nowhere to go except where you are.

The back-bar at TOC is beautiful! With its fine, hand-carved wood and beveled mirror along with the equally beautiful bar itself, it's a great backdrop and foundation to proudly display an impressive lineup of draught beers. Tröegs from Harrisburg, Stoudt's from Adamstown, Sierra Nevada, Anchor Steam and Otto's from State College are just a few of the offerings. If you like craft-brewed beers while in a well-crafted pub, this is one place you should definitely check out. One other thing you'll notice is that the bartenders all wear white shirts and ties - even the women. I love this. It's one more throw-back to a bygone era that fits perfectly with the vintage design and the nostalgic atmosphere of the pub.

The food there is great too! They have a full menu filled with items ranging from soups and starters to burgers, sandwiches, subs and wraps. Plus, they offer plenty of sides, and claim to have "the best wings and ribs in Clinton County and central PA." Quite a claim!

The Old Corner is a classic neighborhood pub with a classic neighborhood vibe. It's little in size but big in spirit. The patrons as well as the staff are friendly and will most certainly turn and look at you when you walk in. But don't worry - after you've been back a few times everybody will know your name and you'll have some great new friends.

Cheers!

Restless Oaks
MCELHATTAN, CLINTON COUNTY

My friends and I have been coming to
Restless Oaks for a number of years
on our way to the Finger Lakes wineries
in New York State. It's always good to
start with a great breakfast before a
day of wine tasting. And since this
place is only a half hour or so from
home, but two hours from the lakes,
it worked out perfectly for us. By the
time we get to the first winery we have
a solid meal in our stomachs and are
ready to sample the fruit of the vine.

The Restless Oaks though is more than a great breakfast stop. It's a full-blown restaurant, museum and
art gallery with a gift store and book shop on the
side. The first clue to the Oaks' amazing multi-
personality is the chainsaw-sculptured tree trunks
inside and out. As a fine artist, I can, on occasion,
be a little full of myself and critical when it comes
to "art" that's associated with the genre of country
crafts, especially when a chainsaw is involved.

JUST A TASTE

Name of establishment:
Restless Oaks Restaurant

Contact Info:
119 Pine Mountain Road
570-769-7385

Owned by:
James and Shirley Maguire

Hours:
Monday–Thursday 6-8
Friday 6-9
Saturday 6-9
Sunday 7-8

Price range:
$3.00 - $23.00

Cuisine / Specialty:
Family Dining

**Offers vegetarian, heart healthy
or organic selections:**
No

Support local farmers:
No

Locally owned accommodations:

Local attractions:
Woolrich Outlet Store
Rails to Trails
Gateway to PA Wilds

I'll admit that sometimes I refer to country crafts as "country crap," but that moniker doesn't apply here. This is art and damn good art at that! Bears, wolves, eagles, raccoons and other wildlife are meticulously cut into huge logs and from massive tree trunks. They're all around the parking lot and the restaurant. The sculptor is an art teacher named Kraig Brady and he's from just down the road in Jersey Shore. Kraig's work is exquisite and it shames me for my uppity attitude. (Check out the "Cool Links" tab on my web site for Kraig's site)

As you approach the entrance to the restaurant, you walk through a long covered wooden walkway and porch. All along the walkway are stones of all sizes with sayings etched in them. There's also a huge set of Toledo Scales at the end of the walkway, and I like to weigh myself before and after breakfast – this would be a very handy item when dieting.

The restaurant is divided into two main parts – a coffee shop and a beautiful dining room. In the dinning room you'll find a high wood ceiling, an enormous wooden beam spanning the width of the ceiling and a huge fireplace. Taxidermy, photos, wood sculpture and artwork adorn the walls, and the sea of wooden tables can accommodate about 100 people. It's hard to talk about Restless Oaks without mentioning wood, but it's not only part of the architecture, art and décor, it's the life blood of the community as well as the owners.

The Maguire family has owned and operated this wonderful roadside restaurant since 1984. Originally from Clearfield PA, the family moved to McElhattan to pursue a logging business and open a saw shop where they planned to sell everything from chain saws to axes. They built a modest log cabin structure for the

shop but Jim Maguire and his son, Jim Jr., went
to a local auction and bought restaurant equipment
instead. Soon after, the Restless Oaks Restaurant
opened its cabin doors.

I had the pleasure of meeting Jim Jr. on a visit
one morning, and he invited me to ride along with
him in his diesel pick-up while he took care of some
things for the logging business. As we drove up into
the mountains behind the restaurant he told me all
about their place, their business practices and
philosophy. When I asked about the sculptures he
told me that instead of spending the entire advertis-
ing budget on ads, they use half of it to invest
in artwork. He said, "People might forget our name
five miles down the road but they may never forget
what they've seen here."

He went on to explain that his mission is "To meet,
greet and feed the folks. Make sure they have a good
time and good food at an honest price and a good
experience the whole time." He talked about his
staff and how he encourages them to greet everyone
as if they are the first customer of the day. "Even
after the 199th person through the door, treat
number 200 like the first. Remember, that even though
you've seen [customers] all day, that's the first
time they see you." I doubt the chain gang has the
philosophy that Jim Jr. has.

He then took me back to the Restless Oaks and gave
me the grand tour and even showed me around the gift
store and book shop where he proudly displays and
sells a series of books by local State College author
Jeffrey Frazier. Jeff writes and self-publishes the
amazingly popular series "Pennsylvania Fireside
Tales." He has even helped me in my pursuits as an
author and publisher even though I'm a potential
competitor (Cool Links member).

Back in the coffee shop, Jim Jr. handed me a menu
and told me about all of the Restless Oaks' offerings,

but on this day I was here for only one thing -
breakfast, and by now I was starving. So I thanked
him, and after we said our good-byes, I took a seat
and ordered up a big helping of eggs, bacon, home
fries, pancakes, coffee and juice. Mmm, mmm!

It was early spring and I was about to embark on a
three day trip up through what I like to call The
"Cinque Terre" of Pennsylvania. The Steed had already
gotten his high octane breakfast earlier but I
needed fuel for this epic journey and downed mine
like a champ. Now we were both ready to go and ride
up through the beautiful Pine Creek Gorge and "The
Five Lands of PA."

Stopping here at the Restless Oaks is always the
right call. The folks here are always happy to see
you, and if you're lucky enough to meet Jim Jr.,
you're in for a treat!

Enjoy!

The "Cinque Terre" of Pennsylvania
PA'S PINE CREEK GORGE AND GRAND CANYON.

A Culinary Quest and Epic Journey from Waterville to Wellsboro

Okay folks, here is where I dig deep into and elaborate on an earlier comment and true quandary – how do I promote a place or an area and encourage people to go there without ruining it in the process? This is a good question because of a real life experience I had in the real Cinque Terre – a beautiful section of the western Italian coast along the beautiful Mediterranean Sea (It's pronounced Ching-qwa tara in English and literally means "five lands" or more simply "five villages"). I discovered this awesome place during my first trip to Italy.

Here, perched above water that's every shade of blue and green imaginable, are five late medieval villages which line the rocky coast just up from Tuscany. All hang precariously on the cliff's edge and are breathtaking upon any approach, especially by sea.

Growing up in central Pennsylvania, I had never seen anything like this or even imagined such a place. It was, and still is, one of the most beautiful places I have ever seen. I fell in loved with one village in particular that was seemingly untouched by tourism. She was cozy and peaceful, caressing my heart with a gentle pace of life and feeling of serenity that one only dreams of. But this wasn't a dream, it was for real and I soaked it in like the rays of the sun that bathed the pink, yellow and burnt sienna dwellings surrounding me. Sadly though, all those lovely attributes where to be stolen away by a travel writer. And my sweet "untouched" village would be no more.

As I strolled through the village for the first time, I felt like I was the first westerner to walk her cobblestone streets and passage ways. There were no souvenir shops here – only the basic little shops for the everyday supplies of life and one small restaurant. A couple of French and German tourists were milling about but they hardly spoke above a whisper because even the soles of our shoes seemed loud and disruptive. Women dressed in traditional clothes sat outside their doors chatting or sewing while little cats tiptoed around in search of a handout.

At one point sometime after noon, the silence was broken only by a woman singing an aria as she was preparing lunch. I caught the rich smell of spices as my vision was filled by scenes of painted doorways and opened windows lined with potted flowers. In fact, I was so moved by this that it inspired an entire collection of paintings portraying these wonderfully picturesque and peaceful Italian hill towns that time had forgotten.

About a year after I returned home, I happened to see a TV travel program in which the host was about to take his audience on a tour of the Cinque Terre. My first reaction was "Darn it, there goes the neighborhood!" and he went right to the place I just spoke about. He too found it quiet, peaceful and undisturbed like it was 400 years ago. He went on and on about its beauty and the fact that few tourists go there and how if you really want to see Italy like she was in medieval times...

Well, I had the opportunity to return to my beloved town in October of 2003. The first indication that something was up, was the five HUGE tour buses parked at the bottom of the village (On my original visit, my little Mini Cooper was the only car, apart from a camper van and some Vespa scooters). Then, before I had even made it into the piazza (town square), I heard the din of people's voices and they were far from whispers. I instantly recognized it as my own language and my heart began to sink into my stomach. I turned the corner to see a hoard of Americans rushing around with their cameras and yelling to each other to come and see this or that. I also saw clutched in their hands, the TV host's guide book.

I made my way through the hoard and proceeded down a tiny street that I had dreamed about since my first visit. All around me were shops selling crap that only Americans would buy. Then, in the middle of the street two tired and bored kids were starting to act up. When their mom finally came over, she took a hold of them and reamed them out. Then they burst into tears and screamed like banshees.

But, the final blow came when a middle aged woman with a fake tan, way too much make-up and holding a polka dot umbrella above her head yelled into a Mr. Microphone, "Alright people! If you want Gelato before the bus leaves you better get it now because we have four more towns to hit before dinner!"

I sat down on a 14th century stone wall, hung my head and tears welled up in my eyes. My beloved village was gone. This was not my sweet innocent love of the past, of whom I dreamed about day after day until now. She was no more – ruined by an overzealous travel writer and TV host. I got up and walked away. Heavy hearted and crushed, I walked back to my car and drove away. To this day I still dream of this village, as she was, as she was when we first met and fell in love. (Even as I've read this piece over again I'm still moved to tears)

Hopefully now you understand my quandary. I want you to experience all that I have written about and support these wonderful places I'm writing about, but without ruining them in the process. Please folks, consider each place you visit as if it was a monastery or holy place. Because in a way, that is what each is. We are blessed by these gifts and they are blessed by us in return, due to our care and support. But, like any love – respect, sensitivity, gentleness and true selflessness are the keys to a lasting relationship.

Most of the places I'm recommending throughout this book are casual but love a vibrant crowd. A few are more intimate and peaceful, and support a more easygoing following. And still others can be a combination of both. But all of these next places are in an environment that is pristine and beautiful much like my Italian village once was. So if I hear about someone leading an obnoxious tour group or hoards are invading these places without care or consideration, I will gather up and burn every last copy of this book!

Please show respect and courtesy wherever you go. Be polite and humble. Walk and speak softly. Don't be demanding or rude, or travel in hoards. And never ever go with a "tour guide" carrying an umbrella and shouting into a personal boom box. God help us.

Thank you! Now let's continue as I set out on a three day culinary quest and epic journey from Waterville to Wellsboro.

It's so easy to blast right past the exit to this sweet winding route that leads you up through the beautiful Pine Creek Gorge into the Grand Canyon and the Cinque Terra of PA. One of the main routes to get to this beginning is 220, a four-lane highway running east to west and a main thoroughfare for cars and trucks traveling across the state. Fortunately there are no huge flashing signs along 220 telling travelers where to turn on to this beautiful road, only a normal exit sign.

Spotting it, I leaned The Mighty Steed into the exit and crossed over from highway to a rural byway. Rt. 44 and her little sister 414 are comparable to some of the roads I've navigated in the mountain regions of Europe (*I will touch more on that a bit later*). For now though, as she (Rt. 44) rises out of the river valley north of Jersey Shore, she's straighter, flatter, less curvy and not as wild and dangerous as little sister a few miles ahead.

The day was brilliant, the air chilly and The Steed was running like the wild mustang he is. As I poked him with a spur of throttle, he reared up and the two of us flew like the wind. The great northern Appalachian range was rising in front of us and with every long sweeping curve they drew nearer and began their caress. This was a special moment and special place indeed. With every mile that passed, I could feel the stresses of life slowly peel away, swirl and get lost in the jet steam of a boy and his bike.

Running parallel to us along the road and almost unnoticed at first was a track of gravel that was clearly an old railroad bed. But this was so pristine and well kept that it could only be one thing – a Rails to Trails path. There I saw a young family pedaling their bicycles along the trail heading north like me. I waved and so did they. The little girl on her pink bike smiled at me and gave that enthusiastic kid wave that just makes all things good. Then on up, I saw two young women pedaling up the grade and looking a little tired. I was tempted to stop but had no room with all my gear on board. Oh well, I just gave them a casual wave and kept going. Plus, unbeknownst to me at the time, a metro-hippy, free spirited artist and golden haired beauty was waiting for us at the end of the journey.

As I cruised further towards the gorge the wide valley began narrow and the mountains began to cozy up even more. I passed by a wide, slow section of the creek and the exposed rocky mountainside on my right had a mini cascade of pure water falling down its face. I had to pull the reins back on the bike and turn him around because I never miss a chance to drink the real thing. There I was, in the front hall of the mountain king – warm sunshine, a crystal clear blue sky above, the mighty Pine Creek below me and gushing fresh spring water falling from the cliffs. Awesome!

I had my fill of water, snapped some pix, checked my map and proceeded north. My five towns and five places to eat, drink and soak in this part of paradise was ahead and the anticipation was high. So with a twist of throttle and a big breath of cold mountain air in his lungs, The Mighty Steed and I made haste to our first stop on this Cinque Terra of PA, the village of Waterville and the Waterville Hotel.

The Waterville Hotel Mountain Cookery and Saloon

WATERVILLE, LYCOMING COUNTY

The Waterville Hotel was built in 1825 to provide lodging, food and drink to lumberjacks and mill workers. Call me old-school, but I just love the architecture, the feel and the vibe of a place that's not pristine and totally preserved. I love peeling paint, weathered wood, rusty or patina metal, wavy glass in multi pane windows and weathered hand-painted signs. The Waterville has all of these attributes but it's not rundown by any means. It's a well-kept antique, with all its character and history intact.

There's a marquee out front that's perpendicular to the hotel and an old illuminated sign hanging from the siding of the second floor that reads "Waterville Hotel Mountain Cookery & Saloon." Across the fascia board of the front porch is another sign, and it was there that I stood mesmerized by five simple words carved out of wood and painted white against a black backdrop – "Home of the Mountain Burger."

JUST A TASTE

Name of establishment:
Waterville Hotel Mountain
Cookery and Saloon

Contact Info:
P.O. Box 57
10783 Hwy. N. Rt. 44
Waterville, PA 17776
570-753-8231

Owned by:
J.R. Bausinger

Hours:
Mon, Wed, Thurs: 11–8
Closed Tuesday
Fri, Sat, Sun: 8–8
Breakfast Fri, Sat, Sun, 8–11

Price range:
$3.25 - $13.25

Cuisine / Specialty:
Hillbilly Cuisine

Offers vegetarian, heart healthy or organic selections:
Yes

Support local farmers:
Yes

Locally owned accommodations:
La Belle Auberge
129 Main St. Wellsboro PA 16901
570-724-3288
www.nellesinns.com

Bear Mountain Lodge
8010 Route 6 | PO Box 216 |
Wellsboro PA 16901
570-724-2428
www.bearmountainbb.com

Local attractions:
Golden Eagle Trail
Pine Creek Rail Trail
Little Pine State Park
PA Grand Canyon
Mid State Trail
Black Forest Trail
Canoeing, Fishing, Hunting
Nesting Bald Eagles

When I regained my senses I walked in to find the bartender giving me the stink-eye! What did I expect? My hair was standing straight up from the wind, I probably had dead bugs on my face (if not in my teeth) and I was toting my black shoulder bag for my computer and stuff. When I say stuff, I mean STUFF! It's like a small office in there! I even carry a snack, water, flashlight, Swiss Army Knife, camera and corkscrew along with a myriad of other "essential" items.

Well, the guy behind the bar must have thought I was a rogue salesman or something because I had to do some pretty fast talking to keep him from grabbing his 12 gauge out from under the bar (actually, he did tell me later that he thought I was a salesman). Turns out though that the guy happened to be the owner and his name is Jan Bausinger and he's a no-frills kind of guy. For example, when I asked what prompted him to go smoke-free at his saloon after 30 years behind the bar, he quickly replied, "My lungs!" He offered no dissertation on health vs. profit or a debate about making all food and drink establish-ments smoke-free. Just, "My lungs!" End of story.

I admit, I had to really bump up the charm and char-isma with Jan. And, if I had any hopes of not getting a good-old-fashioned-country-ass-kicking, I dared not let him see my Clinton '08 button pinned to my shoulder bag. I put the bag at my feet and covered it with my jacket keeping it out of sight.

As I sat at the bar, I contemplated the Mountain Burger. Hmm, was it mountainous? Was it designed to satisfy the appetite of a mountain man? Or, is it simply and aptly named for the topography here at the gateway of the Pennsylvania Grand Canyon? Well, I was about to find out. Jan gave me a menu of his saloon fare and I was impressed. It was quite extensive and everything looked good. Folks all around me were smiling, talking and eating with enthusiasm, so I had no doubt that I too, would be satisfied with my meal.

I half-heartedly perused the menu but the Mountain Burger was what this spiky-haired, liberal flat-lander came in for, and by gosh that's what he was going to get! I dropped the menu and ordered. Asking if the burger came with fries, Jan told me that it did, adding that I had a choice of "German fries" or "Freedom fries". I checked to see if my Clinton button was still concealed and opted with the German fries. Jan then asked me if I wanted coleslaw or applesauce. After learning that the slaw was homemade, I went with that.

As I waited, I took my ultra-mini camera from my shoulder bag and walked around to photograph some of the more interesting things on the wall. When I say "things on the wall" I mean lots of things. Seriously, the walls were covered to the point that hardly any of the wood paneling was visible. There were signs, posters, memorabilia, taxidermy, license plates, bumper stickers and an awesome poster of a Bud girl in ripped jeans and a cowboy hat (lip biting moment).

I got some good photos as well as some dubious looks from the other patrons (just so you know, I traveled incognito to all the places I've written about).
Because, when a "flat-lander" conspicuously mills about in a saloon where they proudly display a sign that reads "My president is Charlton Heston," one no longer has any hopes of incog-anything. Especially a metro-sexual artist wielding an ultra-mini camera and wearing Corona flip-flops (which by the way, was a huge faux-pas since Jan hates Corona and made no bones about saying so)!

I returned to my place at the bar just in time for my Mountain Burger to arrive. It was big, hot and beautiful. The three questions I had pondered earlier were all answered with a resounding "Yes!" It was indeed mountainous, it could easily satisfy a hungry mountain man and it had plenty of everything - meat, fixins', fries and coleslaw. In fact, the

coleslaw was a meal in itself. I couldn't eat it
all. I did however finish the burger and loved every
bite. The beef was fresh and cooked to perfection as
were the fresh-cut fries. The only downside for me
was the beer selection. Jan didn't stock any craft
brews, so I settled for...I can't say.

Jan and I chatted about everything from politics
(no, I didn't tell him) to business and life in
general. He turned out to be a great guy, and very
funny. After paying my bill, I finally told him about
my real reason for being there and he was encouraging about the project. In fact, he was one of the
first people to return my questionnaire for the "Just
a Taste" section at the beginning of every piece.
I finished my beer, packed up my gear, bid everybody
goodbye and walked back out into the sharp sunlight
and the (now) warm spring air. With my sights now
fixed on Slate Run and a cool place that I discovered
while researching via the web, I pointed The Mighty
Steed north and shot the gorge once again.

With the taste of the Mountain Burger and German
fries still lingering on my palate, I just had to
smile. The Waterville Hotel Mountain Cookery and
Saloon is definitely old-school, quirky and conservative. But, there's nothing quirky or conservative
about what Jan has to offer – a great place, great
service, comfort, quality, fun, damn good food and
lots of it! I can't wait to return.

Enjoy!

Hotel Manor
SLATE RUN, LYCOMING COUNTY

After leaving Waterville, I admit
I was not thinking too much about
my next meal. So as The Steed and
I rolled north up Rt. 44 my hunger
was far from impending. No problamo, because the
ride up this next section is sweet and wide open,
and running at a good clip always burns calories.
Plus, I had made plans anyway for a hike so I knew
that by evening I would be ready for the next stop
on this culinary odyssey.

Hiking in Pennsylvania is great, but here in Pine
Creek Gorge at the gateway to the Pennsylvania Grand
Canyon it's amazing! I pulled into a Rails-to-Trails
parking lot and got some hiking gear together. Equipped
with water and some survival essentials, I headed
across an abandoned railroad bridge and up the side
of a forbidding mountain.

The smells of the forest hit me right away and were
of moss, wet earth and most notably, ferns. I took
a deep breath and started the steep ascent. Walking
through the towering hardwoods that stood like
sentinels all around me I felt small and insignificant.

JUST A TASTE

Name of establishment:
Hotel Manor

Contact Info:
392 Slate Run Rd.
Slate Run, PA 17769
570-753-8414
www.hotel-manor.com
htlmanor@kcnet.org

Owned by:
Mark Kauffman

Hours:
Monday – Thursday Noon to 9:30pm.
Friday – Noon to 11:30pm
Saturday 11am to 11:30pm
Sun 8am to 8pm

Price range:
$3.00 to $25.00

Cuisine/Specialty:
American

**Offers vegetarian, heart healthy
or organic selections:**
No

Support local farmers:
Yes

Locally owned accommodations:
Their own place!
10 rooms on location

Local attractions:
Fishing
Pine Creek Rails to Trails
PA Wilds
Hiking trails
Peace and Tranquility

I struggled with each step due to the angle of the mountainside, but when I reached the ridge, I felt as though I had reached the top of the world. I took time to give thanks for this awesome day and sought protection for my journey ahead. When I saw a nice spot I went for a nap, I stretched out beneath a canopy of leaves and I think I fell asleep before my head hit the moss.

I awoke to two squirrels chasing each other around the tree trunk next to me. I looked up at the position of the sun and realized that I had slept for awhile and felt refreshed and good to go. Up there and in the rays of the afternoon sun, the smells were of dried leaves and pine needles and I fell into a daydream. But, it was time to return to the road far below and head for Slate Run and the Hotel Manor.

When I reached the bike the rumbles of hunger were starting. With just a few miles to go, I fired up the Sportster and the blast of his pipes echoed through the gorge. We cruised up the next section of road, which got narrower and with huge drop-offs to the left and loose rock cliffs to the right, there was no room for error. I reached the turnoff to Slate Run, passed Wolfe's General Store and Fly Shop and crossed the bridge.

A grand structure of wood and glass, with a design somewhere between Swiss chalet and classic A-frame, awaited me on the other side. The building rose from its surroundings like a sculpture amidst the gallery of nature. Huge glass windows reflected the lines of the steep angled roof, as well as the immense deck and sparkling creek in the foreground. On the deck were market umbrellas and I could see tables and chairs underneath and most of them were filled with folks enjoying dinner. Slate Run has a population of 174 (including wildlife), so as I pulled into the parking lot of the grand and beautiful Hotel Manor, I figured they were all there that night.

If the outside wasn't amazing enough, the inside just blew me away. At this point, it was clear that everything I was seeing here was new and absolutely beautiful! Since they were so busy, I just walked up to the bar to get something to wash down the dust of the road. I braced myself for the usual rural offerings of only big-batch, small-taste beers, but what I saw almost brought a tear to my eye. It was a sign that read "Tröegs - Proudly Served at the Hotel Manor."

Was I still in my daydream? Or, had I unknowingly passed through a wormhole and came out in a parallel universe where men and women realize the beauty of going local. But maybe I had simply come across a new breed of restaurateur? Well, according to the scientific principle Acoms Razor; the simplest solution tends to be the correct one. So I asked for a cold bottle of Tröegs Rugged Trail and made for the big Adirondack chairs on the porch.

As I sat there enjoying my beer and writing of the days events in my sketchbook, a very classy car pulled up in front of the hotel and an older gentleman got out and made his way to the door. As he approached we looked at each other (as folks tend to do) and I flicked my head up and said "hi." Without hesitation he said, "I know you. You're Ken Hull the artist." I asked how he could have possibly known that. He replied, "I love your work and own several pieces." He introduced himself as Phil Zimmerman, ordered a glass of wine and sat down beside me.

What a cool Guy! It turns out that Phil knew much about this area, even though he was also from State College. He had a cabin farther upstream and was the oracle of enlightenment concerning the place we were at. It seems the reason everything looked so new was because the original old place burnt to the ground a few years back. If that wasn't sad enough, it happened shortly after it was purchased by a young couple from Jersey Shore.

Phil told me how Mark Kauffman and his family took the devastation and used it as inspiration to re-build a bigger and better place. I guess Phil must be some sort of celebrity, or at least a well-liked customer, because owner and Chef Mark Kauffman came out in the middle of the dinner rush to greet him. Phil introduced me to Mark and I saw a rare opportunity. I broke protocol and told Mark about the book. He generously gave me a few moments of his time and I pummeled him with questions. He stayed and talked with me and Phil longer than he should have, and his hostess came out to remind him how busy it was. He returned to his kitchen and we finished our drinks.

Once Phil heard of my journey and that I was camping out that night he offered to buy me dinner. We sat outside under a giant tree that came up through the floor of the deck. Phil ordered the special that night which was Filet Mignon wrapped in bacon and drizzled with a fiddlehead fern and cranberry reduction sauce, accompanied by twice mashed sweet potatoes which were lightly topped with garlic butter. His vegetable was asparagus drizzled with olive oil and finished with shaved Parmesan. I ordered a small pizza.

We enjoyed our meals and chatted for an hour or so before Mark appeared again, this time bearing dessert. He sat with us while sipping coffee and told me more about his place. He is as passionate as they come and lives to serve connoisseurs, fisherman, locals and travelers like me. His place is smoke-free and he uses local produce whenever he can. The Hotel Manor is also a licensed, certified Angus Beef restaurant and Mark said he's open to accommodate all dietary needs.

And if the spacious dining room, the fly-fishing in-spired bar, and the huge deck overlooking Pine Creek weren't enough, the Hotel Manor is also, as its name implies, a hotel. Breakfast is included with your stay and I was tempted to check in for the night. However, I had my heart set on sleeping under the stars. So with the daylight beginning to wane, I thanked Mr. Zimmerman for all his generosity and taking the time to hang out with me. I also thanked Mark for his hospitality (and dessert).

My two new friends watched as I mounted The Steed, fired him up and rumbled back across the bridge. Yes, Acoms Razor proved right. This was no wormhole. It's simply the new breed of restaurant owner who is passionate about his work, who supports local suppliers and businesses, and who has the determination to do something fresh and beautiful even while covered in ashes. And like the mighty Phoenix, Mark and his family rose to the occasion.

Enjoy!

Oh, by the way, as I crossed the bridge to leave, a man was sweeping the winter cinders from the side of the road. I stopped to say "hi" and learned of a wonderful layer to an already wonderful story. It seems Mark was also a modest man. This guy told me that a few days after the fire, when Mark and his family lost everything, the folks of Slate Run and those up and down the gorge as well, got together and had a weekend-long party to raise money for them. By Sunday night the community had raised $40,000 dollars for the young couple and their two children.

I slept well that night.

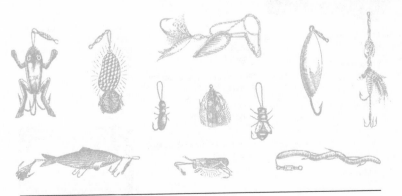

Cedar Run Inn & General Store
CEDAR RUN, LYCOMING COUNTY

Sisters of the Canyon

Sleeping under the stars was one of
those simple pleasures in life that
I'd forgotten about, but the previous
night was a reminder of how truly
wonderful our night sky can be - no
awful high pressure sodium lights to compete
with the gentle white light of distant suns. I wasn't
in a tent either, just a pad, sleeping bag and down
pillow. However, sleeping on the hard ground also
reminded me that my body is no longer eight years
old. It was worth every ache though, and after a
morning walk along the Rails-to-Trails path, the
pain was gone and I was ready to ride.

What lay ahead was a place that I had visited years
ago with "the hot girl who introduced me to snails."
I remembered an awesome restaurant tucked away off
the main road in a charming village called Cedar Run.
We had gone there for dinner one night on the spur
of the moment after hearing about it from a friend
and we just jumped in the car and set out to find it.

JUST A TASTE

Name of establishment:
Cedar Run General Store

Contact Info:
284 Beulahland Road - 570-353-2740 - ddodd@cub.kcnet.org

Owned by:
Don & Sue Dodd

Hours:
Seasonal: April through October
Wednesday–Sunday

Price range:
1 cent to $7.95

Cuisine / Specialty:
Hand dipped ice dream &
Sandwiches

**Offers vegetarian, heart healthy
or organic selections:**
Yes

Support local farmers:
Yes

Locally owned accommodations:
Cedar Run Inn

Local attractions:
Pine Creek
Rails to Trails
PA Wilds - Hiking Trails

I remembered from that trip that its location was remote, but I was confident that I could find it again. With my trusty Gazetteer map tucked in the saddlebag, I rolled back on the throttle and away we went. Phil from the Hotel Manor said to be on my guard because the turnoff to Cedar Run comes up quickly. I took his warning, but the twists and turns of the road and the scenery around it were so mesmerizing that I missed the turnoff anyway by a few hundred feet. I looked down from the high road above the creek and saw though the trees, a tiny cluster of buildings. I turned the bike around in the middle of the very narrow road and then had to make a wicked sharp left down a little paved road and into Cedar Run.

As we rolled slowly over the bridge across Pine Creek it was as if I once again traveled through time. I was no longer in the 21st century or in central PA. I was now in a tiny hamlet somewhere in New England 100 years ago. I slipped into another daydream as I rode over the bridge and into the little canyon village.

I arrived two days prior to the start of trout season, and around these parts not much happens before then.

JUST A TASTE

Name of establishment:
Cedar Run Inn

Contact Info:
281 Beulah Land Road
Cedar Run, PA 17727
570.353.6241
cedarruninn.com

Owned by:
Stan & Charlotte Dudkin

Hours:
5:30 to 8:30

Price range:
$17 to $25

Cuisine/Specialty:
Creative

Offers vegetarian, heart healthy or organic selections:
Yes

Support local farmers:

Locally owned accommodations:
Cedar Run Inn

Local attractions:
Rails to Trails - 58 miles of biking or hiking right next to the Inn. Canoeing, rafting, kayaking available in season on Pine Creek.

The town appeared to be deserted as I parked in front of the Cedar Run Inn and Restaurant. The only activity I noticed was a woman and a young girl across the street, working in a garden behind a white fence and next to the beautiful old general store. The lights were on inside and anxious to have a look, I began to walk toward the store. But the woman, apparently the owner, told me that she was closed and wouldn't be open until the next day. She was clearly in last-minute spring gardening mode and she and her young assistant were both beading with sweat.

I told her I was just out exploring and was thrilled to have "discovered" her village. When I expressed disappointment that the store was closed, she said, "Go on in and look around anyway. I'll be in soon." I thanked her and walked up the steps, through the door and into a bygone era. Though the merchandise was modern, the setting was anything but. High ceilings, handcrafted wood trim, large windows and antique lighting. There was even a faux soda fountain in the back that added to the charm of a store that, as I was to learn later, had served many a lumberman since 1895.

The woman from the garden soon joined me and introduced herself as Sue Dodd. She showed me around and talked passionately about her store. She came to Cedar Run 14 years earlier from Lake Ontario after her husband convinced her to move to this paradise in the mountains of northern Lycoming County. He had been coming there for 30 years, hunting and fishing his way up and down the canyon.

There were less than 15 people living in Cedar Run when the Dodd finally moved there, so right away Sue met Charlotte Dudkin who, along with her husband Stan, owned the Inn across the street. Charlotte told Sue that the old general store was for sale and that she should take it over. Sue acted on the opportunity and is now the shopkeeper, sandwich maker, ice cream scooper and soda jerk for the thousands of tourists, campers, sportsmen and river rats that come there between mid-April and New Year's Day. (Yeah, I said soda jerk, because there's nothing faux about that soda fountain in the back.)The ice cream Sue serves is a brand named Perry's, which she claimed is "the best!" She offers a nice selection of sandwiches for lunch only, and when I asked why she limited herself to just sandwiches and soda fountain fare, she said "It's easy to keep, prepare and there's little to no waste. And when you serve ice cream, everyone leaves with a smile on their face."

With the Inn closed, and not being sure when I'd make it back to meet Charlotte and see her place, I decided to reveal myself to Sue and told her about my book project. She instructed me to follow her and then led me across the little street to the Cedar Run Inn. We entered and Sue immediately called out to Charlotte but there was no answer. She told me to look around while she tried to find her.

As I perused the grand dining room I was taken aback by the simple elegance of it all. It was like I was in a lovingly preserved house of a rich grandmother. The tables were set with linen, china, silverware and beautiful antiques filled the spaces between. There were great old windows that were wide open allowing sunlight to flood the room. Before long, Sue returned with Charlotte and like the perfect hostess she is, Charlotte offered Sue and me a cold drink and seated us at a big round table with fresh daffodils in the middle. We sat and talked as though we were old friends and the two ladies told me about their businesses, life philosophies and what it's like in a place that they called a "best kept secret."

It seems that life there is a simple one during the four months of the offseason, but when the season hits, it hits big! Sue told me that every year right before fishing season, she and Charlotte get together for cocktails and say their good-byes. I asked why "good-bye" and they said that once the fishing season

begins they never see each other except to wave across
the street when they get a break. But in winter they
always have things to do and random people still
stop by. When spring comes and the Mountain Laurel
blooms and the sun hits their little slice of heaven,
the cold and dark of winter is gone and forgotten and
life begins as friends, old and new, arrive again.
For Charlotte this is especially true.

The Inn has provided country hospitality since 1891,
and back then the guests arrived by a train that ran
the whole way up and down the canyon during the great
lumbering boom of the 1800s'. Now as then, the Inn
is a lovely place for food and lodging along the old
railroad line that spans 82 miles. The tracks are long
gone and the bed has now become a Rails-to-Trails
path of smooth, hard-packed gravel.

The Cedar Run Inn restaurant serves an amazing menu
with offerings like chicken Frangelico served with
Cabernet Sauvignon and a praline parfait. They also
offer a generous complement of wine and spirits to
guests only, but if you are there for just an afternoon, Charlotte will be happy to fix you a drink that
you can enjoy out on the porch. The Inn is not only
about food, it's a wonderful place to spend the
night. The Inn provides full accommodations and
breakfast for their overnight guests. They have 13
rooms - four have full bathrooms, four have half-
baths and the rest share two master baths.

Overnighters are allowed to BYOB in their rooms but
not at dinner. However, and I love this part, if Sue

is still open across the street at the General Store and you want Perry's ice cream for dessert, Charlotte doesn't mind at all if you walk over, get some and bring it back to your table or sit on the porch to enjoy it!

These two women exemplify how a community should work together for the greater good. Charlotte does breakfast and dinner - Sue does lunch, soda fountain stuff and ice cream. They are friends, neighbors and business women sharing the wealth and sharing la vie. They're like the sisters of the canyon.

So now imagine hiking, bicycling, floating, driving or motorcycling down the Grand Canyon of Pennsylvania, stopping at an old General Store for lunch and/or an ice cream cone. Then when you realize you're in paradise, you stay for dinner at the Inn. After enjoying an after-dinner drink on the porch, you spend the night and wake up to the sounds of singing birds. While at breakfast in the sunlit dining room, hummingbirds come right up to your window to have their breakfast. After coffee on the porch, you gather your things and set off again down the trail, all the while thinking you should turn around and go back.

Despite their frantic fix-up mode (and technically being closed), the two "sisters" insisted on fixing me lunch. Charlotte happened to have soup made for the coming weekend and Sue made me a sandwich. Both were delicious! As I was about to leave to continue the next leg of my epic ride, Charlotte's daughter came running out from the general store with a big ol' cone of Perry's ice cream. I thanked her and turned back to thank both Sue and Charlotte, who were there to see me off. Sue must have the gift of clairvoyance, because as I was leaving that "best kept secret" she left me with an awesome bit of wisdom. She said, "This is the place to come and heal your soul." As it turned out, that was exactly what I was thinking.

Enjoy!

The Blackwell Hotel
BLACKWELL, TIOGA COUNTY

I rolled slowly back over the bridge at
Cedar Run and back on to Rt. 414. With
my soul healed and The Mighty Steed ready
to run, I gave him a heavy spur of throttle
and we shot like greased lighting across
a big beautiful curved bridge that rises to
meet the pass through the next mountain range. Even
at speed the view from the bridge was spectacular!

Just shy of the top of the pass, I slowed down to a
gentle glide because this is where beautiful little
sister gets really wild and dangerous and I wanted
to take in every bit of her. This part of 414 reminds
me a lot of the D 64 - a section of high mountain
road on the island of Corsica. The mountain roads
there are small - really small! And in Corsica, they
don't use no stinking guard rails. However, this is
lawsuit-happy America and home of the minivan - need
I say more? So with guard rails alongside I looked
out across the great gorge.

On this section there's a towering rock face on one
side (not even a shoulder here), a plummeting cliff
and gorge on the other (no shoulder here, either) and
the drop-off is like a thousand feet. Even though there
are guard rails, if you make a serious mistake here

JUST A TASTE

Name of establishment:
The Blackwell Hotel

Contact Info:
147 Blackwell Square
Morris, PA 16938
570-353-6820
Hotelblackwell@aol.com
www.blackwellhotel.com

Owned by:
Jennifer Linn   Jim Beck

Hours:
7 days a week – 11:00 a.m. until
11:00 p.m. – Closed from 12/15
until 4/1

Price range
$6.00 - $30.00

Cuisine / Specialty:
Pan – Asian, German food in the
month of October

**Offers vegetarian, heart healthy
or organic selections:**
Yes

Support local farmers:
Yes

Locally owned accommodations:
Their Own Place

Local attractions:
The Pine Creek Rails to Trail
Trout fishing
Rafting to Little Grand Canyon
Laurel Festival
Rattlesnake Round

you're dead. But be advised, if you do plummet into
the gorge, you will certainly miss out on some damn
good food in the town of Blackwell - the forth land.

This is definitely a "blink-and-you'll-miss-it" town.
Actually, here in Blackwell there are a couple of homes
that people actually live in year-round. There are
children, dogs and cats and thank goodness a restaurant and pub that welcomes the hungry floaters, hikers,
rails-to-trails bikers, real bikers and travelers,
as well as the 17 locals. The Blackwell is situated
on a little rise right next to 414. You turn up a
fairly steep drive and park at a big gravel lot behind
the restaurant. Like most canyon places, there's a
bike rack available, so I parked The Steed next to
it and headed for the entrance. But once I walked into
the pub from the bright sunlight, I could barely see
anything. After my eyes adjusted to the dim light, I
made out a huge bar below me. When my eyes fully
recovered from the change I was stopped in my tracks.

The bar was beautiful and sunken down a few steps
from the rest of the lounge area. All polished wood,
mirrored and gently lit, it seats over a dozen parched
souls. Today, I was one of them. Unfortunately, the
beer selection was...well, I ordered a Corona and
was lucky to get that. I squeezed and jammed my lime
into the bottle and walked out to their patio.

That place was beautiful! There were plants everywhere
with hanging baskets of flowers hooked to a trellis
overhead. I sat down at a table with my beer and got
out the laptop to make notes and write a little. It
was mid-afternoon, I wasn't hungry and I needed to
update my notes anyway, but here's the thing - I'm
not in a cafe in France or a cool pub in Pittsburgh
or even an indie coffee shop in State College. So
whipping out a laptop in here, where I've already
been pegged as a flat-lander anyway, just drew more
attention to me like down at Waterville. And I know
when people are looking my way and talking about me,
and I know when it's not because of my good looks
and suave appearance. It reminded me of the time my
friend Annie went to Rome for a semester.

Four weeks before she left for Italy she agonized over her wardrobe because she didn't want to "look like an American." Honestly, I can relate because I don't want to be noticed as an American either, especially when our administration is...anyway, Annie was hell-bent on looking like a native Roman and by gosh, she was going to do it.

When she arrived at Fiumicino airport (officially Leonardo deVinci Airport) at 6 a.m. or something ridiculous like that, she was dressed to kill. However she still needed to take the bus into Rome and with a backpack to boot. She arrived at Termini station in the center of Rome and proceeded to take the ancient city by storm.

For her Italian debut, she had chosen a short plastic-like skirt, red pumps with little short lacy socks, a high collared blouse and a cute Gucci backpack (hey, it was still the early 90s). With her outfit in place, she was ready to strut her stuff. All up and down the gran d streets of Rome she got long looks from men, and even a few from women. All eyes seemed to be on Annie, and she loved every minute of it. She told me, "I was sooo damn cool, and everybody knew it." When she finally arrived at the café where she was supposed to meet her friend and new roommate for the semester, she was beaming with delight.

Here was an American girl in Rome, and for all they knew, she was flown in from Milan for the latest Duran Duran video shoot. All eyes were on her at the street side cafe when her friend greeted her and pulled her in close. "Annie, have you seen yourself?" she asked. "What are you talking about and why are you whispering?" Annie replied. "Your skirt, it's stuck up under your backpack!"

It seems Annie's debut in Rome was more like one of those "funniest home video" shows. Apparently while on the bus from the airport, the back of her skirt got caught up in her Gucci backpack, and the two plas-

tics stuck together. It wasn't a Duran Duran moment
after all - it was a derrière moment all the way.
Well, my butt wasn't hanging out at The Blackwell,
but it could have been by the stares I got as I
sipped my lime-infused Corona and pecked away at my
laptop computer. It was all good though, these
mountain folk are super-friendly and very tolerant
of their guests no matter how they look (Have you
ever seen those outfits the bicycle people wear?).

By the time 6 o'clock rolled around I was getting
hungry so I asked for a menu. This ain't your typical mountain fare, kids. It's haute cuisine with a
dash of good ol' mountain cookin'. Let's see, for
appetizers they offered everything from bruchetta to
calamari. For soups they had four-cheese onion and
The Blackwell's chili. Entree's included Southwest-
ern tomato penne, Caribbean chicken pasta, grilled
salmon and a variety of steaks.

I chose to treat myself well on the last night of my
odyssey and went for broke. I ordered the featured
appetizer which happened to be escargot (and you all
know how I feel about that). Then, being the little
carnivore I am, I asked for the Blackwell Steak, a
juicy 16 oz. T-bone coated with a Cajun rub, blackened
and served with mushrooms and onions. I paired it
with a glass of Cabernet Sauvignon and for dessert
it was a sure thing. Crème brulee.

After dinner I was back on the bike once again and
heading toward the fifth land that lay high beyond.
I crossed a little steel bridge as I rolled out of
Blackwell and the taste of crème brulee was still
sweet on my tongue. With the sun now below the
mountains and the temperature dropping, I cracked the
throttle and made haste. I thought about stopping
to put on my leathers, but I was plenty warm inside
thanks to a wonderful meal in a wonderful old-time
hotel/restaurant.

Enjoy!

Wellsboro Diner
WELLSBORO, TIOGA COUNTY

Having literally flown out of Blackwell like a rocket ship aboard The Mighty Steed to get up to the remnants of some sun, I began to notice that with every mile I rode, the elevation rose significantly. By the time I leveled out I had reached a high mountain plateau and the sun was just beginning to kiss the mountains in the distance. I approached a small lake that reflected the scene and serves as a marker to the beautiful town that's but a mile away. As I reached the end of my journey up the Cinque Terre, I rolled into "the fifth land" and the jewel of Tioga County – Wellsboro.

Wellsboro is probably one of the most elegant remote mountain towns in the state. Beautiful architecture, streetscapes and well-preserved Victorian homes line the wide streets that are more like little boulevards with grassy islands separating the traffic lanes. But what I think sets them apart from most other towns, is that in the evening, real gas lamps illuminate the entire length of these center islands. It's like a streetscape from "It's a Wonderful Life."

JUST A TASTE

Name of establishment:
Wellsboro Diner

Contact Info:
19 Main Street
Wellsboro, PA 16901
www.wellsborodiner.com

Owned by:
Nell Rounsaville

Hours:
Monday- Saturday 6-8
Sunday 7-8

Price range:
$1.69 to $12.99

Cuisine / Specialty:
Home cooking

Offers vegetarian, heart healthy or organic selections:
Yes

Support local farmers:
Yes

Locally owned accommodations:
La Belle Auberge, Innkeepers
Nelle Rounsaville and Laura Lee
129 Main St. Wellsboro, PA 16901
www.nellesinns.com
570-724-3288

Bear Mountain Lodge
Innkeeper Jim Meade
8010 Route 6, PO Box 216
Wellsboro, PA 16901
www.bearmountainbb.com
570-724-2428

Local attractions:
Pennsylvania's Grand Canyon
Rails-to-Trails bike path
Beautiful Route 6
Hiking, horse back riding and wagon rides
Rafting, canoeing and fishing
Historic Downtown Wellsboro
Tioga Central Rail Road

I parked the bike and walked around a bit, checking out the variety of storefronts, as well as the pubs, restaurants, cafés and an old movie theater with an art deco façade. The magnificent Penn Wells Hotel still stands on Main Street as a testament to the heyday of lumbering, but the icon I came to see was just down the street - The Wellsboro Diner.

You've no doubt heard the line, "If you build it, they will come," from the movie Field of Dreams, well I think J. B. Judkins might have used a phrase similar to that 80 years ago and he probably said something like, "If I build it and park it in one of the most beautiful places in Pennsylvania, they will come, and come in droves."

Manufactured by the J. B. Judkins Co. in 1938, the Wellsboro Diner is built of steel and porcelain inside and out and has become a veritable institution and landmark. You don't believe me? Visit the diner on any given weekend, pretty much all year round and you'll most likely have to wait in line just to get in the door. Sometimes the line extends around the block.

After a long day of riding I wasn't too keen on camping out again, plus a bank of clouds were starting to move in from the west. I needed to check the weather so I popped open the laptop hoping to find a wireless signal floating around, but nothing. I really wanted to stay near there so I could have a nice breakfast at the diner in the morning which was part of the whole epic journey, but it all kinda hinged on the weather.

Though the diner was due to close in just a few minutes I walked through a little alcove and into the main dining area thinking they would have internet. As I talked with a waitress, I couldn't help but notice a young woman sitting at the counter having soup (she noticed me too, although that probably had something to do with me walking in with an open laptop and asking about wi-fi). I really didn't pay

much attention to her and told the waitress I needed
to check the weather because I might be camping and
coming back for breakfast.

I took a seat in one of the booths and tried to log
on. They had wi-fi all right, but it was a pay thing
so I decided to just wing it and not worry about the
weather. Suddenly, the "soup girl" from the counter
plopped down right across from me. This time I paid
attention – she was beautiful! She had long, curly
blond hair, blue eyes that were like sapphires and
she was dressed in a manner that might suggest a
hippie or an artist...or both, but very chic. I
think my jaw dropped.

She introduced herself as Laura Lee and said that she
had overheard my camping dilemma and told me about
her grandmother's B&B just up the street. "It's called
La Belle Auberge. I have one room available and thought
you might be interested. It's a whole lot nicer than
camping." I said I would think it over, and the next
thing I knew we were having a nice conversation.

I found out that Laura Lee actually was an artist
as well as a poet. She was very bright and a fellow
adventurer and single mother. She also helped her
grandma run the B&B and provided a massage therapy
service for the clients there. But when she told me
this next bit, I went from curious to enamored. "My
Nanny also owns this diner" she said. Well, there ya
go, I was the proverbial fish – hooked and in the
net. I'm sure this was not her intention but...

As she was talking about the diner I was picturing
myself lying out in the woods, but this time not
under the stars but under a veil of clouds and then

possibly soaked with rain. I wisely agreed to stay at La Belle Auberge if Laura Lee joined me for breakfast at the diner in the morning. She said "you know silly, B&B means bed and breakfast and our breakfast is spectacular." I regained my senses and renegotiated for lunch. She agreed and I folded up my computer. She said she would meet me at the B&B in 15 minutes because her little girl was there and she needed to get her home.

I rode the bike two blocks up Main Street and to La Belle Auberge. Wow! It was an example of Victorian architecture at its best. Wrap-around porch, balconies, gingerbread trim, classic wrought iron gate, gardens all around – the works. Laura Lee showed me to my room, which featured a huge, over-stuffed bed and a private bath with a whirlpool tub. But the best part was a tiny balcony off the bathroom where you are surrounded by flowers and can look out over the treetops and at the back garden below (I chose wisely).

As she was getting me settled in, the door sprung open and the cutest little girl on the planet ran in and latched on to Laura Lee. It was her six-year-old daughter. I was prepared to get the typical shy kid routine, but she smiled sweetly, shook my hand and said "Hi!" I noticed that a front tooth was missing and she said "The tooth fairy came last night and gave me this." She reached in a tiny purse and presented a piece of a gemstone. She was smiling from ear to ear and told me how the tooth fairy had made a mess of her house. "She sprinkled fairy dust every-where." I've never been big on kids, but this one was as sweet as they come. And like her mom she was an artist too and she explained that she and her mom spend a lot of time painting, drawing, making collages and throwing pots.

I said nothing of my own art career and thanked them both for their hospitality. After they left, I reclined on my over-stuffed bed and smiled as this whole trip unraveled in my mind. And now I meet a beautiful golden-haired metro-hippy artist with a true indie spirit that rivaled my own at the end of this amazing journey.

In the morning I slipped into the whirlpool just as the sun rose and I literally soaked it all in. It never did rain but I didn't care, I got dressed and descended the grand wooden stairway from the second floor and as I reached the bottom of the stairs, Laura Lee beamed at me and said, "Good morning, Ken. It's a buffet today, so please help yourself." I walked over to the buffet table where an incredible spread was on display – food, juices, coffee, tea, Belgian waffles, quiches, meats, fruits, yogurts, cereals, breads and pastries – all prepared by a young Mennonite woman named Amanda.

I was seated by myself at a table for two, but soon Laura Lee's daughter joined me and we ate breakfast together as we talked about art. She told me of all the art she likes to do and even ran into the kitchen to get some of her drawings to show me. This kid was good! Perspective, beginning color theory and just a good sense of shape and design was all evident in her work. We finished our breakfast and then it was off to school for her.

I hung out hoping to talk to Laura Lee, but she was busy helping Amanda in the kitchen. Eventually she came by and introduced me to her grandma. Nelle, or Nanny, as Laura Lee calls her, is a no-nonsense lady with the charm of a southern belle. She runs two businesses and still has time enough to work her beautiful English garden as well as look after her granddaughter when needed.

I returned to my palatial room and hung out on the balcony and worked on my book. Hand-writing my thoughts are kind of like painting – your thoughts travel from your brain, down your arm, through your hand and pen to take form on the paper. Before I knew it, it was lunch time and Laura Lee appeared to remind me of our agreement. She was wearing a lovely white embroidered skirt and a pale blue wrap-around top that made her eyes glow like jewels.

We walked to the diner by way of the town park and under a canopy of grand oaks and maples. As we neared the diner I saw some folks gathering and before long we were part of "the droves." But I was with the owner's granddaughter, and like rock stars at a NYC night club, we walked right in. The only problem was that there were no places to sit. As soon as a seat opened at the counter, Laura Lee asked me if I would sit there and relax for a bit while she helped out with the customers.

So why do they come in droves anyway? Well, you can start with the décor – it's about as retro as you can get which makes sense because it hasn't changed much since it opened in 1939. Booths, lunch counter, vinyl-covered seats and stools, Formica tops, chrome trim, large windows – the works. Then there are the waitresses buzzing around in a flurry of apparent chaos, but there's really nothing chaotic about it. These women work in tandem like the proverbial "well oiled machine" and move like dancers choreographed by Fred Astaire. No motion is wasted as they negotiate the narrow isle between booth and counter, grill and prep area. Three of the Wellsboro Diner's unsung heroes are Nicki, Nate and Holly.

Nicki has been working at the diner ever since she was a kid and is now the manager. She does it all and does it well.

Grill cook, waitress, crowd control and coach. She
knows the diner inside and out and keeps it all
running smooth for Nelle. Nate, who I dubbed as the
fastest grilled cheese maker in the world, can make
a grilled cheese sandwich faster than I can get
bread out of the bag when I make one at home. Holly
actually wears two hats - a baker's hat and a cook's
hat. She arrives at the diner everyday at 4 a.m. to
make the best damn pies in Tioga County. After she
gets done baking all the pies for the day, she fires-
up the grill and breakfast is served!

Once things calmed down, Laura Lee came over and
showed me to our booth. She apologized for leaving
me alone and insisted on paying for lunch. It was
hard to decide what to order. Most of the offerings
are standard diner fare, including their specialties
- the "Famous Wellsboro Diner Special," which is
a hot roast beef sandwich with mashed potatoes
and gravy and "The Best" prime rib dinner. Breakfast, however, is the big drawing card. Served
all day, you'll find breads, sides, eggs, pancakes,
cereals, fruit, juices, hot coffee, tea and another
Holly masterpiece, sticky buns. I went with the
grilled cheese.

Well, the day was moving on and so I needed to be. Laura Lee walked me back to the B&B, and as I mounted the bike she said, "I've always wanted a ride on a Harley." I said "climb on board," and she hiked up her long white skirt and threw a leg over. I fired up The Mighty Steed, and as I cracked the throttle and jumped to speed, Laura Lee gave out an impressive rebel yell. I smiled and looked into the mirror and saw her golden hair catch the wind.

As we flew west across Rt. 6, everything seemed right with the world – Sun on my face, open road for miles ahead, a full belly and tank of gas and best of all, a beautiful woman with her arms around me and the wind in her hair. Though still full from an awesome La Belle Auberge breakfast and a Wellsboro Diner lunch, I couldn't help but wonder if I could get sweet potato fries with that dinner special? Guess I'll need to find out.

Enjoy!

Cinque Terre Epilogue

My epic journey now complete, I found myself only thirty some miles from my original starting point in Waterville. It seemed like three hundred miles though with the adventure of it all. All the places I visited along the way were different but all had the same spirit of locally-owned eateries – hard work, passion and care in what you do, commitment, welcoming arms and great food that's fresh and at a fare price.

These folks don't have to live in a remote area that really only affords them good business nine months out of the year – they live there because they love it. And you will too when you take the time and explore this awesome part of the state. Like Sue Dodd so beautifully put it "This is the place to come and heal your soul."

My friends, please remember my sad story of a love lost in Italy and please heed my request to visit this land with care and respect. Not only there but in all your travels no matter where you are, treat everyone you meet as a friend because they may in fact, become one.

Look at my adventure – I had entered my culinary quest by way of a Mountain Cookery with a no frills "highlander" who I shared laughs with and had a great time. Then, I came out the end through a classic stainless steel diner with a beautiful woman on the back of my bike riding with the wind along endless mountains and under a sky of blue.

What an awesome journey!

2 O'CLOCK
CHAPTER 2

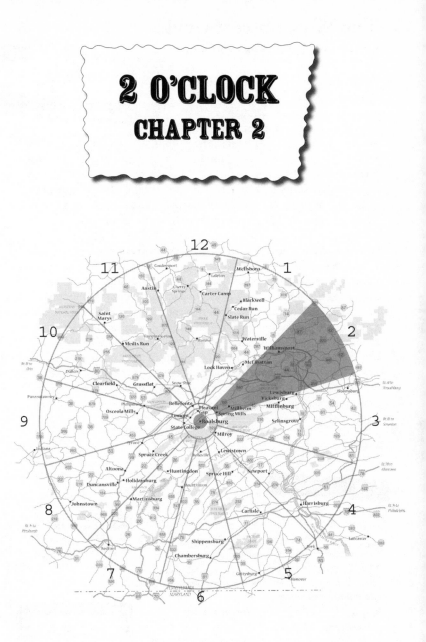

The Water Street Grill
SPRING MILLS, CENTRE COUNTY

In the sleepy little town of Spring Mills, along rural Rt. 45, is a quaint little restaurant that supports my idea about wandering vs. waiting. What's wandering vs. waiting, you ask? The answer is in the form of some questions: Why are people willing to wait for up to an hour at the chain places but won't drive a half-hour to a unique, locally-owned place that serves food prepared and cooked fresh each day?

Did you know that most chain gang restaurants get their food pre-cooked and flash-frozen from a commissary, then trucked in (sometimes from hundreds of miles away) and reheated? So why wait on little benches next to a cash register or outside in a parking lot for 45 minutes to eat reheated frozen food (us old schoolers called those type of meals TV dinners). Why not take a beautiful scenic drive to a place like The Water Street Grill and enjoy the simple pleasures of life by going local, eating fresh and spending some quality time with your sweetie, kids or friends!

JUST A TASTE

Name of establishment:
The Water Street Grill

Contact Info:
118 Water Street (PO BOX 118
Spring Mills PA 16875
814.422.0212
thewaterstreetgrill.com
thewaterstreetgrill@yahoo.com

Owned by:
Dan Schleiden

Hours:
Thurs. thru Sun. 9am to 9pm
Fri & Sat till 10pm, Mon & Wed.
11am-9pm, Tues.CLOSED
Special arrangements can be
made for any day or time

Price range:
$2 to $22

Cuisine / Specialty:
Sandwiches and entrees

Offers vegetarian, heart healthy or organic selections:
Yes

Support local farmers:
Yes

Locally owned accommodations:
The Aaronsburg Inn

Local attractions:
Penns Cave and Wildlife
Trout Fishing

The Water Street Grill was born out of the passion and creativity of Chef Dan Schliden. This talented visionary took an old bank building and transformed it into a delightful BYOB bistro where diners can relax in a casual atmosphere. The décor here is simple but superb. You're surrounded by huge, 12-foot high arch windows, 20 foot high walls, and there's even a walk-in vault which has been converted into a little dining room. The main dining room is a combo of tables and booths and there's even a bar in one corner that customers can use to mix their own drinks.

BYOB (bring your own bottle) is a concept that has been around for a long time, but is now becoming quite chic in major metro areas. I appreciate being able to bring my own alcohol for two reasons: It saves money and I can bring something I know I'll like. I think it's more fun too and is a great option for eateries without a liquor license. I wish more places did it.

Great food, personal and passionate service, very affordable prices and BYOB aside, the next best thing about The Grill is the aforementioned vault. This is my favorite place to dine by far. The vault door is about two feet thick and is propped open all the time, and its entire inner workings are visible through bullet proof glass. Sitting inside the vault is very cool and I could hang out there all night! One evening, a girlfriend and I did almost that.

We booked the vault on a Saturday night and settled in for a long, relaxing meal (like they all should be). Seated at a little table for two, there was nothing but candlelight to illuminate our cozy nook. It was quite romantic, I must say. The candles flickered and caused shadows to jump and swirl against the thick walls of the vault

as though performing a dance just for us. My date's eyes reflected the same warm glow as we raised our glasses of wine in thanks to God, the beauty around us and the blessings of life.

Our young waitress quietly brought us our dinner so as not to disturb us. The food was perfectly prepared and it went well with the wine we brought along. As we settled in for a nice, three-hour dinner, Dan stopped by our table to see how we liked his fare and to compliment us on our desire to take our time and enjoy his excellent cuisine.

This is just another example of why I want you to break free from the chain gang. The gang is just not interested in having their clientele linger – time is money, after all. They just want you to wolf down your order and get out so that the next paying customer can strap on the feed bag. Thankfully at The Grill, as well as most indie owned and operated restaurants, you won't be a number, you won't be herded around a trough, no one will hover over you and you certainly won't be hurried! At The Water Street Grill it's all about chill.

The menu is a simple selection of salads, sandwiches, entrees and desserts. He supports local farmers and uses locally grown produce when in season. He even offers burgers made from local free-range cattle and bison – yes, that's buffalo and they roam nearby. Dan is art supportive too! He often hosts local artists' receptions and hangs their work on consignment.

I was there one night for an opening of two good friends – the immensely gifted Jennifer Kane and the rising star Karl Lietzel. Both were exhibiting their oil paintings – a medium that I find very difficult. (Both artists are listed in Cool Links on my website) Karl's work has recently experienced a rebirth and it shows! Their exhibition at The Grill was a success and once again, Dan's support of going local helped not only the artists, their guests, the community but his own business!

I really love this place and the food is always great. It's always nice to drive down the valley whether by motorcycle or car as the landscapes are amazing. Yeah, it's 20 minuets or so from State College but so what - when was the last time you waited longer than that at a chain place? If you're going by car, it's a good time to chat with your spouse, friends or get in touch with what the kids are up to. It's also a good time to get back to the family meal and spending time with each other over healthy food and good conversation. And this is just the place to do it!

So stop waiting and wander down to The Water Street Grill. Experience and enjoy one of the coolest little country bistros around and get back in touch with the good life!

Enjoy!

Elk Creek Café & Aleworks
MILLHEIM, CENTRE COUNTY

Dreams inspire, they give rise to far off thoughts and great idea's. For some their dreams last only the night but others, the true dreamers, the dreaming never ends. These are men and women with passion and a zest for la vie (the life - it just sounds more beautiful in French) and they take their dreams, by commitment, hard work and faith and make them come alive. Tim Bowser of Elk Creek Café & Aleworks is one such dreamer.

A number of years ago he helped to open a little place called the Equinox Cafe in Millheim. Situated along Rt. 45, this is a one stop light town and not really a place one would invest money and time in to create an eclectic coffee shop. But like my story of the Wellsboro Diner, if you build it they will come. It seems the "Valley Folk" as they like to call themselves, had been dreaming about the same thing. When Tim and associates opened the doors of the Equinox, it was like the whole consciousness of the valley opened and folks poured in.

JUST A TASTE

Name of establishment:
Elk Creek Café & Aleworks

Contact Info:
100 West Main Street
Millheim, PA 16854

Owned by:
Community-owned
Limited Partnership
Tim Bowser, General Partner

Hours:
Wed. & Thurs. 4:00–10:00
Friday 11:30–11:00
Saturday 8:00–11:00
Sunday 10:00–7:00

Price range:
$7.00-18.00

Cuisine / Specialty:
Nouveau Dutchie – Local foods
brewpub

Offers vegetarian, heart healthy or organic selections:
Yes

Support local farmers:
Yes

Locally owned accommodations:
Three Porches

Local attractions:
Millheim Farmers Market
Penns Valley

The place was a Mecca for coffee, simple foods and the best BYOB music jams in the valley (Central PA for that matter)! But wanting to take his dream closer to reality, Tim bought out his partners in 2006 and closed the doors to the Equinox with one last BYOB music bash! This was not just any bash though – it was a "call to arms" (the hugging type).

Tim reached out to his beloved community for help and presented them with the next chapter in his already awesome dream – a full blown brew pub and restaurant. They responded with resounding support and financial backing and the seeds of Elk Creek Café & Aleworks were planted (And if you know anything about Penns Valley, you know it's a fertile land and anything planted here grows strong and hearty).

Before Elk Creek opened I had a chance to sit down with Tim Bowser and talk. He's a great guy – gentle, kind, bright, community minded and a true indie spirit. When I asked what Elk Creek was all about his immediate response was "At the root, it's a gathering place for the community. Here in the valley it's about good food, good drink, good music and good people." He went on to say that the original dream back in 1999 was a brew pub but he couldn't devote the time it needed and a coffee shop was a way to "wet their toes" in the business.

Tim also said that Elk Creek Cafe & Aleworks will not only have craft brew beer, but serve incredible food full time and support local growers and farmers as much as possible. Not only that, but a complete wall would come out and he will be expanding into a huge space now vacant next door. This will allow for a full-blown performance stage, proper PA system and more walls for art. What Tim needed was help.

Local carpenters, plumbers, engineers and sound guys jumped aboard and set out to help make it happen. But finding a brew master and master chef is a little harder. Tim ran a simple ad looking for someone there in the valley that he could train because his initial thoughts were of a low to moderate brewing output. But a guy named Tim Yarrington from New Jersey answered the ad and made a trip up to Millheim to meet the crew.

Yarrington said the expected output would not warrant his level of employment, but he agreed to train someone and help set up the brewing system. This was a huge boost for Elk Creek because Yarrington had received accolades from the Great American Beer Festival as a gold medal brewer. But after several visits to start setting up the brew house, Tim received a phone call from Yarrington saying he and his wife were coming up this time to look for property. According to Tim, this successful brewer of 17 years fell in love with Penns Valley, the people and what was going on there. He also has a young family and the Valley was perfect for raising kids. The two shook hands and Elk Creek Cafe & Aleworks had a full time professional Brewmaster now living in the valley.

Former State College native and Chef Mark Johnson has also relocated to the Valley from a successful tenure in Philadelphia. Because of what Tim and Yarrington were doing, he was willing to jump in too and leave the city. Mark is an advocate of the Gastro Pub Cuisine which is hot in Philly and wanted a chance to spread his culinary wings a little farther. Mark was right in the groove of what Elk Creek is about and was hired. Now owner, Brewmaster and Chef are all locals.

Going local is something Tim is very passionate about. Elk Creek uses nearly 100% local organic meat and dairy. Produce will be an "in season" thing and the beer as you know is brewed and kegged in the back room. They're also smoke free! When I had interviewed Tim he said "It only makes sense" and for him it was also an enjoyment issue. "Why make great food in a great setting and then have someone blow smoke on it?" (My kind of guy)

Speaking of great food, the official cuisine at Elk Creek is called Nuevo Dutchie - a combination of Marks Gastro Pub and what rural Pennsylvania is known for - Dutch style cooking. According to Tim, "Dutch cuisine is a cookery of the land, you used what was available and you used everything except the oink." And this place is as Tim put it so well, "An omnivore's delight." Meat lovers as well as vegans can enjoy a wonderful meal prepared fresh and at a fair price.

As far as the beer, I'm going to restrain myself to near death, because I can't give it all away. But remember, this whole thing was born of a dream. Tim set out to cultivate a gathering place for the community, brew great beer, serve great food, support and showcase local produce, meats, dairy, music and art - all in a sweet place and all with a great vibe.

He told me his "community" is not just Millheim and Penns Valley (that's his home), but like a true dreamer, his reach goes well beyond his grasp and he considers any like minded folks no matter where they're from, a part of his community. He's a true indie spirit whose dream has been made into reality and it's waiting for you in Penns Valley at the Elk Creek Café and Ale Works.

Enjoy!

Bullfrog Brewery
WILLIAMSPORT, LYCOMING COUNTY

This is a place where the journey is almost as sweet as the destination.

Depending on where you're traveling from, that journey can be as calming or as exhilarating as you wish. However, for me and my riding pals, it's all about exhilaration! Well, maybe not so much for the married ones with families, but for us single guys... let's just say we consider the speed limit and posted curve speeds a mere suggestion. After all, if I want to drive five miles an hour under the speed limit while chatting on the cell phone while turning around handing Cheerios to kids in the backseat, I'd just buy a minivan. But I digress.

Since I'm considered somewhat of an "Oracle" when it comes to scenic rides that lead, inevitably, to cool watering holes, I'm always forced to be the ride leader which means I get to choose the route. One of my favorites goes through Amish farmland, rural villages, over three mountain passes, along state parks and

JUST A TASTE

Name of establishment:
Bullfrog Brewery & Restaurant

Contact Info:
229 West 4th Street
Williamsport, PA 17701
bullfrogpubclub@aol.com
570-326-4700

Owned by:
Bob, Harriet, & Steve Koch

Hours:
Mon.- Thurs. 11:00–11:00, Fri.
& Sat. 11:00–Midnight, Sunday
9:00–2:00 brunch, 2:00–4:00
lunch, 4:00–10:00 dinner

Price range:
$2.00 - $20.00

Cuisine / Specialty:
Pub cuisine

Offers vegetarian, heart healthy or organic selections:
Yes

Support local farmers:
Yes

Locally owned accommodation:
The Hampton

Local attractions:
Little League Museum

132

across a mighty river. There are sweet curves and straight-aways that allow you to fly like a rocket and views that are worth stopping for. There's even a dip in the road where, if you go fast enough, you can actually become airborne. That one might not be so good for the dads or the mini-van folks, but... come to think of it - a mini-van becoming airborne would be awesome!

Anyway, when we take this route, my buds instinctively know where we're going to end up, and there is much rejoicing! With the sun to our backs as well as the wind, we head out to one our favorite brewpubs.

The Bullfrog Brewery, in an old but lovingly restored building in downtown Williamsport and has become a noted microbrewery, a first-rate restaurant and a great place to hang out, which explains its popularity as a destination spot for locals and travelers alike. Upon entering Bullfrog the first things you're likely to notice are the huge copper brewing tanks beneath the 20 foot high tin ceiling. The din of conversation and laughter, as well as the clatter of cutlery against porcelain, makes you feel as though you've stepped into a friend's house at Thanksgiving. Once you venture inside further, you'll see a grand bar to your left with giant, stainless steel fermentation tanks behind. A big chalkboard lists the brews currently on tap, and this presents a difficult part to the visit - deciding what to choose.

For me, it's not so hard since I'm a confessed "hophead" and always go for the bitter ales. My esteemed colleagues are men of similar good taste, but it's always fun to switch it up once in awhile and have everyone get something different so that we can have a sampling of each.

The Bullfrog not only produces some of the finest beers in the state, but it has even won a gold medal at the World Beer Cup. All of their brews are made in-house, with a long history of great recipes, quality ingredients, and a knowledgeable staff. From dark to light, wheat to classic, and fruit to hops, Bullfrog's beers are all damn good!

But the beer is not the only thing that brings folks in. The owner Steve Koch also knows the beauty of "going local," and all his baked goods arrive fresh from local bakeries, his produce is grown locally when in season and the beef even comes from a free-range co-op. They serve popular pub fare and some nice original dishes as well. I love the fish and chips but admit that sometimes it's just as hard choosing what to eat as it is deciding what to wash it down with.

We're always happy with the quality as well as quantity at Bullfrog. However, I always try and encourage moderation. When we're just off from a long, challenging ride and are as famished as we are parched, me and the boys always try to spend plenty of time eating, having a cold one and enjoying a few hours of just hanging out, telling stories and having some laughs before we mount up again.

As stated, Bullfrog has many great selections and the dilemma I mentioned earlier about what to choose is evident from their current beer list that I pulled down off the net.

Billtown Blonde: A lightly colored ale with a delicate floral aroma and flavor reminiscent of Williamsport's first breweries. It's clean and crisp with just a touch of lingering sweetness leading to a dry, balanced finish.

El Hefe: This Bavarian-styled Hefeweizen combines the flavors of banana, clove, bubblegum and citrus in a wonderfully refreshing summertime ale.

Blue Collar Brown: Cask-conditioned, this ale has a luscious brown body and is lavishly brewed with American grown Centennial hops. This beer is a salute to Williamsport's working men and women and is rich in flavor but low in alcohol and is served from a 45 degree cask room via a hand pump.

Edgar IPA: Redesigned to be a bigger, better IPA than before. This one is a tribute to the macabre, Baltimore poet - Edgar Allan Poe - and his short story Hop Frog. But be careful, this frog will bite you!

Susquehanna Oatmeal Stout: A big, burly oatmeal stout full of chocolate, caramelized malt and coffee flavors. This stout has a rich feel and a smooth, roasty finish.

But what about the food? Well, you're going to have to check that out for yourself. Being somewhat of the Oracle I mentioned earlier though, I feel obligated to impart a little fable before I sign off.

One day a very handsome young man was riding his motorcycle through a wicked sweet section of high country road. While leaning into a turn, a frog hopped out in front of him. Having to decelerate like a bullet hitting Kevlar, he brought his bike to a complete stop to avoid smashing the little frog. Just then, a gorgeous blond mountain nymph with blue eyes and with a scent of sandalwood walked slowly out from a deep bed of ferns. She opened a wooded box and the little frog hopped in. She smiled at the rider on his steel stallion and said, "Thanks for stopping." She then threw a leg over, took hold of his waist and the two road off into the sunset.

Oh, and the frog? He stayed behind to open a brewpub.

Enjoy!

3 O'CLOCK
CHAPTER 3

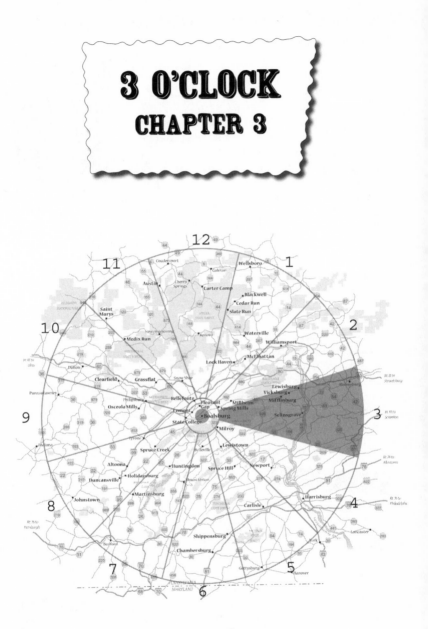

Scarlet D Tavern & Mifflinburg Hotel
MIFFLINBURG, UNION COUNTY

*"Love, if she leaves you, will re-
turn to you if it is meant to be."*

These words have been spoken forever
as a way to make someone feel better
at the loss of a love. For me and in
this case it's not the love of a real
woman, it's the love of a lady that
captured my heart with her food,
drink and peanuts! Seriously.

Rolling down Rt. 45 east one sunny day, I rode through
the town of Mifflinburg. As I've done for the past
several years, I looked toward the vacant old building
of The Mifflinburg Hotel and where the Scarlet D Tavern
used to be, lamenting the days of old.

With a little tear in my eye, I would remember Saturday road trips there to drink Guinness and eat
their in-house roasted peanuts. You see, back in the
day, the owners of the "D" roasted their own peanuts
and patrons were allowed, even encouraged, to throw
the shells on the floor. By doing so, we were told we
were actually conditioning the old wood plank floor

JUST A TASTE

Name of establishment:
Scarlet D Tavern &
Mifflinburg Hotel

Owne by:
Nancy J. Buck

Contact Info:
264 Chestnut Street
Mifflinburg PA 17844
570-523-7800
mifflinburghotel@dejazzd.com
Mifflinburghotel.com

Hours:
Weekdays 4pm to 11pm
Fri and Sat 11am to 11pm
Sun 11am to 9pm

Price Range:
$6 to $39

Cuisine / Specialty:
American

**Offers vegetarian, heart healthy
or organic selections:**
Yes

Support local farmers:
Yes

Locally owned accommodation
Our own hotel or our sister hotel
Norman's Lewisburg Hotel

Local attractions:
Knoebels

with the oil from the peanuts. Memories also included the atmosphere, which was old time and unhurried and the food was always good. But sadly, Scarlet's doors were closed, the peanut roaster shutdown and the old girl just sat empty, cold and lonely.

I tend to humanize inanimate objects and give them emotions too, and so it was the Scarlet D. When I passed by the papered-over windows, I often imagined her as a beautiful woman whose friends and lovers were not allowed to come to her anymore and the door to her heart was locked up. However, like that old saying – if it's meant to be...

I now sit here again in the Scarlet D, writing these words and enjoying a Guinness and a huge turkey club with fresh cut fries! Yes, love does conquer all and once again the Lord shines upon this project (and me). I'm with Scarlet again and I thought she was gone forever. Life is good!

In January 2007, thanks to the new owner of The Mifflinburg Hotel, Norm Buck (Bucky), Scarlet's heart and doors opened once again. Once again the love poured out with the same affection as they must have had back in 1834. Bucky was a successful businessman, popular musician, loving husband and father. Despite his early death, he had the vision to give new life to this old but beautiful tavern.

Unfortunately the peanuts are gone and a giant mutant projection screen TV fills one entire wall. Hopefully they will only have it on for major events since I think it diminishes the old time feel of the place (in my opinion, I feel TVs, MP3 players and especially cell phones, are a major contributor to the death of conversation in restaurants and pubs). Other than the aforementioned TV, Scarlet's pretty much the same old girl, just dressed better.

The wood floors, beams, trim, bar and doors look like they've all been sanded and lovingly polished. The

ceilings are painted and tiny sprinklers which use-
fully don't compliment, actually blend in but re-
assure you that you're safer than before. The upstairs (which I never knew even existed) is totally
renovated and partly exposed with a loft opening
that allows customers access and a great view of the
place. Hanging ceiling lamps and wall sconces gently
light the room although the huge plate glass windows
make the lights almost useless, as they bathe the
space in the warm, bright and natural sunlight with
their southern exposure.

The old bar has scratches, gouges and some nearly
invisible initials. Kaleena, the bartender, told me
that years ago, patrons would sit at the bar and
scratch their fingernails into the soft wood. There
are probably a hundred gouges, some little and
shallow, and some big and deep. Kaleena showed me
a place with three long shallow gouges, side by
side. She said that that was her favorite because
the person who put them there was apparently falling
off their barstool and dug in to avoid the fall(more
likely avoiding the loss of a beer).

Please make sure to stop by and visit The Scarlet D –
she loves visitors and patrons! Belly-up to the old
bar and order a good beer and a bite to eat. Check
out the scratches and strike up a conversation.
Listen for echoes of Bucky's old band and envision
piles of peanut shells under each bar stool. Yes,
it was meant to be. Scarlet left us for a while,
but the old girl is back and her love flows out for
us once again!

Enjoy!

The Daily Grind
VICKSBURG, UNION COUNTY

I love surprises!

As I was whizzing toward Lewisburg aboard The Mighty Steed, I passed through the little village of Vicksburg. Out of the corner of my eye I thought I saw a coffee cup sign in the window of an old building. Since I'm always on the lookout for cool places, I'll pull over for just about anything. Sometimes I find nothing, sometimes I hit the jackpot. Thank goodness no one was behind me because I had to bring the bike to a quick halt on this busy road so I could go back and investigate.

I thought there was no way a little town like this could support an indie coffee shop and that the sign was just a decoration someone put on their home to tease me. Well au contrare mon Fraire! I drove slowly past again, looked, and sure enough it was a coffee sign hanging behind a huge glass window that read: The Daily Grind. As I was to find out later, this place is not only popular with the locals, but folks come here from all over (and it's not just a good cup o' joe that brings them in).

JUST A TASTE

Name of establishment:
The Daily Grind

Contact Info:
6404 Old Turnpike Road
Vicksburg, PA 17883
570 9663481

Owned by:
Theresa Koch

Hours:
Tuesday-Saturday 9am-7pm

Price range:
$6.00 and under

Cuisine / Specialty:
Coffee & Tea

Offers vegetarian, heart healthy or organic selections"
Yes

Support local farmers:
Yes

Locally owned accommodations:
The Vicksburg Inn B&B

Local attractions:
Buggy Museum – Mifflinburg
Local Farms
Antiques

At first I couldn't figure out where to park, but then I saw an entrance to a back lot. I pulled in, powered-down The Steed and walked in through the back entrance. Not knowing what I was to find there, I was taken aback as I surveyed the massive room before me. It must have been 20 by 60 feet, open and uncluttered. Down the center, there were black enameled tables and chairs that contrast nicely with the dark amber of the old pine floors which were beautifully preserved. In the middle of the room is a little oasis-type setup with a big couch and a love seat flanked by little fig trees. Beyond that is another set of tables and chairs. And at the very front and outside is a big ol' porch. In nice weather it provides a place to sit, drink your tea or coffee, and watch the motorists speed by.

If you enter from the back as I did, you will immediately notice the solid wood counter running along the wall. The owner told me that it was an original fixture from the country store that used to be there from 1885 to 1958. Its surface is well worn with marks and scratches from nearly 75 years of sales (I love when someone appreciates old-school craftsmanship and takes the time to restore it). Along the opposite wall, running the long length of the shop, are shelves filled with merchandise – mostly local arts and crafts!

It turns out that the owner, Theresa Koch, is an art teacher herself and is very passionate about using her coffee shop as a venue for local artists. Not only that, she supports and encourages the local music scene too. Every first Friday she hosts Irish Music Night and opens her doors to players and listeners alike to interact and enjoy. All are welcomed and all are encouraged to play an instrument. This Irish music session brings musicians from the Vicksburg area as well as visitors from as far away as State College and Harrisburg to jam the night away.

Yeah, The Daily Grind is a sweet place, all right, and the art, music and community thing just puts it over the top. For me, as an artist, this place inspires me like a well-executed painting. The old and new combine to create a cool space that doesn't just stop at a coffee shop, but goes beyond and embraces the arts all around. As a lover of unique places to eat and drink, as well as an advocate for indie businesses, a place like the Daily Grind gives me hope. All in all, this "blink and you'll miss it" place is definitely worth a look. Actually it's worth hanging out for a spell.

So, when you see the Village of Vicksburg sign on Rt. 45 slow down and put on your turn signal right away because you'll be pulling over in a few seconds. Also, when you walk in, don't act surprised like I did. Just smile and count your blessings that passionate individuals like Theresa are standing up against the chain gang and offering the best that their hearts, hands and passion can give you. Please go and support her!

Enjoy!

Elizabeth's An American Bistro
LEWISBURG, UNION COUNTY

Here is another exception to my
"rule." Why? Well, Elizabeth's is a
little bit upscale for this book,
but the fact that you're even reading this means something must have
convinced me otherwise. Besides the
food, service and atmosphere being
fantastic, there's something else
that makes Elizabeth's a *going
local* kind of place.

During my trips to Lewisburg, my
heart always warms up a bit when I
see the Campus Theater along Market Street. It's
an art deco style movie theater built in 1941 and
is in an ongoing process of being lovingly restored
by a committed group of local supporters. The beautiful vintage marquee made up of thousands of caba-
ret lights and bold red letters is like a beacon
to me of a bygone era. But the era is not gone
thank goodness.

I was there with some friends when they flipped the
switch for the newly restored marquee, prior to a

JUST A TASTE

Name of establishment:
Elizabeth's An American Bistro

Contact Info:
412 Market Street
Lewisburg, PA 17837
570-523-8088
elizabeths@elizabethsbistro.com
www.elizabethsbistro.com

Owned by:
Liz Long-Furia & John Furia

Hours:
Wednesday to Saturday
Lunch 11:30 to 2:00 PM
Dinner 5:00 to 9:00 PM

Price range:
$8.00 to $30.00

Cuisine / Specialty:
Innovative American cuisine
from ethnic origins

**Offers vegetarian, heart healthy
or organic selections:**
Yes

Support local farmers:
Yes

Locally owned accommodations:
Lewisburg Hotel

Local attractions:
The Campus Theater
Bucknell University
Antiques
Shops
Covered Bridges

special showing of the original cut of Casablanca! This was not just a classic film being shown at a classic theater, this was a vintage film being shown at a classic theater. What's the difference, you ask? The difference is that this particular roll of movie film was one of only four original prints from the movie-making process. This film was only one generation removed from the actual celluloid that was rolling as Humphrey Bogart, Ingrid Bergman, Claude Rains, and Paul Henreid stood in front of the camera and gave one of the greatest ensemble performances of all time.

From this first generation print, all 400-plus copies were made and distributed throughout the world. On loan to The Campus Theater from the Library of Congress in Washington, D.C., this film saw the light of day as well as the light of a projector for the first time in over sixty years! We were in awe as we watched the nearly flawless film on the immense screen of the Campus. No cracks or snaps caused by dust, just incredible picture and sound quality that must have been as if you were right there on location with Bogie.

It was a night and experience that will live in my heart and mind, much like the love Rick and Ilsa must have had as she flew to America, or the warmth that Captain Renault felt when Rick said to him, "Louis, I think this is the beginning of a beautiful friendship." And so it is with the Campus Theater. Though it's an hour away, it will be a friend that I will always be eager to visit.

What does all this nostalgia and gushing over a theater have to do with a posh restaurant across the street? Let me enlighten you.

As I sat one evening at a finely appointed table, in the lovely old house at 412 Market Street that is Elizabeth's, I opened the menu and was blown away by the offerings: Autumn Greens Salad, field greens, toasted walnuts, Denmark bleu cheese, roasted butternut squash and apple cider vinaigrette. Grilled Strip Steak, savory Vermont cheddar-herb bread pudding, charred spinach and a roasted shallot-red wine demi glace. Grilled Atlantic Salmon, warm roasted mushroom, haricot verte and Israeli couscous salad, peppery greens and white truffle vinaigrette.

They also have a lunch menu that takes the typical and makes it unusual: Southern Grilled Burger, choice of Vermont cheddar, fresh mozzarella or goat cheese then topped with charred red onion, smoky bacon and Southern Molasses BBQ sauce and paired with Creole French fries. Artesian Bread Sandwich, grilled chicken, bruschetta salad, arugula and balsamic aioli served on our daily artisan bread accompanied with an Italian-style bean salad.

But those menu features are still not what really caught my eye (although my stomach was in love) and what got Elizabeth's in this book. It's that she offers a very cool fixed price meal with a side of *going local*! What made my heart melt a little is that "the side" offered you two tickets to the Campus Theater! That's right, for an extra $5.00, you and your date can dine in elegance enjoying food that will knock your socks off and then walk across the street to enjoy, no, experience a movie. This friends, supports a deep doctrine of the *going local* gospel – community, and how by being good to your neighbor you bring good to all, including yourself.

Yes, here's an elegant bistro that partners up with an old-time theatre to offer its patrons an evening of culinary art, architectural art and film art! Yeah, Elizabeth's might be a bit upscale for the type of places I'm writing about, but it's undeniably awesome!

If I were writing a review about fine dining, I would tell you about my incredible meal (I went with the salmon) and the delicious wines I enjoyed with it (a really cool "Wine Flight" thing). I would tell you about the charming atmosphere and beautiful décor. Then about the friendliness of the staff and even mention the folks at the table next to mine who were celebrating a birthday – when I offered to take their picture just to be nice, they secretly told the waitress to save a piece of cake for me for my dessert (it rocked!).

But since I'm not reviewing fine upscale restaurants, I guess you'll just have to go to Elizabeth's and find out for yourselves. Make it a date night and go for the dinner-and-movie deal. Once you've tried Elizabeth's American Bistro and taste the quality of her cuisine, I'll bet you'll want to put your arms around her and say, "Lizzy, I think this is the beginning of a beautiful friendship."

Enjoy!

Herwig's Austrian Cuisine
LEWISBURG, UNION COUNTY

If you've checked out the Happy
Valley section already, you're
not seeing double and this isn't
a typo. This is, however, one of
the very few situations that I will
mention a place that has more than one location.
I did this for a few reasons. Herwig's in Lewisburg
is a franchise not a chain - franchises are indie
owned and use an authorized method and practice
of the original place and ownership to do business
and serve customers. This situation also supports
the movement of community I'm mentioning throughout
this book.

My good friend Herwig "Brandy" Brandstatter the big
(Austrian) cheese, came to me while I was set up
promoting this book in front of his restaurant at
Arts Fest in State College. He asked "Ken, would you
have space in your book to mention Herwigs in Lewisburg? Just a sentence or two, that's all?" I asked
him why he wanted me to mention a place that was
basically a competitor. "I think they could use

Name of establishment:
Herwig's

Contact Info:
406 Market St, Lewisburg, PA
(across from the Campus Theatre)
Herwigsoflewisburg@Hotmail.com
www.herwigsoflewisburg.com

Owned by:
Barbara and John Price

Hours:
M 11:45 am - 4 pm
T - Th 11:45 am - 7 pm
F - Sat 11:45 am - 8 pm

Price range:
$5.50 (sandwiches);
$7.50 – $14.95 (entrees)

Cuisine / Specialty:
Austrian

**Offers vegetarian, heart healthy
or organic selections:**
Yes

Support local farmers:
Yes

Locally owned accommodations:
The Pineapple Inn

Local attractions:
Slifer House
Packwood House
William Cameron Home
(old homes / museums)
Reptiland

the help. You know how hard it is to get a new place going." So with that preface, let me introduce you to "Herwig's Lewisburg."

This Herwig's is located right on Market Street, the main drag (Rt. 45) through Lewisburg. It's a cozy place and the décor is really nice and features art by local artists. I love the feel and vibe here! It's got a great sense of style yet simply put together. The colors are warm and little wooden booths line one wall. The menu is pretty much the same as Brandy's place, but with the addition of varied soups, salads and sandwiches.

One day I was walking by and a family was standing outside reading the menu that was posted outside (I love this practice of posting menus outside an eating establishment - I think most people are a bit timid when going in a small place and this affords them "a taste" without feeling like everyone is looking at them - just my thoughts). Anyway, while they were looking over the menu, I stopped and told them how great the food was and how the owners dreamed of doing this restaurant.

Well I guess my short dissertation worked because they were there when I stopped back later. They were all packed into one of the little booths but they were having such a great time. They were chewing one second and laughing the next! Hands were waving around expressing points and while others were stealing food off each others plates. I walked over and asked if my recommendation was okay. "Okay?" they said. "This is some of the best food we've ever had!" I guess I did well. Oh, I think it's the owner of Herwig's Lewisburg that did well - I just helped get the folks in and that's what I'm doing here with you.

Former chemist, John Price and his wife Barbara moved back to Lewisburg where they met in college. Bucknell University is a prestigious private school and it's easy to pick up on that as you look around town, surrounding neighborhood and campus. John and Barbara loved to drive to State College and eat at Herwig's, but they dreamed of having one in Lewisburg - maybe their own.

After several trips to SC, John and Barbara became friends with the Brandstatter family (not a hard thing to do). Eventually, John asked Brandy about a place in Lewisburg and if maybe he could take a shot at it and open his own place. Brandy agreed and in 2006, Herwig's Austrian Cuisine in Lewisburg opened for business!

Please, if you're in Lewisburg and want to try something really special, unique and good, stop in. Take a seat in one of the little wooden booths and be prepared to experience authentic Austrian food prepared by a dedicated local couple.

Enjoy!

The Lewisburg Hotel
LEWISBURG, UNION COUNTY

You know that urban legend that claims that McDonalds puts some sort of chemical in their food, and that after a time, if you don't return, the chemical releases itself in your brain and causes this crazy desire for their burgers or fries? You can't shake it, you must go and eat. I think it's fun to envision scores of people heading, zombie-like, toward McDonald's with their bodies stiff and their arms straight out in front of them as they repeat "Ronald, Ronald" over and over again in a creepy sci-fi movie.

Well, thank goodness this place is not a transfatty wasteland of "meat-like" substances with a clown as its mascot. But I do question whether or not The Lewisburg Hotel puts something in their signature soup that draws its customers back time and time again. The crab bisque here is so damn good it's addicting! Seriously, they should offer a 12-step program for those of us that just can't get enough. The only bad part about eating this delicious bisque is when the spoon scrapes across the empty bowl.

JUST A TASTE

Name of establishment:
Norman's Lewisburg Hotel

Contact Info:
136 Market Street
Lewisburg PA, 17837
570-523-7800
www.lewisburghotel.com

Owned by:
Nancy J. Buck

Hours:
Mon - Thurs 11am to 10pm
Fri and Sat 11am to 11pm
Sun 11am to 9pm

Price range:
$6 to $39

Cuisine / Specialty:
American

Offers vegetarian, heart healthy or organic selections:
Yes

Support local farmers:
Yes

Locally owned accommodations:
Our own hotel or our sister hotel
Norman's Mifflinburg Hotel

Local attractions:
Knoebels Grove

Every time this happens, I have to fight the desire to lick the bowl. Hey, kids and even adults do it with cake mix and stuff, so why can't I do it with my crab bisque? Well, I guess if I were at home... but not at a nice restaurant. Who came up with all this "manners" crap, anyway?

Like its sister, the Mifflinburg Hotel and Scarlet D tavern down the road, the Lewisburg Hotel offers two types of dining in two equally beautiful spaces. The formal dining area has two rooms with linen and silver on the tables and a menu to die for. It features soft lighting and floral wallpaper, a hand-carved wooden ceiling and lace curtains. There's also a grand fireplace that provides a soothing ambience as you dine on appetizers like Panzarella salad, Charmoula, shrimp cocktail, and smoked salmon. For entrées, there's Angus Filet with Sambucca or Pecan Crusted Red Snapper, just to name a couple. Is your mouth watering yet?

Adjacent to the dining room is a pub-style room with plenty of seating, including comfortable booths along one wall. Here they offer both a casual atmosphere and a kickin' pub menu, which just happens to include "a certain bisque!" They also offer a nice selection of beers on tap including two of my favorites - Sierra Nevada Pale Ale and Boddingtons Pub Ale (which is like the blonde version of Guinness) and their bottled beers include Tröegs of Harrisburg which is a staple in my fridge.

Like a lot of people, I prefer the pub for lunch and the dining room for dinner. I once took my German friend Julia there for her birthday and we sat in the dining room. She had only been in the states for a month or so and she was amazed at the quality of food and the beautiful décor of a place "in the middle of farm country." When we took a walk after dinner and she was impressed with how beautiful Lewisburg was, particularly the architecture, the little shops and the old movie house. We also walked the back streets, which are lined with beautiful old homes and gardens.

The Lewisburg Hotel is also an actual hotel and the rooms there are decorated in the grand style of a bygone era. Someday I'd like to spend a weekend in Lewisburg and stay at the hotel and just hang out in town. I'd eat at all the great restaurants, do some shopping and antiquing, pick up art supplies at Brushstrokes, pub-hop, enjoy the cafés, take walks around the neighborhoods, go to the Packwood Museum, check out the galleries and catch a movie at The Campus (whew, that's a big day). The grand Lewisburg Hotel, the matriarch of a grand town, offers more than just great food and accommodations, she offers you her friends and neighbors and they're all calling you to come and visit.

Enjoy!

Selin's Grove Brewing Co.
SELINSGROVE, SNYDER COUNTY

Well if my friend Charlie from Otto's in State College says he loves this place, it must be amazing. I must say, I love this place too. I first stumbled upon SGB several years back because someone told me of a great little brewpub in Selinsgrove in a big old stone house on the main drag. Heck, I didn't really even know where Selinsgrove was, but the lore of handcrafted brews and the recommendation was a good enough excuse to fire up the bike and go for it. I headed out one summer's eve and rode down a beautiful stretch of country road on my search for the Selin's Grove Brewing Co.

The warm August sun was on my back and the evening wind was blowing east, as though helping me along on my journey. Since the wind was going my way, 55 mph felt like 15 mph and the ride seemed effortless ("55" written there was used for legal purposes only).

I arrived in Selinsgrove and cruised up the main street looking for the brewpub, but couldn't find it. It was

JUST A TASTE

Name of establishment:
Selin's Grove Brewing Co.

Contact Info:
121 North Market Street
Selinsgrove, PA 17870
admin@selinsgrovebrewing.com
www.selinsgrovebrewing.com

Owned by:
Steven Leason & Heather McNabb

Hours:
Wed & Thurs Noon-11pm
Fri & Sat Noon-Midnight
Sun Noon-8pm

Price range:
Under $9

Cuisine / Specialty:
Fresh Soups, Salads and
Sandwiches

**Offers vegetarian, heart healthy
or organic selections:**
Yes

Support local farmers:
Yes

Locally owned accommodations:
Pottinger House B & B
Selinsgrove Inn

Local attractions:
Susquehanna University
Shops & Galleries
Bicycling, Kayaking and Canoeing

a beautiful main street though, with a 19th century commercial streetscape and many old buildings of brick and stone. I pulled into a parking space on the street and looked around as I had a feeling I was close. I saw some folks walking down the street and I told them I was from Boalsburg and not familiar with Selinsgrove, and could they tell me where the brewery was. They pointed right across my face and said "right there." The building was literally right across from where I was standing. I nodded my head and grinned to myself for my ability to find good pubs. I like to call it pubdar.

These guys were really nice, and in fact, were on their way to SGB as well and told me to just follow them. One of the young women said "Come on, I'll buy ya a beer." I gladly dismounted The Mighty Steed and walked with them across the beautiful tree lined street and down an ivy laden stone "stairway to heaven." With just one look I knew exactly why Charlie loves this place so much, and I hadn't even had one of their beers yet! The outside of SGB is like a little Garden of Eden except that everyone is wearing clothing and there are no snakes. God is there for sure though – it's got a great atmosphere that's relaxed, cozy, sweet and serene.

Now I know why I "felt" it but didn't see it. The brewpub is in the basement of this grand old stone building across the street from where I pulled over. I was to find out later that the building happened to be a former state Governors mansion. Only a little sign along the sidewalk gave any clue to the existence of a pub. But, if you approach from the alley behind, it's a little easier to find because of a bigger sign and a parking lot full of cars.

I followed my leaders inside and one of the couples went directly behind the bar. The young woman, the ones who offered me a beer, said "What ya have?" as she stood behind a sweet line-up of taps. A bit perplexed, I asked "Do they have a Pale Ale here?" She

said "Yeah, an IPA, is that ok?" She then poured
that IPA like a seasoned pro and brought the foamy
head up just proud of the rim. She brought my beer
over to me and the guy she was with came too. "I'm
Heather and this is Steve," she said. "We love
Boalsburg and wanted to do this there, but nothing
was available at the time so we ended up here."

It turned out that these two were the owners and
the brewers! They showed me around and told me about
the mansion's history, how they "ended up there" and
how the building was built in 1816 by Pennsylvania's
third (and only three term governor), Simon Snyder,
for whom the county was named. The building is re-
markably intact and is also on the National Historic
Register. The Selin's Grove Brewing Co. is housed on
the ground floor in the governor's kitchen, complete
with two walk-in fireplaces.

Heather then went on to give me an insider's tour
(This was like six years ago before this book was
even a twinkle in my eye. Heather, Steve and crew
are just nice people and treat everyone well, even
if they're not writing a book). She told me more about
the brewery and explained "We started out in 1996
with a tiny 3 bbl (barrel) brew house which we
squeezed into a 9 by 13 foot room in the basement
here (it was tiny, Heather and I had to squeeze
through in a few places). Here we toiled away on
our amazing little system and made some incredible
beers, but just not enough. We would come back
from our annual week-long vacation to a near empty
lineup and angry staff and customers."

"In 2003, we started renovations on our four bay 1930s
cement block garage and by August of 2004, we started
brewing. The 7 bbl direct-fired brew house we use
today is secondhand from Avery Brewing in Colorado.
The remainder of our equipment we picked up ourselves
in Pittsburgh from the Foundry in the Strip District.
We were concerned that the new system would change
the beer and it did, for the better! Now we can offer

more styles of beers, add more taps, have more room to be creative and have more natural light and ventilation. We are so happy!"

They should be, and so should you when see this lineup of beers (from their website fall 07).

Captain Selin's Cream Ale: smooth delicately hopped ale using a bit of corn to give it its golden color and clean distinct taste. 4.5% ABV

Wilder's Hefeweizen: German style wheat beer with lots of heat malt and a distinctive yeast strain to create an unforgettable thirst quenching beer.

India Pale Ale: traditionally made strong & highly hopped so it would keep on its long journey, from England to India during British rule. Ours is a wonderfully bitter beer with a spicy aroma, some fruity characteristics and a lingering hop finish. A great aperitif! 7.2% AVB

Stealth Triple: body warming golden Belgian style ale, traditionally brewed by monks. Our Triple is made with Belgian candy sugar and a special Belgian yeast strain. We carefully age it to round out this beers complex characteristics. (Limit 3) 9% AVB

Organic Baltic Porter: 100% certified organic ingredients; domestic malts and New Zealand hops, this strong style of porter developed in the countries surrounding the Baltic Sea in the late 1700s. Ours is soft, velvety and full bodied with hints of cocoa, toffee, finishing with an underpinning of roast. 9% ABV

If that's not enough, Heather and Steve offer some of the best lunch and dinner selections around. The cool thing about SGB is that they offer incredibile food in an incredibile simple format. Just a teaser would be appetizers like hot soft pretzels and a hummus plate, vegetarian three bean chili, curried

chicken salads and a mess of sandwiches that will have you saying "Man, it all looks so good, I don't know, what should I get?"

With first class beer and amazing food at Selin's Grove Brewery, I was happy too - a sunny summer's eve, beautiful rolling hills and roads, memories of past pleasures and fireworks, meeting Heather and Steve, having a wonderful dinner, great beers, a tour and the good company of the SGB friends/patrons. It was truly a ride of discovery and experience I'll never forget. And how can I? I return to the Selin's Grove Brewing Co. several times a year and each time the experience, as well as the beer and the people, are great. I hope to go with Charlie some day but like the McNabb's he's always brewing something.

These days you don't see Heather and Steve as much because they've been brewing offspring too - they have three kiddos now! But that won't stop this brewing couple - they've still got their hands deep in the "mash" and their hearts deep in the community.

So, from a tiny brewing operation in a back-basement to a full blown brew-mansion with its very own Garden of Eden, the Selin's Grove Brewing Co. is truly a slice of heaven!

Enjoy!

Note: Heather McNabb is my new "poster girl" for *going local* and supporting the notion of community (even when it's competition). When I sent her a letter telling her of my book and asking for her information for the "Just a Taste" section, she sent me this email reply.

From: heather mcnabb [mailto:admin@selinsgrovebrewing.com]
Sent: Saturday, July 07, 2007 12:30 PM
To: Ken
Subject: Re: NOT SPAM - A book about your place. Please don't trash.

Great idea Ken!

Since you've last been to downtown Selinsgrove we have some outstanding establishments I strongly recommend you add!

'Mrs. Green Jean's' , a natural & local foods merchant and deli opened up fall 2006 & is a wonderful place run by a husband a wife team, Stacey & Chris, she scouts out amazing local products, makes organic pizzas and sandwiches, her husband has a bakery called 'Rip Rap' and his breads are organic, we now use his crusty sourdough at the pub. Non smoking.

Emma's opened in April of 2007 and is owned by our former cook Emma Renninger, who just got her degree in holistic diet (or something like that, very cool) and beau Nick Charles (an Alaskan fishing guide). They feature local grass fed meats, local raw milk cheeses, seasonal local produce, whole grains, a full menu, very nicely done, relaxed atmosphere, kid friendly, Non smoking. Oh yeah, another cool thing about Emma Renninger is she is willing to make foods for people with dietary concerns and if I am not wrong has a side business of helping people with dietary issues.

Kind Cafe - Been around for a about 5 years and in my book is the BEST coffeehouse in central PA, owned and operated by two brothers Troy and Brent Spenkle, top notch organic coffee, local art constantly shown on the walls... and any other surface that suits, great soups and sandwiches, local music, poetry readings... great place, awesome people. Troy is an artist who's metal sculpture works can be enjoyed throughout this seriously funky place. Non-Smoking.

Irene's -opening this summer, upscale fine dining in a beautiful, spacious old bank building, Italian & French cuisine, will feature local foods as well, will have beer & wine.

And YES...my answers will follow!!

Hope all is well.

Heather McNabb

****

4 O'CLOCK
CHAPTER 4

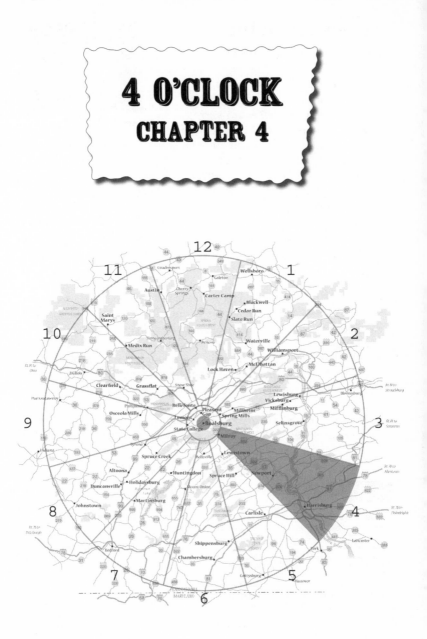

Honey Creek Inn
MILROY, MIFFLIN COUNTY

Some days it's just good to be
inside and in the comforts of
an enclosed vehicle like my
truck. On super cold mornings
like this you can turn on the heat, crank up the
tunes and take a nice drive over the mountains for
breakfast. After a few miles you're almost too hot
and have to back the heat down or open a window.
You're sweating at this point and laughing as those
crazy idiots on their motorcycles pass you looking
like something between an icicle and a frozen turd,
hanging on to the handle bars hoping not to crack in
half at the first bump in the road.

Well all that visualization and mind control wasn't
working as I crested Seven Mountains on Rt. 322 aboard
my motorcycle in mid February and freezing my "you
know what's" off. Okay, the sun's out, it was a beautiful day, the roads were clear and I was hungry for
one of the most delicious hot breakfasts known to this
belly. The fact that the thermometer was just at 40°
was no reason to be a wuss. But at this point and
with my lips nearly frozen, the only thing I could
say to comfort myself was a barely audible "mommy."

JUST A TASTE

Name of establishment:
Honey Creek Inn

Contact Info:
4698 U.S. Highway 322 (old)
717-667-2314

Owned by:
Betty J.M. Lawhead, Cindy
Beckenbaugh, Sandra Ake

Hours:
M – Sat. 6 AM – 3 PM
Sun 6:30 AM – 3 PM

Price range:
Under $10.00

Cuisine / Specialty:
All American Home Cooking

**Offers vegetarian, heart healthy
or organic selections:**
Yes

Support local farmers:
Yes

Locally owned accommodations:
Aurandt – Lawhead House
717-667-4226

Local attractions:
Amish Farms
Antiquing
Belleville Market - Wednesday s

Actually it wasn't that bad because what I was really envisioning was the breakfast that was waiting for me only a few mores miles away at the Honey Creek Inn. Picture if you will, a big bowl of hot baked oatmeal with a touch of brown sugar and steaming milk poured over top. Then, two scrambled eggs, bacon, pancakes and coffee to accompany it. This is what kept me going and what keeps me coming back to the Honey Creek.

The HCI is on the old 322 through Milroy, but not too long ago this was the only 322 and part of the only highway corridor between Harrisburg and State College. This particular section around Milroy was known as "The Missing Link" because on either end of this stretch of 322 the highway was four lanes and wide open, as you came to the bottom of Seven Mountain's south side, it went into a little two lane rural road through town and then back to a four lane to Lewistown.

For years folks were wishing the state would connect the two highways and make it one smooth motorway all the way to our capital. Well they got their wish, and with one section still under construction at a place called "The Narrows" beyond Lewistown, it's a clear and fast shot to Harrisburg. The downside of this highway/bypass thing is that whole towns are bypassed. Once thriving businesses along a once busy main road are now barely noticed and some are even dying.

Note: If you're reading this book, chances are you're a bit like me and try to travel those old original routes as much as possible. When I do, there's nothing like an old well seasoned place along the road for a good ol' country breakfast.

I pulled in to the Honey Creek Inn and instantly smiled with the smell of bacon wafting through the air. I walked in and my glasses instantly fogged over from the moisture of a griddle covered with steaming pancakes! I took my seat at a little booth in the middle of it all hoping to absorb some heat from happy patrons and their hot morning meals.

The first thing I asked for was a piping hot cup of coffee to wrap my hands around and begin to thaw myself out. My server was a young woman named Ashley and she brought it right away. I settled in to enjoy my surroundings and began to peruse the menu even though I knew what I wanted.

The décor here is country for sure with lots of wood, some antiques, quilts as wall hangings and a very cool player piano towards the back that actually works with the drop of a quarter. The clientele is very young to very old and all seem to be in good cheer. Why not, the food here is always good, the portions pleasing, the prices right and the staff efficient and friendly. I swear Ashley was practicing for the Miss World Waitress contest and she made all the grades and then some.

It's no secret among my friends that I can be a little "high maintenance" when it comes to eating out. So this young woman had her work cut out for her, but, she didn't miss a beat and took very good care of me. She came back to take my order and I went with what I had been meditating on the whole way there - baked oatmeal, eggs, bacon, pancakes and coffee. I was warming up, and this was starting out to be a wonderful day!

One of the great things about the HCI is that folks are so busy eating and chatting here that they don't seem to notice strangers writing in sketchbooks. This is good because I don't get a lot of stares and subsequently become distracted, taking longer to write than usual. I was well into a page when my breakfast

arrived. Everything looked great and I did my cere-
monial preparations to my oatmeal. For those of you
unfortunate enough to have never enjoyed or even
heard of baked oatmeal, let me be the first to tell
you and then you better get to the HCI to try some.

The first time I had it was in a little restaurant
in Lititz PA. I kept noticing everybody getting
these bowls of something looking like hard oatmeal.
I asked the waitress about it and she told me it was
their specialty. I couldn't resist and had to try
it. It's basically just cooked oatmeal, then baked
and served with butter, milk and brown sugar. Being
high maintenance, I ask for my milk to be whole and
heated. I sprinkle only a little brown sugar on top
because it's pre-sweetened already. I'm AC/DC with
the butter so you should try it yourself - my friend
Miki from Lititz always goes for butter.

The Honey Creek Inn is not just a great spot for
breakfast, they do it all and they're always bustling with customers eager to get their bellies full
at a fair price. The owner Betty Lawhead puts in a
long hard day with the help of her two daughters
Cindy and Sandra. Betty not only runs this great
restaurant but also owns and operates a beautiful
B&B just down the road as well.

So, if you ever take the old 322 coming from or going
to Harrisburg and you want a really good old fashioned
breakfast at an old fashioned price, stop in at the
Honey Creek Inn. Tell Betty I sent you and ask to try
the baked oatmeal. Get the milk heated and put a
quarter in the player piano, sit back and enjoy your
meal. And remember, when you take the interstate the
only thing you see is interstate. Take the old routes,
go local and support places like the Honey Creek Inn.

Enjoy!

Espresso Yourself
NEWPORT, PERRY COUNTY

Whether you enter Newport from
Old Rt. 22 or bigger, faster Rt.
322, you have to cross a bridge
that spans the mighty Juniata
River. I think bridges are cool
to begin with because there's
just something about crossing a
river or even a large stream
that evokes a feeling of history for me. There was
a time when a river crossing meant a major operation
for even the most rugged pioneer types. Of course,
I'm not guiding a pack mule, or floating a raft. I'm
only looking for a cozy coffee shop in another little
town forgotten by the speeding travelers along the
super highway – A place where the indie spirit is
alive and well, and where *going local* is not just a
concept but a practice.

I had no idea where this coffee shop was, but as soon
as I rolled into the main square of Newport I spotted
a neon sign that read: Gourmet Coffee. I couldn't
really see an actual business sign but I figured it had
to be the place I was looking for. I parked the bike
out in front of the old building with huge windows.

JUST A TASTE

Name of establishment:
Espresso Yourself Cafe

Contact Info:
8 South 2nd St.
Newport, PA 17074
717)-567-9882
espressoyourselfcafe@pa.net
www.espressoyourselfcafepa.com

Owned by:
Cheryl & Rick Miller

Hours:
Tues-Fri. 7am-7pm
Sat. 7am-2pm

Price range:
To $8.95

Cuisine / Specialty:
Café

**Offers vegetarian, heart healthy
or organic selections:**
Yes

Support local farmers:
Yes

Locally owned accommodations:

Local attractions:
State Park & Campground
Antique shops
Arts Counsel

Inside I could see tables filled with patrons sipping out of huge ceramic cups, eating big beautiful muffins and engaging in spirited and jovial conversation that are all telltail signs of the new era of the coffee shop. As I approached the door, I looked above my head and there was a handmade sign and the confirmation I was seeking.

Let me ask you a question. What if everybody bought their home furnishings from Pottery Barn and chose the exact same pieces? Or, all your friends cooked from the same cookbook and bought their ingredients from the same store? Can you imagine how boring that would be? So why would a couple that dreams of opening a coffee shop in their home town make it exactly like the one in the next town over? They wouldn't. They'd make it different. They would "trick it out" with what they think is cool and do it with a spirit of passion, vision, creativity and love.

Everyone in this book lives and breathes that same spirit but they all exhale differently. Case in point is a coffee shop called Espresso Yourself. Just that name says it all.

After I took a seat and settled in, I looked around. Cool hardwood floors, tin ceiling, wrought iron tables and chairs, and lots of art on the walls. I noticed a guy working on a laptop across the room so I figured they even had wireless. When I went to the counter to order some coffee and a muffin, I was greeted by a young girl who took my order for a double espresso chocolate steamer and a fresh cranberry muffin. Just as I was ready to go back to my seat, the owner appeared from the kitchen and introduced herself as Cheryl. She told me to make myself at home and, when she saw my laptop, she said that internet there was free and I was welcome to use it.

Only a couple of minutes after I sat down and started making notes, my coffee and muffin arrived. As I was enjoying these, I couldn't help but feel good there – was it because of the cute older couple sitting at a table by the front window acting like it was their first date? Was it the two couples at the other side laughing and sharing stories over a late lunch? Maybe it was all the art on the walls that appeared to be locally done, or maybe it was all of the above. I finished my coffee and muffin and decided to take a look around.

Through a large opening in the wall I entered another huge room. This one was a lot more sparse but at the far end was a "nook" consisting of a bunch of pillows on a carpeted floor. It was the kind of space you would find in an Arabian Sheik's tent. At the other end of the room there were a number of these funky painted picture frames and clocks on the wall and I was to learn that they, along with the rest of the artwork displayed, were created by local artists.

Walking back to my table was a whole display supporting local endeavors. Here I found articles and publications on everything from art and sustainable agriculture to holistic living. Not only that, but when I had a chance to read through the menu, I noticed they offered vegetarian and even vegan selections. Later, when I talked with Cheryl and her husband, Rick, I came to realize how passionate these two were about going local.

Folks, if you all want the same furniture, eat from the same cookbooks and want to go to Starbucks, fine. But if you want to see how the locals do it, then you've got to break the chain and check out these indie places like Espresso Yourself. You won't see the same décor, order from the same menu, drink the same drink, or be part of a demographic that appears in an annual corporate report.

No two works of art are exactly alike and artists usually paint from the heart to evoke an emotion and a feeling that reaches inside you and touches your senses. Owners of indie places are a lot like those artists, and some are even like the rebel bikers that "trick out" their rides to set them apart from all the others. Maybe someday the rarest coffee shop will be the chain-gang, cookie cutter type, and maybe if we all just "Espresso Ourselves," it'll happen in our lifetimes. I sure hope so.

Enjoy!

McGrath's Tavern
HARRISBURG, DAUPHIN COUNTY

This is where living in such a rich region of awesome indie-owned restaurants, pubs and cafes can be frustrating. I've only been to this pub in downtown Harrisburg one time in my life and it was a few years ago. So as I write this, I confess that the memory of my visit is a little spotty, but it left such an impression on me that I just had to include it.

My friend, fellow foodie, actor and beer snob cohort, Gino, was living in Harrisburg at the time when I told him I was coming for a visit he said "I know how much you like cool, locally-owned places buddy, and have I got one for you!" That's how I found out about McGrath's Tavern.

When Gino and I, along with some of his thespian girlfriends (groupies), went to McGrath's during my weekend trip to the capital, the place was packed! I remember an impressive lineup of taps and lots of happy patrons clustered around the main bar.

I thought we would never get a seat, but Gino signaled for us to follow him. He then walked past a massive bouncer and disappeared. I walked over to see where he'd gone. There was a long narrow staircase leading to a second floor.

It's hard to pin it down in words what it is about McGrath's upstairs that sticks in my memory, and even though it's as Irish as an American pub can get, I can only think of that French phrase *je-ne-sais-quoi* which means "that certain something." Well, upstairs at McGrath's had that certain something in spades - old handmade brick walls all around, soft lighting, old tables and chairs, posts, beams… very old-world. I also seem to remember the space having a little bar of its own.

Because of this one and only experience, I recently looked up McGrath's on my favorite website for finding pubs - PubCrawler. On this site, people can review and comment on pubs from all over the world. Just go to **PubCrawler.com**, type in the city and state and if there are any reviews you can check them out. So if you want some solid, updated info about McGrath's, including a review by a very famous and prominent beer book author, check it out on PubCrawler or go directly to McGrath's own site which is great.

Good beers, good food, good friends, cool atmosphere and good cheer. All these elements combined to put me and my friends into a groove that lasted well into the night and memories that are still sweet to this day. Cool old pubs like this in city centers are always a good find, but McGrath's has that...I wish I knew the Gaelic version of *je-ne-sais-quoi*, but the only Irish I know is *céad míle fáilte* (a thousand welcomes) and Guinness of course! At McGrath's Tavern you'll not only get a properly poured Guinness, but *céad míle fáilte* as well.

Enjoy!

Tröegs Brewery
HARRISBURG, DAUPHIN COUNTY

The beauty of writing and
publishing my own book is
that I can do whatever I
want! If I want to include a
place that's not a restaurant, pub
or café, but simply a place in which I happen to
love the product they create, that's my prerogative
(so there).

My cheapskate friends (which are most of them) know
that on any given day my fridge is stocked with beer.
Of course, I am the biggest cheapskate of us all by
far, but a man must set his priorities. I don't drink
soda, milk, sugary fake fruit juice, or most varieties
of common cold beverages. What I do drink as my uni-
versal cold "anytime, any occasion" beverage is beer.
And not just any beer my esteemed foodies and beer
geeks, only damn good beer. How can one be the co-
founder of the Self Proclaimed Beer Snobs Club and
allow oneself to be subject to drinking big batch
small taste swill that prides itself on its funny ads
more than its quality and flavor? One can't. So one
(this one) must maintain his reputation and only
stock the very best.

JUST A TASTE

Name of establishment:
Troegs Brewing Company

Contact Info:
800 Paxton St.
Harrisburg, PA 17104
717 232 1297
www.troegs.com

Owned by:
Chris and John Trogner

Hours:
Gift shop hours: Mon-Fri 8–5pm.
Sat. 12–4 pm.
Brewery tours and tastings every
Sat. at 2 pm

Locally owned accommodations:
Milestone Inn
www.milestoneinn.com
2701 N Front St, Harrisburg
(717) 233-2775

Local attractions:
Hershey Park
State Capital
Civil War Museum

As I said, I love this brewery, but I must confess I know little of their history and how they rose to such dominance in the craft brew world (or my fridge). So rather than try and make stuff up (like that's a no-no in this book), I'll let the boys themselves tell you. The following was cut and pasted directly from their Website.

"Chris and John Trogner have been working hard to get Central Pennsylvania on the brewing map. Since 1997, these Mechanicsburg natives have been hand-crafting world-class beers that combine traditional English brewing techniques with the eclecticism of new American brewing. But how they reached this point is as compelling as where they are headed.

Chris and John, 18 months apart in age, were simul-taneously intrigued by the art of handcrafting beer while living some 1,750 miles apart - Chris in Boulder, Colorado and John in Philadelphia. John, the older brother, often found relief from his not-so-satisfying work in the Philadelphia real estate market at the nearby Dock Street Brewpub. At the same time, Philadelphia was proving to be a booming beer city with dozens of neighborhood bars that cared as much about beer as they did about food. Chris was drawn to Colorado for the skiing opportunities, as well as educational ones. In between the two, he found himself in the midst of craft-brewing nirvana as more than 100 breweries appeared throughout the state.

As Chris and John would talk, a flicker of an idea gradually turned into a full-blown business plan. The brothers had always dreamed about starting a business together, and now they had brewed the per-fect idea. John moved to Boulder, and within days secured a job cleaning tanks at the Oasis Brewpub. Over the next three years he would learn the brewing business from the inside out. Along the way, he took brewing classes at the University of California at Davis, and Chicago's Siebel Institute of Technology.

With John knee-deep in yeast, hops and barley, Chris focused on marketing, sales and management classes. He also managed a restaurant to determine whether a brewpub or a brewery would be a better business model. The brothers decided to leave the food to someone else and focus on beer. After graduating, Chris went to England to take an intensive brewing class at the University of Sunderland. The brothers needed to decide where to build the brewery; and while Colorado offered the right audience, it also meant a lot of competition. After a lot of thought, Chris and John decided to return to their roots and use their brewing skills in the Mid-Atlantic States.

The Tröegs Brewing Company was established in 1997. Today, the brewery produces seven different beers including **Hopback Amber Ale, Troegenator Doublebock, Rugged Trail Nut Brown Ale, Tröegs Pale Ale, Oatmeal Stout (seasonal), Sunshine Pils (seasonal), and The Mad Elf (seasonal)**, and distributes its product in Pennsylvania, New Jersey, Maryland, Delaware and Virginia."

There you have it. This isn't a place to sit down and buy a good beer, but you can taste all the fine brews that the brothers make at a brewery tour every Saturday at 2 p.m. Also, if you've never tried a local craft brewed beer I encourage you to try what committed independent breweries are doing. Like the Straub family, Chris and John Trogner take pride and passion, along with water, yeasts, hops, malts, barleys and a whole lot of hard work and turn it into a beer of excellence.

Stop by my place sometime and raise a glass of Tröegs with me. Like I said, my fridge is always stocked.

Enjoy!

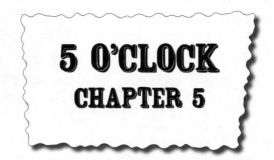

5 O'CLOCK

CHAPTER 5

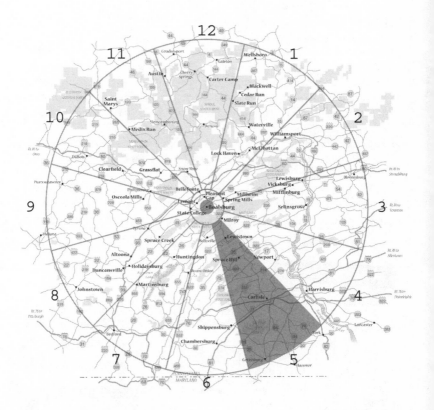

Waterfront Tavern
LEWISTOWN, MIFFLIN COUNTY

Folks, it's hard to have the right words. I don't mean for this place – I mean something abstract, something deep. What I'm trying to say is how life can be so beautiful when you just let go and see where you might end up. To be able to accept disappointment when your plan doesn't work out, but then look beyond that and what you wanted in order to be given something different and maybe much, much better.

It's a Friday night at about midnight and I'm about to recount for you an evening that was one of those when serendipity once again took hold of me, pulled me in tight and gave me a big kiss on the lips when I wasn't even flirting with her. As I sit here transcribing my scribbles from my sketchbook into my laptop, my heart is still warm and the smile I've had on my face all evening is still aglow.

It all started this afternoon. I got out my map and plotted my evening recon trip to find a small brewpub on the outskirts of Lewistown in Mifflin County. I

JUST A TASTE

Name of establishment:
Waterfront Tavern

Contact Info:
6398 Belle Avenue
Lewistown, PA 17044
717-248-9094
bratty@waterfronttav.com
mifflincountyliving.com

Owned by:
Donald M. Chapman
Mike Britt
Todd P. Fink

Hours:
M – Sat 11 AM – 11 PM
Sunday 1 PM – 10 PM

Price range:
Lunch $5.95 - $10.95
Dinner $11.95 - $22.95

Cuisine / Specialty:
Fresh Sautee Cooking
PA preferred restaurant

Offers vegetarian, heart healthy or organic selections:
Yes

Support local farmers:
Yes

Locally owned accommodations:
Dragonfly Inn – Juniata County
Numerous B&Bs in Belleville, PA

Local attractions:
Juniata River
Amish in Big Valley
Raystown Lake
Brookmere Winery
Oldest R.R. station in USA
 (Lewistown)

hopped on The Mighty Steed and headed over the mountain. Since my last visit to this pub the roads had been changed and I ended up on a back country road that wasn't the right one but it paralleled the one I wanted. I knew, due to my in-brain GPS that if I could just connect with a crossroad I would only need to hang a right and I'd be good to go. Well I proceeded to go up, down, curving right, curving left, passing fields and farm animals and then being brought to a near snail pace by some old dude who must have thought that the 35mph speed limit was only for experienced NASCAR drivers.

Well my sense of direction paid off because I came out exactly where I thought I would and only three miles passed the brewpub. I turned onto the main road, cracked the throttle and was there in no time. The problem was there wasn't any "there" anymore. The brewpub was closed and by the looks of things it had been closed for a long time. As I sat there with my shoulders slumped it was like one of those "cricket" moments (you know, those moments in cartoons when the character finds himself somewhere he doesn't belong and all goes dead silent except for the sound of a lone cricket). Well this was one of them. I was hungry, thirsty and hearing crickets. I realized my journey was a bust and I felt really disappointed and a twinge of anger because I had come all that way for nothing.

I thought about heading home. My plan didn't work out and I really didn't have any good options. Somewhere between feeling sorry for myself and wondering about what to do, I vaguely remembered a place my folks told me about a year or so ago. It was called the Riverfront or something and was in downtown Lewistown. I figured it probably wouldn't pan out anyway, but I turned the bike away from the ghostly former brewpub and headed for town.

Saddened by the loss a local pub and leery of a place I only heard about, I just hoped I could get some

dinner and a decent beer (the latter being only a
dream at this point). As I approached downtown I
turned right, crossed the Veteran's Memorial Bridge
and over the mighty Juniata River. I spotted a
restaurant just on the other side, precariously
suspended above the waters edge and could see from
the bridge that the place looked open. Not only
that, but by the number of cars in the parking lot
it was very popular too!

From the entryway I could hear the sound of joyful
patrons, smell the scent of cooking, and see through
the window that every table was full. The sign
outside the door said Waterfront (not Riverfront
like I thought) and I knew I was in the right place.
But, little did I know then that by the end of the
night the place would be in me.

As I walked into the crowded tavern this huge guy
with an ear to ear smile and bright welcoming eyes
lunged right at me. He took hold of my hand, gave it
a firm and sincere handshake and said "Welcome to the
Waterfront, glad you could stop in! It's pretty busy
and I don't have a seat for you right now, but how
about a drink or beer? As soon as something opens up
I'll seat you!"

I felt like the President!

This had to be the manager if not the owner because,
who does that!? Where was the last place you went
to where you were so genuinely greeted and offered
a drink while you wait by the manager? I told him
I could sure use a good beer and he showed me his
draught selection. There before me, shining through
like a searchlight in a thick fog of thirst was one

of the most beautiful tap heads that I could have asked for, Tröegs of Harrisburg! I sighed and knew that God must have arranged this night long before I even said goodbye to the cats as I left home.

Well, it turned out the guy who greeted me was in fact the owner himself! And from my brief experience with him, he was also an ambassador to how things should be when you go out to eat. The whole time I kept thinking he knew - he knew I was there to check out his place for possible inclusion in my book. But there was no way, no way he could have known. Heck, I didn't even know I was going there that night either. No, he was the real thing - I was his guest and he was delighted to have me at his tavern!

Folks, this is were passion, commitment, manners, good business skills and a shear love for what you do, all combine to make everyone who comes in your door feel like the President! He even introduced himself and asked my name and where I was from. I hate to sound like a broken record but, Who Does That? His name was Mike Britt and he was a strapping guy and a former Law Enforcement Officer whose love for food and libations just happened to be taken into custody by an early retirement.

As I said the place was really busy but he insisted on showing me around like a little kid who just built his best tree house ever! He showed me up-stairs, which was a beautiful non-smoking dining area and my eyes went straight to a table set right in front of a huge floor to ceiling window that looked out across the river and the lights of Lewis-town (a real date pleaser for sure). Then, we went back down, through the bar/dining room and outside to the immense deck that is suspended high over the riverbank. The deck was buzzing with patrons and the view as well as the vibe was amazing! I will wager that this is one of the sweetest outdoor seating areas this side of Italy.

Three levels provided plenty of different views as all were enjoying the warm summer night. After my "Presidential" tour, Mike said "Ah, there's the seat at the end of the deck I reserved for you" and walked me over - it was the only open table in the house! It was under a giant umbrella and bathed in the warm light of the setting sun. When I sat down I had a view to die for, or as their motto says, "A View to Dine For." Mike then ran down the list of specials and highly suggested his rib rolls as an appetizer which he had just learned the recipe for on a trip to Florida. I sat my beer down, ordered the rib rolls and settled in for a night I'll not soon forget.

All around me were happy faces and laughter, really pretty women and guys out having a good ol' time. Families with children were there too along with couples on a date - just a great group hanging out in a great place. I pulled out my book and started writing feverishly as I didn't want to miss a single vibe.

My rib rolls came and they were...Damn Good! As always, I took my time and savored both appetizer and beer. Mike also told me about a dinner feature of broiled Tilapia over three types of potatoes and surrounded by sugar snap peas. It sounded too good not to have, so after an hour or so, I put my request in for the feature.

When it arrived it was being carried by my server Tanya who was so nice and asked if I was journaling. I said "yeah, kinda" and she suggested I try the house Chardonnay to pair with my fish. I did and it was like love at first sight! As I wrote, ate, drank and soaked everything in, an overwhelming feeling rose up inside me and knew this was where I was to be that night. Yes, serendipity kissed me tonight, but the Waterfront took me home with her!

This is what I was talking about at the beginning of this piece - how life can be so beautiful even in the midst of disappointment. It's when you just let go and see where you might end up and be able to look beyond what you thought was good to be given something different and much better. It's now 3 a.m. and I'm starting to fade, but tonight was my night to learn a lesson. Life is beautiful when you let go and let her take you by the hand. Especially when she leads you to the Waterfront!

Enjoy!

Spruce Hill Lunch
SPRUCE HILL, JUNIATA COUNTY

When I want to impress my friends with my "guru" prowess or turn their culinary world upside down, or when someone asks me to name the most unique place I'm writing about, there's one that instantly comes to mind - Spruce Hill Lunch.

It all started years ago on a crisp day in October when I was searching out Pennsylvania's vast collection of covered bridges. While down in Juniata County to find the longest in the state, I discovered this little gem. It didn't look like a restaurant but more like someone's home. There was what appeared to be a garage/gas station next door and a parking lot between. A sign outside read Spruce Hill Lunch and I just had to check it out. Plus it was lunch time so it was destined.

When I walked through the door of this roadside luncheonette I felt as though I traveled through time again. If the men would have been wearing Fedoras and the women would have had hairdos like Marlene

Dietrich or Betty Grable,
I would have surely thought
it was 1946. But I hadn't
gone back in time.

Now years later, a few things
have changed but a few have
remained the same. The building,
parking lot, old empty gas station next
door and the sign reading Spruce Hill Lunch
were all well intact, but what changed was on the
inside, and isn't that the best place for change?

People are constantly trying to look like something
they're not, or tying to change their outside when
their inside remains the same - in some cases, not
so good. Christian Scriptures talk about a "renewing
of the mind" and the "transforming of hearts." The
Dali Lama speaks of this in his acceptance speech
after receiving the Nobel Peace Prize. "True happiness comes from a sense of peace and contentment" he
says, and I bet he would agree that it's not from a
huge wardrobe or a wrinkle free face.

I took that little philosophical detour there for a
reason and that reason will be made clear at the end.
For now though, let's step inside Spruce Hill Lunch.

What a sweet place! It reminds me of an Amish kitchen
and dining area. On my first visit, I remembered the
place to be a bit cluttered and more walls. Now it's
all open, bright, clean and simple. Many little windows
surround the room and all the vintage tables are all
nicely set. There's a small lunch counter to one side
of the room with soda fountain stools. Down from that
is another counter but this one displays a variety
of things from local art pieces to baked goods and
jars of handmade maple syrup.

As I was looking around, I was greeted by a guy wearing an apron, a welcoming smile and seemed delighted
that I had come in. He introduced himself as John

and said that he and his wife Deb were the new owners as of a little more than a year ago. He asked if I wanted a cold drink and suggested one that was the special of the day, a maple syrup and lime fizz. It sounded refreshing and I took him up on his offer and looked around some more.

Spruce Hill Lunch is just one room with eight tables, counters and kitchen. At the counter you can sit and watch the goings-on of the kitchen and if you choose to sit at a table you'll find them as vintage as I said - padded vinyl backs and seats tucked and buttoned, tops covered in old school Formica and chrome steel frames underneath. They even have tables outside but, it was so hot out and the air condition- ing felt so good that I parked it by one of the windows inside. I had a great view and could look out across the beautiful farmlands and beyond to the majestic and mighty Tuscarora mountain range. What an awesome sight!

As I sat enjoying my fizz, folks started coming in for a Friday lunch and it filled up fast. It was so good to see people coming in and they were of all ages and walks of life. There were the two construc- tion guys who made a bee-line to the counter. Then there was the elderly couple and grandkids, a busi- ness duo and a group of two couples who were riding monster Honda Gold Wings. John came by with a menu and told me of the daily specials. "Sesame stir fry with brown rice and a cup of creamy carrot and cashew soup or stuffed manicotti with soup." I said I would think about it and look over the menu. They offered burgers, cheese steak, pizza, wraps, burritos and a few entrees'. I went with the stir-fry special.

As I waited for my lunch I couldn't help but feel good there. John and Deb along with their two sons were so attentive and efficient. Deb buzzed around always with a smile and always eager to help even when she was busy in the kitchen. John was so friendly and sincere as he went from table to table asking customers if they were enjoying themselves and their meals.

My stir-fry came and it was beautiful! The veggies were fresh, bright, colorful and done just the way I like - hot but still a bit crunchy. The chicken was somewhat shredded which was cool because it blended in with the veggies and allowed for some in every bite. The taste of the sauce was great and the chicken, amazing! And although it was a large portion my appetite didn't allow for much savoring time because I was starved.

As I was finishing up my meal, I remembered John saying something about soy protein when he was describing the stir fry and I though he meant the chickens were free range and were fed soy beans. Little did I know that the chicken I just enjoyed so much wasn't fed soy, it was soy. Turns out the Spruce Hill Lunch is completely vegetarian! My chicken wasn't...chicken? The cheese steaks are not steaks? And what about the American staple they offer - hamburgers? Nope, none of those were made of meat.

Believe it or not, out in the middle of rural central PA there is the sweetest vintage luncheonette serving an entire vegetarian and vegan menu with the same passion, commitment to quality, and success as their carnivorous colleagues. Not only that but this wonderful family are followers of Hare Krishna. They don't wear saffron robes or shave their heads. They don't chant as you eat (which actually I would prefer over a certain "Roadhouse" where the wait staff line dances while you eat a heart-attack-waiting-to-happen dinner) and, John and Deb don't hand out any tracks or booklets.

Honestly, you would never know of their faith, only of their kind, friendly, and welcoming spirit, their passion to be an indie restaurant serving and doing what they hold dear as a healthy way to enjoy God's gifts of food. And, in a very subtle way, live out their faith and way of life. Remember that "philoso-phical" stuff from before and how I said it would be clear at the end? Well, here's a quote from the Hare Krishna website: "The self within is by nature joyful. So we don't need any material stuff to 'make' us happy. We just need to purify ourselves and uncover the happiness that's already there."

What a wonderful mantra to live by no matter your individual faith. At Spruce Hill Lunch there is a joy that's apparent and a menu that will please you, fill you and keep that "self within" happy and very healthy!

Enjoy!

Market Cross Pub

CARLISLE, CUMBERLAND, COUNTY

Sometimes things are better from the source. Here's what the folks at Market Cross write about their place on their website.

"What's in a name? Well, in the case of the Market Cross Pub, quite a bit. The name Market Cross is taken from across the Atlantic, the town of Carlisle, England. Its history spans over two thousand years.

The Celtic Britons were the first to arrive, naming their new settlement Caerluel. Unfortunately for the Britons, the spelling of the town was not the only change to come. Eventually, the Romans arrived and took Caerhuel as their own, renaming the city Luguvalium. For the next 300 years the city served as the northern-most outpost of the Roman Empire. When Romans withdrew to defend their own empire in the 5th century the city was left open to invasion, and invade they did. In those days, everyone had an interest in expanding their empire; the Danes, Vikings, Scots and Normans all controlled the city at one time.

JUST A TASTE

Name of establishment:
Market Cross Pub & Brewery

Contact Info:
113 N. Hanover St.
Carlisle PA
717-258-1234
and
105 W. King St.
Shippensburg PA
717-532-3967
www.marketcrosspub.com

Owned by
JoAnne & Jeff Goss

Hours:
11 am to midnight 7 days/week

Price range:
Food $5 - $25
Beer - $2.50 & up

Cuisine / Specialty:
English Fare –Fish & Chips, Cottage Pie, Shepperds Pie as well as American Favorites

Offers vegetarian, heart healthy or organic selections:
Yes

Support local farmers:
Yes

Locally owned accommodations:
Carlisle House in Carlisle
Dykeman House in Shippensburg

Local attractions:
Army War College & Heritage Center
Local History from 1750's
Arts and Antiques
Dickinson College
Shippensburg University
The Gord Farm
Hershey Park
Penn National

Finally in 1092, William Rufus claimed the city for England, but apparently not for Scotland. A permanent state of war existed for the next few hundred years and the ownership of the city fluctuated between the two nations. During this continuous turmoil, a monument known as Market Cross was erected in 1682 at the town square. The Market Cross still stands as the main gathering place in modern Carlisle.

With this symbolism and the appreciation for the communal nature of English pubs, our efforts have culminated into the Market Cross Pub, established April 1, 1994. The Publicans welcome you to a "taste of our English heritage." The Market Cross Pub offers you good food, a fine assortment of beers and ales from around the world, and the friendly atmosphere of English Pub life."

Recreating the friendly atmosphere of pub life is just part of why I love this place! Sure, they have a very nice lineup of draughts, including Tröegs, and a killer selection of bottled beers like other good pubs, but here at Market Cross they brew their own too! The brewery is located in the rear of the pub and is equipped with a 10 barrel open-fermentation system that was brought over from England in 1933. They produce a variety of ales and porters, one of which is a personal favorite of mine – Olde Yeller IPA. By now you must think I care more about beer than food, but I'm also a die-hard foodie.

Foodies are those of us who dig food more than most, like my friend Rogers McLane (also a beer snob) who talks about food the way art buffs talk about the Dutch Masters. And here at the Market Cross Pub, they don't just know beer – they create a veritable gallery of great food offerings: Starters, soups, salads, sandwiches, "Royal" sandwiches, homemade English fare, a "From the Grill" section and a very nice entree menu. One time when I was there I counted about 75 different menu items, including the old Brit standard – fish and chips.

Some of the other English fare: Cottage Pie, which is seasoned ground beef layered with green beans, cheddar & mashed potatoes, Shepherd's Pie, the same but with lamb, carrots, a sauce and mashed potatoes (sans cheddar), Potato Pastie, which is mashed potatoes and cheddar wrapped, then baked, in a light puff pastry & served with a side salad, and Beef Pastie, the same but with ground beef, sausage & cabbage. They also do Bangers & Mash, spicy American-style sausages served with seasoned mashed potatoes, peas and Coleman's English mustard.

And that's just the English fare. You will be delighted with the rest of the menu and I would venture to guess that if a bloke or bird from the old country were to be teleported to the Market Cross Pub, they wouldn't even know they'd left England.

Enjoy!

6 O'CLOCK
CHAPTER 6

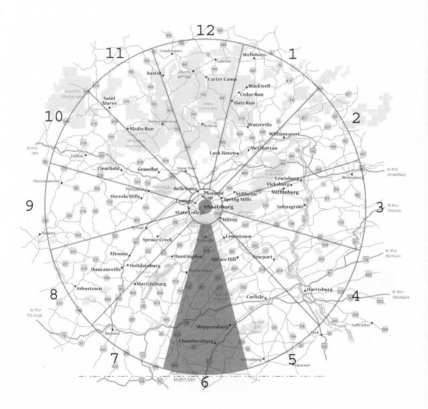

The Niche
SHIPPENSBURG, CUMBERLAND COUNTY

Sometimes the one you pass by is the one you were looking for in the first place. And sometimes it takes a friend to point it out.

It was a spectacular day in early September. The morning air was crisp and the sun was shining bright with not a cloud in the sky. I had planned for several days to make a trip down south (PA) to check out some towns and pos-sible places for my book. I had even made a list of potential finds and the day of reckoning was at hand.

It also happened that my friend Alain was visiting me for a few days on his way to an art show in Michigan and although I almost always travel alone, I thought it might be fun to bring a friend. Fortunately my buddy McC keeps his big Yamaha parked in my garage and since Alain is an accomplished rider and McC was nice enough to let him take his bike, Alain joined me for the day.

I first met Alain at the State College arts fest a few years ago. He's a fellow artist and his work is amazing. He paints these wonderfully colorful street scenes

JUST A TASTE

Name of establishment:
The Niche

Contact Info:
9 West King Street
Shippensburg, PA 17257
marciechapline@yahoo.com
717-530-3663

Owned by:
Marcie Chapline & Mark Beard

Hours:
9 AM – 2 PM, 5 PM – 10 PM,
Mon – Sat.

Price range:
Lunch $6 - $9
Dinner $15 - $25

Cuisine / Specialty:
Healthy lunch, fresh-baked breads
and "casual" fine dining

**Offers vegetarian, heart healthy
or organic selections:**
Yes

Support local farmers:
Yes

Locally owned accommodations:
The Dykeman House

Local attractions:
Shippensburg University
Michaux State Park
Gettysburg
Amish Country

of Paris, and since he's French and lives right in the heart of Paris, he's perfectly qualified. He's also qualified to handle the back roads of PA on a bike, having logged thousands of miles on those crazy rues that he so beautifully paints. We fired up the bikes, headed south, and set out together on a day of discovery, food and fun.

Since we started out early, some breakfast for the journey to Shippensburg seemed like a good idea and the first town we hit was Mount Union in Huntingdon County. Asking a local, I found out about a little "hole in the wall" called Coffee Café on Jefferson St. This was a great little place with a simple and very inexpensive menu. Our waitress was so nice and even called Alain "honey." We filled up on the good ol' American breakfast of eggs, bacon, toast and home-fries, bid them adieu and continued south.

What was already a great ride on Rt. 522, turned to an awesome one once we hung a left at Shade Gap. Here we picked up 641, 997 and then 533 and I thought Alain was going to wee wee himself as we weaved in and out of sweet turns and over amazing mountain passes into Shippensburg. I'm sure cruising up the Champs Ellysees checking out la femmes, or riding across Point Neuf in the shadow of Notre Dame is very cool but, leaning a bike over at 50 mph around a tight uphill mountain curve would maybe beat them both (especially if said la femmes were watching at little café tables while going around said curves).

Pulling into the borough of Shippensburg Alain and I took to the streets on foot to see what this historic town had to offer. As we walked in the sun along the main drag we passed a place called The Niche. Alain stopped to read the menu which they had posted out-side (very "Euro") but since it wasn't on my list I kept walking. Alain called me back and said that he thought this might be a good place. I took a second look and even walked inside for a glimpse. Nice, but

I thought my list was going to yield a better place. Alain tried one more time to convince me but I passed it up.

Up and down we went, and in and out of my "list" places. Yeah, some were nice, especially The Black Horse Tavern in the Shippen Place Hotel. But there was something I was looking for and hadn't found it yet. One more time Alain (very politely) suggested we try The Niche, and this time I gave in. We walked across the street and into the dimly lit bistro and sat down.

Once seated, I started to pick up on a vibe I missed when I first walked in. Warm colors on the walls, dark wood and just a cozy feel all came together to set a mood that was beginning to be more what I was looking for. Opening the menu brought another step towards that with selections like Cajun shrimp and sweet potato chowder, handmade chicken Caesar salad and a crab cake sandwich. I ordered the soup and sandwich combo so I could sample both. Alain ordered the day's special of a stuffed and roasted Portabella mushroom sandwich. I was informed by our server that The Niche was BYOB but unfortunately Alain didn't bring a nice Boudreaux with him and we sadly ordered water.

Our lunches were delicious and after Alain generously paid the bill I asked our server if I could talk with the owner. She smiled and said "How may I help you?" It turned out she was her. We had a nice conversation and I had the chance to ask her all about her place and her philosophy. It turned out she was a big supporter of *going local* and hoped that her attempt at bringing great food and a cool place to her town would be well received. As far as Alain and me, it would be for sure. And as we walked out, I thanked my friend and thought how glad I was that he had come along for the day. He helped me find what I was looking for, and it was The Niche after all.

Enjoy!

Heavenly Grounds
CHAMBERSBURG, FRANKLIN COUNTY

This is a sweet place, bright and full of local art. The atmosphere was typical coffee shop, with comfy chairs, eclectic furnishings and very chill. Besides the local business crowd getting everything from straight coffee to funky  frozen lattes, the young clientele curl up in big sofas and chairs with cappuccinos in one hand and expressing themselves with the other.

When I had the chance to speak with the owner Susan Hedges, she told me that she had moved to Chambersburg from Richmond VA and wanted to go into business for herself. She said "A coffee shop seemed easy enough," and that was all the more reason she needed to get one going. As you've read in this book, most coffee shop owners talk of dreams, passion and a desire to break out and do something creative. But like people who just fall into their niche without all that artsy stuff, Susan just saw an opportunity and took hold of it.

JUST A TASTE

Name of establishment:
Heavenly Grounds Coffeehouse

Contact Info:
15 N. Main Street, on Memorial Sqare
Chambersburg, PA 17201
(717) 264-5222
www.heavenlygroundscoffee.com
heavenly@heavenlygrounds
 coffee.com

Owned by:
Susan Hedges, Owner

Hours:
Winter hours: 7am–5:30pm M-F,
9am–5pm Sat, closed Sunday

Price range:
Specialty coffee $2.50 - $4.50

Offers vegetarian, heart healthy or organic selections:
Yes

Support local farmers:
Yes

Locally owned accommodations:
Craig Victorian B&B
756 Philadelphia Ave (Rte 11),
717-263-3371

Local attractions:
Gettysburg & Antietam battlefields

After finding an old building Susan and her daughter, along with an all female staff, set about the task to make a coffee shop and place of business, art and a community gathering space. She is a woman of faith and therefore tries to seed that into the spirit of the place by creating an air of peace and serenity. Susan said it's hard work to run a business, but she seems happy to give it her all.

Heavenly Grounds is situated on the main square of Chambersburg. This square by the way is beautiful and reminds me of many town squares down south – maybe that's why Susan feels so at home here. There's old buildings surrounding it, the Town Hall is right there, but the main feature is a large lovely fountain right in the middle. And, there's a lot of history there too.

Chambersburg is southwest of Harrisburg in the Cumberland Valley, part of the Great Appalachian Valley. The borough is the county seat of Franklin County, Pennsylvania (my dad's birthplace county). The settlement there began in 1730 when water mills were built along the creek that now runs through the centre of the town. Its history includes episodes related to the French and Indian War, the Whiskey Rebellion, John Brown's raid on Harper's Ferry, and the American Civil War.

Along with history, Chambersburg now has a terrific little coffee shop where business, youth, artists and community can gather in a place that's truly heavenly.

Enjoy!

The Cottage Pub and Restaurant
CHAMBERSBURG, FRANKLIN COUNTY

Getting the word from a local is the way to go when you're out exploring. However, it doesn't always have to be when you're out looking for it or even asking for it in the first place.

I live outside State College which is home to Penn State, which is home to Penn State Football, which is a venue for perhaps thee biggest tailgate party in the world! One weekend I was parading around the acres of tailgaters wearing a giant beer coaster/sandwich board promoting this book. When I had the opportunity to "preach my gospel" about *going LOCAL!* I felt a tiny bit like Billy Graham or Martin Luther King. Folks from all walks of life would gather round and say things like, "that's right brother" or "Yes, we love the mom and pop places too." Most were very supportive and excited, and many of them wanted to share their favorite places with me.

One particular group captured my attention when they said they were from Franklin County, because that is

JUST A TASTE

Name of establishment:
The Cottage Pub & Restaurant

Contact Info:
572 Wayne Avenue
Chambersburg, PA 17201
717.264.8543
thecottagepub@comcast.net
fattommyscottage@comcast.net
www.gotothecottage.com

Owned by:
Tom Boock

Hours:
Sun.–Wed. - 11 a.m.–12 a.m.
Thurs.–Sat. - 11 a.m.–2 a.m.

Price range:
$6.50 - $24.99

Cuisine / Specialty:
American Style cuisine; steak, seafood, pasta

Offers vegetarian, heart healthy or organic selections:
Yes

Support local farmers:
Yes

Locally owned accommodations:
Lillies Garden Bed and Breakfast
65 Norland Avenue
Chambersburg, PA 17201
(717) 262-2252

Craig Victorian Bed & Breakfast
756 Philadelphia Avenue
Chambersburg, Pennsylvania
717-263-3371 or 877-236-3399

Local attractions:
Civil War history is all around
Chambersburg
Gettysburg battleields,
Antitam National Park

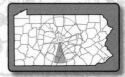

the county my dad was born in. I moved in closer, accepted a beer and giant chilidog and listened closely to what they liked in their own backyard down south. Topping the list was a pub and restaurant that came with rave reviews from the whole gang! They told me about The Cottage Pub and Restaurant in Chambersburg – that it was a great place, had a huge PSU following, had good beer and is smoke free! I finished my beer and giant chilidog, thanked them several times, accepted a beer to go and bid them goodbye. As I strolled through the mass of humanity I was already mapping out a route south in my head.

I arrived in Chambersburg late in the afternoon of another Penn State football Saturday and went straight to The Cottage Pub and Restaurant and the place was hoppin'. I could hardly get to the bar but amazingly got a seat and ordered a Tröegs Pale Ale. At the far end of the bar were a group of guys battling it out on the grid-iron of banter and sitting beside me was a big guy who could have been a running back. He turned out to be the general manager of The Cottage and next to him was a pretty young woman who was the owner's assistant.

Jimmy Spadaccino and Mary Caldwell were so nice and talked with me like I was one of the regulars. I asked Jimmy about the place and he took the time to talk with me for quite awhile. When I asked about any history, Mary jumped up and ran to the back. She reappeared with a single sheet of paper on which was a brief history on the place. Rather than interpret, I'm just going to let you read it for yourself.

"Seventy four years ago with little more than a fresh keg of beer and a few picnic tables, Nellie Goble began to build a small piece of Chambersburg history and named it The Cottage. Attracting workers from the Chambersburg Engineering Company,

the corner of Wayne and Coldbrook Avenues soon became
the place to relax after work and drink a few beers.

Since 1933 The Cottage has had a succession of owners,
all of whom have added their own unique signatures
to the establishment. Throughout it all, one thing
has remained the same; The Cottage is still one of
the area's most popular gathering places."

Now, I wanted to find out what makes this place stand
out from the chain gang, what keeps folks coming back
and why I'm not wheezing despite the crowd and that
I'm sitting at a bar.

In March 2007 The Cottage went smoke free! Owner Tom
Boock decided the health of his staff as well as his
loyal customers was important. What he didn't realize
(like most bar owners) is that his business actually
improved because of this. "Our business shot up by
a lot" Jimmy said. I asked if anybody got mad or
stopped coming. "Yeah at first, but only a handful,
but even those folks came back. We offer a fall NFL
package, we feature Penn State football and have a
huge Nittany Lions and Steelers following. Those folks
just couldn't stay away! What was amazing was how
many people overflowed from the restaurant to the bar
now that we're smoke free and offer the same menu
on both sides."

What a place, I thought. But Jimmy wasn't done. Without prompting, he proudly told me how The Cottage
goes local! "We use three different local suppliers.
We get our poultry from Farmers Produce and our meats
from Steely's Meats, both here in Chambersburg and
our produce comes from Dave's Produce in Hagerstown
Maryland. We take pride in that and in our food."

With that I had a look at the menu. Soups like Cottage
Crab, Black Angus burgers, specialty sandwiches like
the Nellie Goble - tender roast beef sautéed with
mushrooms topped with provolone and served on a hoagie
roll. Wraps, pasta dishes like Cajun Chicken Alfredo

and a killer entrée lineup starting with Fat Tommy's Baby Back Ribs and ending with a "make your own Surf & Turf. But what The Cottage is famous for is their wings, 720 pounds of them a week my friends and all from a local supplier. With Tröegs on tap, smoke free, cozy, super friendly staff and patrons, sweet pub room, beautiful dining room, PSU and Steelers supportive and all about going local, it's hard to beat a place like this!

The Cottage came to me without asking, without scouting and without the help of the internet. It came to me by a group of dedicated Penn State fans in the middle of a sea of motor homes and EZ-Up's. It came by folks eager to share their favorite places and bring support to their locally owned eateries. I've heard about many places while working on this book - most great, some just okay. For me, The Cottage was one of the great ones. "We Are...Penn State!" even in Franklin County!

Enjoy!

7 O'CLOCK

CHAPTER 7

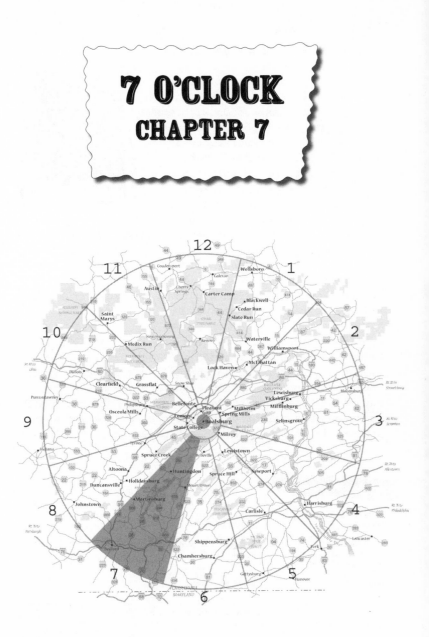

Boxer's Café
HUNTINGDON, HUNTINGDON COUNTY

This place is a Knockout! Ha ha! Actually that's the only thing this place has in common with the sport. Just the opposite is true. This Boxer is somewhere between hippie, scholar, workin' man, biker and just plain folk. It's a place that embodies vision, passion, preservation, quality, value, friendliness, and a true indie spirit. Actually named for their love of Boxer dogs, Tony and Paula Seguin opened their pub in 1990. Born and raised in State College but not being able to cope with the high rents there, Tony and Paula looked beyond their front yard to the wonderful and affordable beautiful backyard to their south.

Huntingdon is the county seat and is a really beautiful place! It was founded in 1796 and sweet Victorian era structures line the main street where trees and grass blend in nicely with handmade brick and cut stone. The Courthouse is stunning and is a grand backdrop to an arbor courtyard that greets you when approaching from the southeast on Pennsylvania Ave.

JUST A TASTE

Name of establishment:
Boxers Cafe

Contact Info:
410 Penn Street
Huntingdon, PA 16652

Owned by:
Paula & Tony Seguin

Hours:
Mon – Sat 11 am until ?

Price range:
Under $10.00

Cuisine / Specialty:
Soup and Sandwiches

Offers vegetarian, heart healthy or organic selections:
Yes

Support local farmers:
Yes

Locally owned accommodations:
Solvang

Local attractions:
Rothrock Outfitters
Swigart Car Museum
Raystown Lake
The IRIS Film Festival in September

Huntingdon is also home to Juniata College, a private, top-notch university that brings not only diversity, but a young and hip vibe to a somewhat sleepy town.

Boxer's Café embraces this vibe but is also "grounded" in the ways of Mother Earth. Here, super nice, friendly, and some dreadlocked young women move about the tiny pub transporting everything from pints of Guinness to plates of burgers and other tavern fare. The bar, which Tony explains with pride, was brought by water canal from Baltimore Maryland. This bar however did not start its life as a fountain of alcohol, but a fountain for youth – It was a soda fountain in the midst of a family-run drug store. Young Huntingdon boys and girls would plop down on the high stools after school and on Saturdays to enjoy the ice cream soda delights that defined an era.

Now, Boxer's is a fountain that soaks in young and old, academic and hippy, business people and bikers, college kids and locals with an equal welcome that is rare to find these days. As soon as you walk through the door you'll see the happy faces of folks eating and talking as they enjoy the great food and drinks while everything from Beatles to Bob Marley plays over the sound system. And all this is comfortably tucked into a space not more than 12' by 40'.

Only at a place like Boxer's can this kind of mix of people, culture, music and lifestyle co-exist in such a rural setting. But it may have more to do with Tony's passion for quality craft brewed beers and a simple but wonderful menu of foods. A combo that is sure to please just about everyone from everywhere! There are always 6 to 7 top notch hand-crafted beers on tap and Tony always keeps an extra tap just for Guinness with pours that are always perfect.

The offerings on the regular taps range from domestic to imports. But, you will not find any big batch beers here! No, we're talking Pilsner Urquell from the Czech Republic, Victory Hop Devil from Downing-town, Tröegs from Harrisburg and Sierra Nevada from California, plus many other quality brews that are rotated often. Sometimes I think they get Otto's in too when Charlie can find the time to bring it out. And, if that selection brings a smile to your face, you should see the variety of bottled beers. Tony must stock a hundred different brands and styles - if you want it, they probably have it.

My pals and I make a "Boxer's Run" a lot during the summer on our bikes. We love Boxer's, and it is nice to be there with friends - it's just that kinda place. The food is awesome, the prices are right and the staff is great. You cannot enter Boxer's without an instant sense that all is well in the world at that moment. You also cannot leave unhappy and still hungry.

Tony and Paula have taken a little old time drug store and soda fountain and transformed it into a gathering place for the community and travelers alike. Stop in, order-up a burger and beer, chill and sit a spell. Let the vibe of Boxer's touch your heart, let the groove bring you back to earth and let the food and drink knock you out! Boxer's is calling you to the mat - don't fight it!

Enjoy!

Mamie's Café
MARTINSBURG, BLAIR COUNTY

I heard about this place from
an unlikely but very reliable
source, my friends Mark and
Jeff, the Beer Geeks. Some may
assume that my esteemed colleagues don't frequent
"dry" establishments but, they do and that's what
makes these dudes geeks to begin with - they appreciate, embrace, and support the indie spirit whether
it's wet, dry, baked or brewed. Beer advocates as
well as wine connoisseurs have a knack for sniffing
out unique, cool and cozy places - Mamie's has all
those adjectives and more!

I arrived one sunny morning aboard The Steed to find
Mamie's Café located along the main drag of Martinsburg in an old building with windows along the
entire front. A vivid red and white striped awning
hangs high above the sidewalk and black ironwork
flanks the steps leading in. As I approached, there
seemed to be two different sides to this place, but
both seemed connected.

I noticed that the left side was filled with people
at tables and the look was subdued and the colors

JUST A TASTE

Name of establishment:
Mamie's Café

Contact Info:
110 East Allegheny Street
Martinsburg, PA 16662
814-793-9122
mamiescafe@earthlink.net

Owned by:
Karen Wyland

Hours:
Mon. thru Fri. 6 a.m. to 7 p.m.
Sat. 6 a.m. to 6 p.m.

Price range:
$1 to $10.00

Cuisine:
Home Style and Baked Goods

**Offers vegetarian, heart healthy
or organic selections:**
Yes

Support local farmers:
Yes

Locally owned accommodations:
The Clubhouse Bed and Breakfast
327 High Street
Williamsburg, PA 16693
814-832-9122

Local attractions:
Lake Raystown
Horseshoe Curve

soft and muted – this was the look of a cozy coffee shop. The right side was bright and bustling with folks standing in lines holding bags of goodies. The décor here was of stainless steel, ceramic, baker's racks and bread baskets. This was a cool bakery for sure and I opted for this side to walk in.

As soon as I did I knew why Mark and Jeff told me to check this place out! You know how some places take awhile to warm up to? Not here, not for me. As soon as I entered Mamie's I caught the sweetness (and it wasn't the enormous rack of sticky buns either) and knew I was in a great place. High ceilings paneled with decorative tin, white walls and white and red checkered tile floors. These floors were covered with racks and racks of fresh baked goods, cakes, muffins, pies, doughnuts, cookies, whoppie pies (or "gobs" as they're called in this neck of the woods), and of course, those luscious gooey treats – sticky buns.

What made Mamie's a bit unique was that the workings of this bakery were right out in the open for all to see and smell. In front of the oven was just a 4 foot high counter with an apron clad woman standing behind it. She was very busy but when I walked up, she looked at me and with a nice smile asked if she could help me. I looked over to see what she was making.

There before my pastry loving eyes was the most delicious looking fruit tart that I've ever seen! She was just adding the raspberries to finish it off and gently set it up on the counter right in front of me. She asked again if she could help me, but I was transfixed on the tart – It was like my first day at a nude beach on the island of Corsica.

There I was standing in water that was every shade of blue and green imaginable on sand that was as white as snow. Near me was an older guy whose language was clearly Italian and not the native French, so I struck up a conversation with him to practice my Italiano. Before I knew it he asked me if I would like to meet his family. We walked out of the water and back to his blanket. After a brief intro, he asked me to sit down next to his daughter. What happened next is a bit like the fruit tart encounter – sort of.

This young woman of around 25 years old was a combination French, Italian, super model and topless! Though I would never want to watch it, I wish someone would have been shooting a video of my face as I spoke to her (remember, this was my first visit to a French beach where topless is the norm).

Note: Just try this test sometime. Get about 2 to 3 feet from a friend, look them in the eye and start talking. Then, about every 2 seconds, drop your eyes down to their chest for another split second and then, look back up to their eyes. Ask if they notice. The response every time will be "Yeah, are you kidding?"

So there I am talking with this young woman in broken French/Italian and completely tongue tied. And then, knowing full well I was doing it, but completely unable to stop myself, I was constantly staring at... She was sweet and polite and never let on I was making a total fool of myself.

So it was with the woman behind the counter at Mamie's Café. I stood there speaking with her but all my attention was on the beautiful and voluptuous fruit tart sitting on the counter. As we talked my eyes kept dropping down and I began to fantasize about it and not paying attention to what she was actually saying to me. She had to have noticed but she was also sweet and polite never saying a thing.

I ordered a latte and saw an opening in the brick wall that separated the two large spaces that I noticed from outside. I walked through and was totally impressed by the décor and feel. Luckily a high table opened up by the front windows and I sat down and began to write in my sketchbook to make notes of the cool vibe. After a bit of writing and seeing all the delicious food being served around me I decided it was time for a late breakfast.

The woman making the fruit tart took my order but her hands were deep in dough so when she called on her daughter Valerie to help me I realized this must be Mamie herself. I asked her and she said she was the owner but her name was Karen and Mamie was her grandmother.

I returned to my table and within a few minutes my veggie omelet arrived, hot and accompanied by Karen's homemade bread which was thick and toasted to perfection. The omelet practically melted in my mouth – I think it might be the best one I've ever had. It was huge but super light and fluffy, full of veggies and cheese and damn good! I settled in with my breakfast and remaining latte, continued writing and enjoying la vie at Mamie's.

After a two hour breakfast, I paid my bill and introduced myself. Karen held out to me the most wonderfully gooey, soft and warm, brown sugar and cinnamon coated hunk of goodness I ever tasted – her famous sticky bun – for free! She didn't even know why I was there at this point, just my name. She just must have been proud of her buns! Ha ha.

As we chatted I told her about my purpose there and it was all she could do to talk and keep up with the folks coming in and out for baked goods, pastries, breakfast and lunch. She did tell me that the reason she is there is because she had always dreamed of opening a bakery and café but never could take the risk. After losing both her husband and son to cancer she realized life was just too fleeting and risks where nothing compared to the joys of life. She decided to make her dream come true and live life while she could.

A few years back Harvard University did a survey of folks over 80. They were all asked if they were to do it all over again what would they do differently. The number one response was "take more risks." Karen Wyland took her dreams, rolled them out, added a cup of passion, two tablespoons of courage, a pinch of risk, a dash of grit and a whole lotta love. Then, warmed it all in her heart and offers it up everyday for you and me at Mamie's Café.

Enjoy!

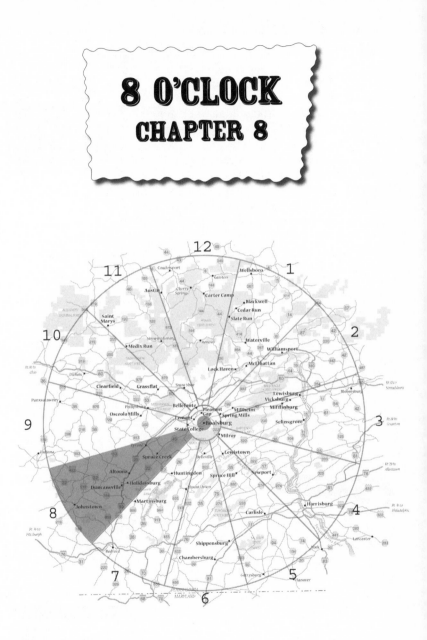

Spruce Creek Tavern
SPRUCE CREEK, HUNTINGDON COUNTY

At the head or end (depending on which way you're traveling) of beautiful PA Rt. 45, and sitting above the confluence of Spruce Creek and the Little Juniata River, is the small hamlet of Spruce Creek. With lovely Bed and Breakfasts, world-class trout fishing, a great fly fishing shop, church and post office, all this little country town needs is a great place to eat and gather with locals. Well fortunately, they have one – it's awesome, and it is called The Spruce Creek Tavern. This place is legendary!

My sister Kathy told me of the SCT and that it's known as the French fry capital of the world (at least central PA). She told me, "They peel and cook over 200 pounds of potatoes per week and serve them hot, golden brown, piled high and on cafeteria lunch trays." That in and of itself is legendary, but the legend became reality one summer evening many years and a lot of fries ago.

JUST A TASTE

Name of establishment:
Spruce Creek Tavern

Contact Info:
Rt. 45
Spruce Creek, PA 16683
814-632-3287

Owned by:
John Carper

Hours:
Closed Sun. & Mon.
11:00 to 8:00 ?

Price range:
$1.25 grilled cheese
$9.00 shrimp

Cuisine / Specialty:
American

Offers vegetarian, heart healthy or organic selections:
Yes

Support local farmers:
Yes

Locally owned accommodations:
Carper's Spruce Creek B&B

Local attractions
World-class trout fishing
Indian Caverns
Lake Raystown

On this fateful eve, I mounted The Mighty Steed and rode the twenty plus miles west through beautiful farmlands and mountains to check out this place for myself. Arriving at a large gravel parking lot, I barely had room to park the bike because of all the cars. A big sign along the road indicated I was at the Spruce Creek Tavern and the words below reading "Famous Fries," were one more conformation of the legend.

Once inside, I had to take a seat at the bar because every table was full. As I sat there, I perused the menu. Back then, they offered fries in four different sizes - Single, Handful, Basket, and The Tray. I assumed the "Single" was for the kiddos. I ordered a beer, a burger and because I was a bit hungry, went with the Basket size.

You've seen those red plastic basket things you get fries in, right? So, even I could easily down a basket of fries I thought and have room for dessert. As I was enjoying my beer and taking in the "ambiance," the kitchen doors opened and the wonderful smell of freshly cooked fries came and kissed my nose. Just then a woman (who turned out to be the owners wife) emerged from the steamy, peel-laden kitchen and in her right hand, and held in the classic waitress pose, was a brown lunch tray piled at least 6" high and from edge to edge with the crispiest looking, most golden brown, deep fried, long skinny sticks of starchy delights that I have ever seen!

My eyes popped open like that first time I saw a girly magazine at the ripe old age of 13 (I started young). Jaw dropped and eyes wide, I sheepishly asked this waitress, "Is that the tray size?!" With the smile of a new mother cooing her baby, she said, "No sweetie, it's just the Handful." With that single wonderful experience, The Spruce Creek Tavern is and always will be my French fry capital of the world. But, it's not just the fries and good food at the SCT that

make it legendary – it's the character (and I don't
mean the feel of the place) that makes these next
stories so funny and endearing.

One Friday night, my best buddy Mike and I rode out
for a mess o' fries and a couple cold ones. We had
taken the long way and arrived starved and parched.
We walked in, and as always, the place was packed.
A small table was just clearing out in the center of
the room and we waited like sharks in a pool of fat
kids while the waitress cleaned it off. We took our
seats and didn't bother with the menu as we frequent
SCT many a summer night, especially aboard our bikes.
We placed our order of beer, sandwiches, and of
course, the Basket of fries (even Mike and I can't
handle The Tray without help).

The owner John was working at the bar as usual and
his tee shirt that night read, "This place insured
by Smith & Wesson." John is a classic! No fuss, no
muss, more fartsy than artsy and just a good ol' guy
running a good ol' tavern. As I said, the place was
hoppin' so John had to pinch-hit and bring us our
order of food and what happened next will also go
down in the "anals" of history.

As John approached our table with our bounty of
fries and two ice-cold beers, I looked up at him and
said, "John, you're our best friend!" (a bit tongue
and cheek but mostly out of kindness). Without
missing a beat or breaking stride, he set down our
order, looked me square in the eye and said, "Yeah,
and you're full of shit too!" He then just turned
around and walked away. It was all Mike and I could
to not to bust out laughing. True story.

That might paint John as a hard nose but he's actually a big softy at heart. For example, and on yet another ride to SCT, my friend Shawn said he would be buying that night so I didn't grab any extra cash before we left home. Well, to make a long story short (like I've been doing) Shawn forgot to get extra cash himself (Spruce Creek is not a metropolitan area. It has no ATM machine and no bank). It turns out that we had, to the penny, just enough to pay for the food and beer but nothing for a tip. We discovered this while at the bar paying the bill. We told John of our dilemma and that we had no money to give the young waitress. John turned around, took three dollars out of his cash register, handed it to me and told me to put it on the table. While I stood there half dazed, he said, "Hey, it's only money and we're all in this together. Plus, she's a good kid."

Try that one at the chain places folks.

I walked out of the SCT that night with a whole new view on things. Shawn and I climbed back on our bikes and put the sun to our backs. With full stomachs and warm hearts we cruised home along clear waters teaming with trout, roads that bend and curve and mountains alongside that rise up to touch the sky. There's much more to the Spruce Creek Tavern than "famous Fries" I thought, it's about a mom and pop place where the bottom line is not the business of making it rich, but living out the riches of life when running your own business.

And so the legend continues. Enjoy!

The Knickerbocker Tavern
ALTOONA, BLAIR COUNTY

My first visit to this cool tavern was the result of my own advice - I asked a local.

I was out riding on a sunny summer day, exploring the back roads and byways southeast of home. Around the outskirts of Altoona, I pulled over for gas and realized how hungry and thirsty I was. Not about to eat or drink anything from a "mini fart," I asked a guy at the pumps with me where a unique and locally owned place might be. I have always heard that angels roam among us, and this encounter proved that true. The guy told me that just down the road and around a few bends at the corner of 6th Ave. and Burgoon Rd. was a place that had great food, character and 12 micro brews on tap and maybe one hundred other quality beers in bottles. I thanked the guy (angel), fired up the bike and made haste.

As I pulled up to the curb, I saw a big awning hanging from the building that read The Knickerbocker Tavern. The building was not much to look at from the outside, but I knew I was at a great place before I even went

JUST A TASTE

Name of establishment:
The Knickerbocker Tavern

Contact Info:
3957 6th Avenue
Altoona, PA 16602
(814) 942-0770
www.knickerbockertavern.com

Owned by:
Terry and Lillan Reed

Hours:
Mon–Sat: 11:00 a.m. to 2:00 a.m
Sun: 10:30 a.m. to 2:00 a.m.

Price range:
Food: $1.25 to $14
Drink: $2 to $35

Cuisine / Specialty:
Classic American Cuisine, Tavern

Offers vegetarian, heart healthy or organic selections:
Yes

Support local farmers:
Yes

Locally owned accommodations:
The Altoona Hotel
  An American Bistro
3830 5th Avenue, Altoona, PA 16602
(814) 944-5521.

Local attractions:
Horseshoe Curve
Altoona Curve Baseball
Lakemont Park
Railroaders Museum

through the door - Two Harleys, one Ducati and a black vintage Honda were parked on the sidewalk in the front of the brick building and just next to the front door. I sheepishly parked in a regular street space because I was new there and didn't want to have to experience another "scene" (more on that in a bit).

I walked in, and the owner welcomed me with a smile and said, "Go ahead and pull your bike up on the sidewalk with the rest of them. That way we can keep an eye on it for ya." That was all it took, then and there I fell in love with The Knick.

In all my travels to Europe, I've always envied the bikers and scoot riders because everywhere, even the crowded sidewalks of Paris and Rome, they allow both scooters and big bikes to park on the sidewalks. In front of cafes, in front of bars, and even in front of chic restaurants along the Champs-Elysees, Europeans embrace fuel-efficient vehicles and saving space for cars to park. I actually think they like having motorbikes on the sidewalks because it adds an exciting, young, and romantic spirit to the already hip vibe.

(Here comes the "scene") I tried this little Euro-parking method at an upscale (uppity) place in State College once, not long after hanging out with some bikers in Nice (one of the hippest towns in the world). Within minutes of walking through the door of the State College restaurant, I was stopped by the owner and told to get my bike off the sidewalk and away from his building (seems that this place considers itself a bit above the Cote d' Azure). But here at a little tavern in Altoona, there was no scene just la vie (the life) and they embrace it!

I was delighted to join my brothers parked on the sidewalk and those in Europe, even if it was only in spirit. I pulled The Steed up alongside the Ducati and with an ear-to-ear smile, went inside. I thanked the owner and took a look around. An old

antique bar to my
left and big cushy
booths to my right,
a beautiful lineup
of beers on tap and
a cooler filled with
the mother lode of
imported and craft
brewed delights just
like the angel said.

I sat down at the
bar and opened the
menu to find a wonderful variety of tavern fare as
well as salads, entrees and desserts. I ordered up
a Weyerbacher Simcoe Double IPA (say that ten times
fast. But do it before you drink one, because it's
strong - 9+% AVB I think) and a big ol' bacon cheese-
burger with fries (had to try and balance out the
beer). All were big and damn good!

A few other guys were sitting at the bar and we
chatted about everything from beer to food to bikes.
Oh, and I think politics were in there too somewhere. Anyway, I mentioned how cool it was that the
owner allowed motorcycles to park on his sidewalk
and how Euro that was. The guys told me that the
owner's wife was from Sweden and he spends a lot of
time over there and is a bike enthusiast - the
Ducati was his!

During my meal, two of the guys told me about a big
party they were having the following weekend and
invited me. It turned out they were partners in a
local beer distributorship and would have no shortage
of good brews at the party. I thought that was incredible that they would invite a stranger to their
party but, then again, this is the kind of thing to
expect at The Knick. Not only can you park your bike
on the sidewalk and not get kicked out, but you can
enjoy great food and beer, a cool atmosphere and
make some new friends too!

Terry Reed, his wife Lillan and their son Bjorn own and run the place that way because that's how a place should be run. Not with an uppity attitude and little room for expression. The Reeds also run their place with passion. Whether it's the European influence of Lillan or the fact that Terry is a biker, it really doesn't matter. What matters is that they get it! They get what this book is partly about – that life is too short to be worrying about bikes on the sidewalk or what percentage of the target demographic is spending the most money. The Knick is about a time honored and proven way to do business that's more like "Keep it local and keep it real."

In fact, here's what they say on the front of their menu: "Our mission is to strive for the best possible food and service, from our extensive collection of fine beers to our menu selection ranging from the popular to the unique. The Knickerbocker Tavern is committed to quality, value and your complete satisfaction." Nice!

On any given day, evening or night, you will find the place full of young, old, hip, not so hip, newbie's, regulars, afficionados and just regular folks. Not only that, but you'll feel welcomed and appreciated even if you don't ride a bike and park it on the sidewalk – or wear Prada! They really *go local* at The Knickerbocker Tavern and love you just the way you are.

Now it's my turn to tell you to go "just down the road and around a few bends at the corner of 6th Ave. and Burgoon Rd."– I guess there's a little "angel" in all of us!

Enjoy!

It's June 23, 2007 and it's absolutely beautiful today! I've returned to an old flame – The Knickerbocker Tavern in Altoona, PA. It's been awhile since I've been here and quite a bit has changed, but for the better! Right now I'm sitting at an immense outdoor terrace basking in the sun of afternoon. All around me on the terrace are old brick buildings with windows set deep into the brick. It creates a kind of outdoor/indoor feeling. But one look up into the azure blue sky and you know you're outdoors. Grand market umbrellas provide spots of shade for the patrons and create a play of sun and shadow.

The folks all around are laughing, chatting and enjoying la vie. Cool Latin Music plays as the wait staff dance and weave around the tables bringing beer, food and great service to their guests. Now as I'm enjoying my Blackened Salmon Caesar Salad, the music just changed to French. If I don't listen to the language of others around me, or look up at the Tröegenator Doublebock sign in one of the old windows, I would swear I was somewhere in Europe.

Why did I wait so long to return to this place? Life I guess. But life here is worth returning to more often, as it is truly la Vie for me!

Saint Drogo Coffee Pub
HOLLIDAYSBURG, BLAIR COUNTY

This little place is just
another reason to get lost, or
at least off the beaten path.

While out on a reconnaissance mission to write about
a place I remembered from my past, I got off of main
Rt. 22 and cruised through the town of Williamsburg
PA. My trusty Gazetteer map showed a combination of
winding roads ahead and several little villages.
However, I was on the south side of a long mountain
chain and my destination was on the north side.

When I arrived at the first village, it looked to have
about a population of five, and that included the lowly
cow in the field and a couple of chickens pecking
around by the side of the road. I saw a sign indicating
another road to the right that I hoped would get me
over this mountain range which seemed to be hemming
me. I leaned The Mighty Steed into the turn, and as
I looked across my left shoulder down this beautiful
valley, the mountains went from green to purple as
they met the horizon miles off in the southwest.

JUST A TASTE

Name of establishment:
Saint Drogo Coffee Pub

Contact Info:
519 Allegheny Street
Hollidaysburg, PA 16648
(814) 695 5700
Djc0322@hotmail.com

Owned by:
Donny Chwatek

Hours:
M–F: 7am–5pm
Saturday: 8am–4pm
Sunday: 9am–2pm
Open Mic Night: Every Thursday
7:30–10:30

Price range:
$2.00 – $7.00

Cuisine / Specialty:
Café & Light Fare

**Offers vegetarian, heart healthy
or organic selections:**
Yes

Support local farmers:
Yes

Locally owned accommodations:
Iron Corbel B&B
703 Allegheny Street
Hollidaysburg, PA 16648

Local attractions:
Horseshoe Curve
Chimney Rocks
Canal Basin Park
Rails to Trails
Blue Knob Ski Resort/State Park,
Altoona Curve Baseball Club
Lakemont Park

Gaining altitude quickly, the road became narrow, curvy, sweet, dangerous
and full of surprises - just like a good
woman! I crested the top and down the
other side to the next valley. I was going
along, happy as a clam (I have no idea
what that means - clams seem so boring)
when I saw a guy cutting firewood along
the road. I stopped to get the poop on
whether this road would take me where
I thought it would, and he acknowledged
that it would. With a crack of the
throttle and a thunderous roar across
the quiet rural valley, I was off to
historic Hollidaysburg, PA.

As I slowly cruised down the main street of Hollidaysburg, I realized what a beautiful town it was.
Prior to that, I always used the highway around it
because I was always going somewhere else. Well
today I had nowhere to go except a little café in
the heart of town.

Beautiful old homes lined the street and as I got
into downtown the housing turned to brick row-homes.
At the main intersection of town, I spotted the sign
I was looking for. In a window was a beacon for all
hungry and thirsty travelers - a neon sign reading
"OPEN!" I pulled into a parking space right out
front and counted my blessing to have it because it
was Saturday and the place looked busy.

Let me just digress here for a moment.

Hollidaysburg is cool, I've already established that.
But one thing there puzzled me. The parking meters
in front of the café and a few others around me had
big bold signs on them which read "12 minute parking."
What's that all about? It's like the town council
hired some dude to park there, run in to the cafe,

get a coffee, pay for it and then get the hell back in his car while a little man with round glasses and a pocket protector stood by with a stopwatch yelling "faster, faster!" God forbid, you might order a double shot cappuccino with hazelnut syrup and a pinch of cinnamon!

Sorry, I just had to get that out.

Anyway, I parked, fed the (12 minuet) meter, walk over and opened the door to Saint Drogo Café – the place I had remembered and hoped was still there. It was, and what a cozy place! The vibe was peaceful and the décor soft and cushy. All the tables were cool but different – some were low, some high, some big and some small. But what caught my eye were the tables in the windows.

On each side of the front door were huge bay windows and in each one had high-top tables. They had side-walk seating but my ride was kinda cold and I needed to warm up a bit and the sun shining through the windows was perfect! I was hungry and needed a good coffee, so I sat down and checked out the menu. It was great, but what made my appetite increase and my heart be glad was what was behind it.

The owner Donnie Chwatek totally supports *going local*. He buys as much fresh and locally produced foods and stuff as he can. He's an advocate for sustainable agriculture, organic meats and produce. Donnie backs all that up by buying most of his stock from local suppliers. He even offers Gaffron Sunrise Bakery delights and Irving Bagels – both from my neck of the woods.

I ordered a grass-fed beef sandwich wrapped within a whole wheat tortilla and filled with fresh veggies and a cup of soup on the side. As I enjoyed my

lunch, my senses were enjoying the surroundings. I looked around at large plants here and there that complemented the space. The sound of light conversation and music filled the room and the smell of fresh ground and brewed coffee hung pleasant in the air. Local artists hang out there and I met one that day. He said that local musicians play there frequently and later that day, one band would be recording a CD in the café. They even sell some local artists work including jewelry and paintings, and this is just the beginning.

Some other amenities inside are wi-fi and a laptop for customer use and a nice flat screen television stands in front of a really deep cushy love seat – headphones are available so as not to bug the others. Cool floor lamps, games, books and of course a complete coffee concoction list makes Saint Drogo Café well worth getting off the beaten path.

Enjoy!

U.S. Hotel, Restaurant and Tavern
HOLLIDAYSBURG, BLAIR COUNTY

Here's where history, tradition, family, passion and support all converge at a hidden corner just outside of Altoona. The U.S. Hotel stands adjacent to a large rail yard and boasts quite a colorful past. It was built in 1835 by John Daugherty and apparently was a haven to the weary traveler and provided "entertainment for men."

The hotel and town was in its heyday back when the iron industry was booming. Water canal transportation kept the goods and people flowing in. The goods, people, and iron then flowed out towards the west and on to the great steel mills in Johnstown and Pittsburgh. Fire destroyed the building in 1871, but that didn't stop a young German immigrant named Englebert Humperdink. Ha ha, just kidding! Actually, his name was Englebert, but his last name was Gromiller (Engelbert Gromiller, hum, I'm sure he quickly changed that to Bert Miller after a few beatings).

Being a friend of Bert must have been sweet because he came from Germany as a Brew Master! He established

JUST A TASTE

Name of establishment:
U.S. Hotel Restaurant & Tavern

Contact Info:
401 S. Juniata Street
Hollidaysburg, PA 16648
814.695.9924
info@theushotel.com
www.theushotel.com

Owned by:
Karen Yoder

Hours:
Open seven days a week

Price range:
From $6.95 to $25.95

Cuisine / Specialty:
American

Offers vegetarian, heart healthy or organic selections:
Yes

Support local farmers:
Yes

Locally owned accommodations:
Wye Motor Lodge
Duncansville, PA

Local attractions:
Horseshoe Curve
Canal Basin Park

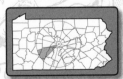

a brewery on the premises and the whole Juniata River basin rejoiced. Then in 1905, the cut block barroom was added to the brick structure. This section is still the bar room today and boasts such original relics like a hand-carved mahogany back bar, beveled silver mirrors, hand-leaded stained glass windows and a brass foot rail, under which flows a still active water trough spittoon. It's actually one of the last working spittoons left in the state!

After World War II, Bert's family sold the place and the hotel changed hands several times in the next half century and began falling into disrepair. The grand but deteriorating brewery had to be destroyed (what is this salty liquid draining from my eyes?). Then in 1987, Joe, Karen and Jason Yoder set about the task of restoring this grand old hotel and bar. Today, it offers room after room of lovingly restored floors, walls, and ceilings, just like they must have been in 1835!

The day I stopped in, I was very pleasantly greeted by the owner's granddaughter, Karri. You would have thought this sweet young woman was the owner herself. She beamed as she showed me around and described how passionate her family is with the place. As we walked through, she told me that their dining rooms can accommodate just about any occasion, business meetings, rehearsal dinners, weddings, birthday parties, and just about any special event.

She went on to say that the chef prepares daily lunch and dinner features and uses the freshest ingredients possible. She even stopped at a table while on our tour to check in on some customers. They couldn't say enough about their meal and complimented Karri on the service too! Karri smiled and said "I'm so glad you're happy - that's our goal."

I think Karri is a shoe-in for membership in the chain breakers club! She's what's going to keep this kind of sole-proprietor establishments open for future generations to enjoy and appreciate. And you should have seen how proud she was to inform me that they serve Johnstown Brewing Company beer on tap in the bar! Way to go U.S. Hotel!

Between burgers, wings, ribs and fish and chips for lunch to an outstanding dinner lineup and JBC beer, you can't go wrong. Just check out some of these samples from the menu: appetizers like Hotel Bruschetta, Spinach and Artichoke Dip and Drunken Mushrooms and Oysters Rockefeller. A few soups include French Onion, the du Jour and Hotel Turtle Soup – Yikes! Entrées include Fettuccine Alfredo, Lobster Ravioli, Stuffed Chicken Saltimbocca, Veal Roulade, Stuffed Filet Mignon, Prime Rib, Smoked Salmon, Mahi Mahi and Grilled Tuna and Portabella.

I was desperate to have something, but regretfully, I couldn't. I had to keep on rollin'. The day was short and that ol' lonesome highway was calling me back. A place like the U.S. Hotel is a find, and is so close to home! I really hated to leave but you know what? This place seems like a good old friend – no matter how short your stay is you know you're always welcome back anytime and for any reason.

Enjoy!

Marzoni's Brick Oven & Brewing Co.

DUNCANSVILLE, BLAIR COUNTY

This is a relatively new
brewery and restaurant just
south of Altoona. It sits
in the middle of a giant
parking lot, along a major
chain lane, is not much to
look at and very "chain-ish."
So what's going on here?

My esteemed colleagues, The Beer Geeks, who write
beer columns for local papers, recommend Marzoni's
and frequent it often. So, how can such a place for
beer purists' look and feel so much like a member of
the chain gang? Hmmm, curiosity got the best of me
and I decided to go in and check it out.

The bar here is huge! Three sides for patrons and
the end for wait staff to pick up orders. I took my
seat at the far side and settled in. My bartenders
Jamie and Christy where attractive, friendly and
very informed about all the beers on tap. Christy
suggested that I try the sampler - eight, six ounce
glasses of their complete offerings. This was not a
good idea. Forty eight ounces of beer in one short

JUST A TASTE

Name of establishment:
Marzoni's Brick Oven & Brewing Co.

Contact Info:
165 Patchway Road
Duncansville, PA 16635
www.Marzoni's.com

Owned by:
Bill and Nancy Campbell

Hours:
Sun – Thur: 11–11
Fri & Sat: 11–midnight

Price range:
$6 - $26

Cuisine / Specialty:
Craft Beer & Brick Oven Dishes

**Offers vegetarian, heart healthy
or organic selections:**
Yes

Support local farmers:
No

Locally owned accommodations:

Local attractions:
Railroad Museum
Horseshoe Curve

afternoon in this peanut body had DUI written all over it! I declined, but chose just one of their IPA's and ordered a pizza. The beer I chose was Avalanche IPA which they describe as "aggressively bitter with a floral hop aroma," weighing in at 6.9% AVB.

Honestly, I don't like when ale is described as "bitter." I've experienced too many folks who turn their nose up to an IPA because they think "bitter" means it tastes like a lemon or aspirin. Avalanche IPA is far from tasting like either one, on the contrary it's very tasty and damn good! I would scratch the word bitter and just use hoppy. The hops in this beer dominates and grips your tongue for sure, but not out too aggressive – It's more like your kid when they wrap their entire body around your ankle – they don't easily let go, but that's ok, it's fun and feels kinda good!

As I chatted with Christy I inquired about why the place felt like a chain but was clearly an indie brew pub. When she told me that Marzoni's is owned by a member of the chain gang, I felt like I had just been violated! All I wanted to do was to go home and take a shower! I expressed my shock and dismay to her and she calmly took the opportunity to tell me how this seeming atrocity could be, and her explanation sparked an epiphany.

Christy told me how a manager of a Pennsylvania based chain restaurant was also a passionate home brewer. He eventually convinced the "head office" to try opening a brew pub where he would be the Brew Master and they could run the restaurant. Fortunately they agreed and Marzoni's was born or shall I say "unchained."

Though owned by a chain, housed in a chain-like building and having a chain feel, I must admit the beer is damn good, the bartenders know their stuff and my pizza was great! Brew Master Bill Kroft is certainly passionate about his brew and does a terrific job. He offers a wide variety of beer styles for a wide variety of tastes. And the residents of Blair Co. now have the opportunity to say NO to the big batch small taste beers and embrace quality and goodness!

There's a moral to this story, and it's a little like a story out of the bible.

One day Jesus' disciples came to him and reported that a group of people were healing and performing miracles that weren't a part of their group. His disciples were indignant towards them but Jesus being the awesome dude he is indicated that as long as they're doing good for people, that was cool. In his own words, "If they're not against us, they must be for us."

So, my friends, it is the same with Marzoni's and the "head office." For whatever their reasons are, whether for pure profit or jumping on the brew pub bandwagon, the result is that they're brewing quality beer and bringing it to people who might not otherwise experience quality craft brewing. This can only help the cause.

Enjoy!

Johnstown Brewing Company
JOHNSTOWN, CAMBRIA COUNTY

It was on the cusp of fall when I arrived at the Johnstown Brewing Co. - the day was absolutely perfect and it was just beginning! The weather that morning when I left home on The Mighty Steed was a bit cold and a lot foggy. About every mile or so, I had to use my left index finger like a little wiper-blade on my glasses because of the moisture in the air. My pants were getting wet and my leather jacket shed beads of water.

That may not sound like fun to you, but for me it's wonderful! Not only was I confident that the fog would clear, the moisture would be gone and I would be toasty warm in the bright sun. But also, I was simply a boy on his bike with not a care in the world except to visit a wonderful brew pub ahead. Life was/is truly good!

I arrived at JBC and parked under the shade of a giant pine tree. When I looked around, I saw a building that seemed to be built like a combination Adirondack lodge and country club - it was beautiful! All the walls

were of mountain stone and the roof appeared to be slate. The gable ends were wood sided with grand stone chimneys running up the middle and then extending through the roof. It was backed up close to a forested hillside but the front was situated due east overlooking a huge grassy lawn. The main entrance seemed to be on the backside under a cool carport thing, so I walked on in.

I was greeted by a lovely woman who seemed to be the owner by the way she presented herself and by the way she talked about the place and their offerings of beer and food when I inquired about both. She was also as attractive as she was friendly and personable, so I thought she might be the hostess as well.

Her name was Susan Lovette and it turned out that she was one of four owners and she was actually the general manager. I hoped to have an opportunity to talk with her so I let her know of my project right away. She had been on her way to the office so she asked me to just have a seat at the bar and she would be with me to talk as soon as she could. Just before she continued to the office, she poured me a beer that just went on tap that morning - their Irish Red.

Despite the really nice bar area, I took my beer out on the side terrace to soak up some sun and enjoy my beer. This lovely red ale was nicely hopped and quite good! In the remaining days of September, it was a perfect match to the Maple leaves in the distance whose tips were just beginning to turn red as well.

While I was enjoying the weather and my beer, another woman walked out to the terrace and introduced herself as Karen Lovette - the sister in-law of Susan, and the actual hostess of JBC. Karen asked if I wanted a tour of the place and learn a bit about what makes JBC not just a great brew pub but a tribute to the community!

The place was huge on the inside and was split into two levels, both with their own personalities. Upstairs is called the "Upper Works" and is a fullblown restaurant with a sweet little bar off to one side. Big and bright, this space affords views out across the hills and valleys and is totally smoke free!

Downstairs is the "Lower Works" and the main pub. This space is as cool as it gets - low ceilings, darker, steel memorabilia, big and beautiful bar and a vibe that rivals any pub I've been to in England or Ireland (and I've been to a lot!). This is where you go if you want to eat or drink in an atmosphere of fun, friends and camaraderie. And, it's where the Mug Club hangs out (more on that later)!

Karen told me this place was a former country club as I thought, but not for just anyone though, but for Bethlehem Steel executives. Back in the day, big steel honchos would come here for fun and play while the workers sweated it out in the mills. Bethlehem Steel was the lifeblood of Johnstown and like most western PA cities, steel ran through the veins and pride was the beating hearts of the men and women who made it all happen. Today, this place honors them, the workers.

I doubt that Karen worked the mills but you couldn't tell that from her passion to share it all with me. She pointed to a chilling and moving lineup of hard hats hanging with pride from the main beam in the Upper Works (and these were the real thing - names still on the fronts of some, and others with marks and dings from close calls with the steel). Then in the Lower Works, Karen showed me these wooden patterns which were used to bend hot steel. Some of these things were normal size and some absolutely huge! They were so cool and very unusual, and some-

thing I'd never seen before. Everywhere I looked there was something to throw me back to a time when blood, sweat and pure muscle created everything from the skeletons of skyscrapers to the rivets and bolts that held them together.

After my tour, Karen went back to work and I sat down and looked over the beer menu. There in front of me was a beer I just had to have. Not an IPA mind you, but a Kolsch style beer. But, it wasn't the style I was concerned with this time, but the name - Dam Beer! Seriously, that's the name - South Fork Dam Beer!

For those less informed on PA history, this Dam Beer is named after the South Fork Dam that collapsed in 1889 and devastated the town of Johnstown. 2,209 souls were lost along with countless homes, businesses and animals. 900 bodies were never found. Obviously the people of Johnstown take that flood very seriously. They have an awesome museum dedicated to it downtown and the site at South Fork is a National Park Service National Memorial.

Johnstown has been through a lot so they deserve a good beer, needless to say, this beer was damn good! In fact, when Susan arrived back at my table, she told me that their patrons love to belly up to the bar and say, "Give me a damn beer" (my kind of place)! Try doing that in a froo-froo chain bar and you'll probably be asked to leave. Here at Johnstown Brewing Company, they'll not only give you a Dam Beer but the whole place will most likely raise their mugs to you!

Speaking of mugs, Susan told me that they have a "Mug Club." Mug after personal mug line and fill one entire wall behind the bar in their Lower Works. When there's a special, the staff puts little notes in each and every mug to let their customers know.

Mug Club members, as well as you and me, have some really amazing beers to choose from – all with names that invoke the pride of Johnstown and the industry that made her strong. They also serve two styles of root beer for kids and those taking the great and selfless responsibility to drive their happy friends and neighbors home.

They serve great food here. Everything from simple appetizers like Wire Mill Wings to Laurel Highlands Lobster Bisque. They also offer lots of things like burgers and pizza, with main courses like Titanium T-bone Steak and Axle Plant Asian Chicken Salad. You can eat and drink in both levels, and in good weather you can enjoy yourself on the wonderful deck outside.

Johnstown Brewing Company is a true family thing. Susan, Karen and their husbands Pat and Ralph along with non-family member Sean Hallisey – their awesome Brew Master, work their butts off running a place where passion and commitment along with dreams and vision run together. When I told Susan a quote from my first art mentor, "It's a hell of a way to make a living, but it's a great life," She nodded in agreement.

This is a place you've got to visit! It's a brewery, pub, restaurant, museum and just a wonderful space to hang out in. The owners have given up any sense of a "normal" life, to bring the best they can provide you, and honor the community that has afforded them this chance. They've come from all backgrounds but are now grounded in one common goal – to burst forth to you, their neighbors and friends, a flood of good eats and great cheer.

Now, get me a Dam Beer!

Enjoy!

9 O'CLOCK
CHAPTER 9

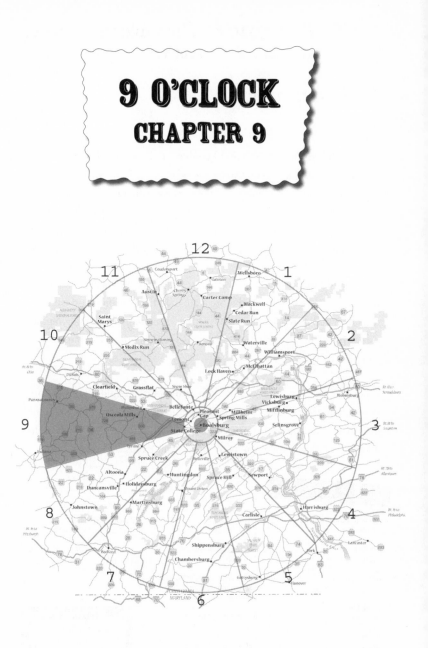

VFW Post 5020 & The Golden Cantina

OSCEOLA MILLS, CLEARFIELD COUNTY

A 24 hr. Odyssey

Scene I

It was Saturday March 10th and I couldn't wait two more weeks till spring to set out on a recon trip for the book aboard The Mighty Steed. The morning sun was shining and the forecast called for a high of 53°, and since my cutoff for cold weather riding is 40°, I was good to go! What I chose not to acknowledge was the prediction of rain showers – I was just so eager to fire up the bike for a ride longer than around the block.

Over breakfast I consulted my PA state map and Delorme Gazetteer. I planned my basic route on the big state map then verified and confirmed the smaller roads with the Gazetteer. I memorized the beginning routes (reducing the need to stop at every intersection) and the basic compass directions.

I had decided that today would be pure uncharted exploration – no pre-determined towns, no prior recommendations, not even a clue if I would fine something. Up to this point I had no listings for my 9 o'clock region and without this chapter the book wasn't going to be complete.

JUST A TASTE

Name of establishment:
Golden Cantina

Contact Info:
613 Lingle Street
Osceola Mills, PA 16666
814-339-6699
suesum@verizon.net

Owned by:
VFW Post 5020

Hours:
Mon.-Sat: Lunch 11:00 a.m–2:00 pm
Mon, Wed, Fri: Dinner 5:00-8:00 pm
Bar food available:
11:00am-9:00pm daily

Price range:
$3.50-$12.00

Cuisine / Specialty:
American

**Offers vegetarian, heart healthy
or organic selections:**
On request

Support local farmers:
Yes

Locally owned accommodations:
Whispering Sisters
Philipsburg, PA

Local attractions:
Museum with local artifacts
  across the street
Garvey car museum within 1 mile
Hiking trails nearby
Local fishing streams

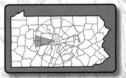

I stoked-up my coal stove, put on my cold weather riding gear, packed a snack, said goodbye to the cats and fired up the bike. A guy walked by just as I was ready to go and asked where I was headed. I said "wherever I end up I guess." He smiled with a bit of envy as I rolled back on the throttle and set out on the historic 28th Division Highway – Rt. 322.

The air was a bit "nippley" but my polypro and heavy leathers shielded me well. It was a beautiful morning though and the open road was ahead. The Steeds belly was full of high octane fuel and with the cold air ramming up his nostrils he was running in top form. With the morning sun on my shoulder, wind in my hair and the anticipation of a cool pub or café to come, I thought to myself "I can't believe I'm getting paid to do this!" Then it hit me, I realized I was not getting paid! In fact, because of this project and wanting to devote full time to it, I took a leave from my painting, closed my gallery and was living totally by faith (and my folks!).

As I cruised west along Bald Eagle creek the sun burned off the remaining fog that had settled there overnight. Black silhouettes of barren trees began to appear as a beautiful Egret swooped and caught its breakfast right next to me. Further on, I hung a right onto Rt. 350 north that would take me up into the heights of the Alleghenies. I cracked the throttled and blasted up Tyrone Mountain like a leather clad jet pilot!

Cresting over Sandy Ridge at 2, 042 feet, I kept a sharp eye for the smaller road I needed to take to continue my journey west. I sensed that it was coming soon and when I spotted the crossroad sign ahead I brought the bike down to the speed limit. Making the turn I saw a sign reading Osceola Mills 4 miles.

I pulled into town just as a bank sign went from 52° to 12:16. I was hungry for sure but my foodie radar wasn't picking up much here. The streets were quite – no artsy cafés, no neon signs of good beers and the sidewalks were totally void of pedestrians accept one old dude walking slowly out of town. It seemed kinda dead there.

Practicing what I preach though, I pulled over to ask that guy if he knew of a place that served up some good grub and beer (I figured asking for a Gorgonzola cheese steak and an India Pale Ale was out of the question). He took one look at me and ran like a little kid from a plate of broccoli! No seriously he didn't, but he did look a bit scared. He was helpful though and very friendly – as I would soon find the whole town to be.

First he pointed to a pizza shop and I grimaced. Then he told me of a VFW (Veterans of Foreign Wars) post just up the street and said the food there was home cooked and delicious! Well, the timing of this information and my rumbling stomach was perfectly in sync. But the problem was I was neither foreign or a veteran and I wasn't about to put a VFW in my book (I wasn't practicing what I preach – being open to fate). The lure of food and a cold one however, was more than I could bear so I said thanks and rode away.

I parked the bike outside VFW Post 5020, put on my best warrior face, practiced my salute and sheepishly opened the door. Well like all small town pubs, as I walked in every head in the place turned and looked straight at me. I confidently walked up to the bar (actually I was close to wetting myself) and said "Uh, I'm not a veteran. Is it okay for me to be in here?" The place went dead silent! Not a sound from anyone, just imaginary crickets chirping away. Finally, a young woman behind the bar said "Are ya 21? Let me see your ID."

I took my drivers license out of my pocket and placed it on the bar. As I did, all eyes were still locked on me like snipers ready to take out a target. Thankfully I cleared check point Charlie – actually it was check point Susan (who was also the manager) and she said something about signing in. What? I thought. Sign in for what?

Out of the corner of my right eye I saw two old timers staring me down and as I reached for the sign-in book. One of them burst out and said

"You don't sign it she does! You can be here as long as you're twenty one and a member signs you in, but just as a guest!" I jumped back, thought of something funny to say and hoped I wouldn't be Court Marshaled. Honestly, I don't remember what I said accept everybody laughed and I quickly made a beeline to the bathroom to check my pants.

While in the restroom I overheard one of the old timers say to the other "I bet he's with the PLCB!" From what I could gather in later conversations, they (the post) have a special standing or something with the Pennsylvania Liquor Control Board and they need to be very cautious of those they serve or they might lose the bar. I also found out I could only be a guest there two more times and then have to become a member myself. That was ok with me because I figured I would be out of there after lunch and probably never be back.

I returned to find the only empty seat at the bar to be right next to the old timers who must have been former CIA agents by the way they were watching me. I then asked them if somebody was sitting at the stool and the "agent" on the far side said "Yeah, you!" I laughed with one of those short laughs that's somewhere between scared and really nervous.

I put my pack on the floor, sat down with my map and thought about a beer. Susan asked what I wanted and when I spotted a Saint Marys original (Straub) on the tap docket I ordered a mug. She drew a perfect pour, set it down and said "that'll be 90 cents." What, 90 cents?! Uh, did I wormhole back to the 40's? No, this is what happens when you get out of the city and its haute cuisine.

I took a sip, settled back, and in my usual style with which I was born into through my dad, started right in with conversation and banter with the two old timers as well as the bartender and the rest of the crowd. Before long we were all laughing and joking, telling stories and spinning tales. I asked the old boys their names and all I got was "H. J. Kephart" and "R. E. Crain" – no first names (I might be the PLCB ya know).

It turns out that the two presumed agents were actually the two guys who started the club back in, are you ready for this, Nineteen Hundred and Forty Six! That's right, 61 years ago. Wow! The two of them returned home from WW II in the Pacific theater and for $16,000 dollars bought a clockmaker and watch repair shop and applied for a charter with the esteemed Veterans of Foreign Wars. They received their post assignment and set up The Gold Stripe, a bar and lounge catering to any vet of a foreign conflict.

Well having watched the HBO series Band of Brothers, my view of WW II and the veterans who fought in it has been changed forever. What I once didn't think much about and hadn't much respect for (a generational thing I guess) I now have an incredible respect, and every time I encounter a Veteran of that conflict I want to salute them. My heart goes out to these men and women who gave their commitment, hearts and sometimes their lives to a war worth fighting. So I immediately started chatting with them about their experiences.

Despite their previous apprehension of me, they began telling me stories that would make Spielberg sit up and take notice. Get this, Mr. Kephart told me that he was in Pearl Harbor the day of the Japanese invasion – December 7th 1941 the "day that will live in infamy." Then he started to tell me where exactly he was when the first bomb dropped. His sidekick Mr. Crain jumped in and said "He was downtown in a cathouse, you know, a house of prosti-tution!" The whole bar busted out laughing!

Those two guys then proceeded to let fly an exchange of insults and banter that could only be achieved by years of true friendship and mutual respect (or at least I hoped that was it). What I saw and sensed in those two, was the bond that could only be achieved by being kids together, going to school together, fighting a war together, going into business together and growing old together.

When I asked how old they were, Mr. Crain told me he was 81 and Mr. Kephart only gave me a math equation – he said "I'm 22 + 60." He then went back to his story about the day "the war came to America." "I was in my barracks" he said. "I heard the sound of a plane approaching but that was normal. What wasn't normal was the sound of the motor itself. It was clearly not an engine that I recognized and then it hit! The fuel depot right next door to me went up like you wouldn't believe. We jumped so high that we almost hit our heads on the metal ceiling of he barracks. I ran outside to see the Zero fly out of a fire ball and then bank sharp to the right. At that moment all hell broke lose and the harbor was under full attack by the Japanese air force. If their infantry would have followed up with a land assault, the island would have belonged to the Japs! They didn't thank God."

I just sat there jaw-dropped. The only thing I could muster up to say was something like "No Way!" Mr. Crain then said "I'm tellin' ya, he was at a cathouse!" I didn't know whether to laugh or go over and give Mr. Kephart a hug. However, since I was already under suspicion, that move would have had me out on the sidewalk for sure.

Scene II

After a bit more banter, lots of jokes and some outright lies, I had to order some food. It was now 2pm and my stomach rumbling turned to quakes. Susan brought me a menu and I asked what she recommended. Of course everybody chimed in with their favorites, and everything came with rave reviews! Susan even brought out the head cook Joanie to tell me herself what she thought. After Joanie's statement, "My chili took a blue ribbon in a local contest," what choice did I have? It was March, I was still a little cold from the ride anyway, and chili sounded just perfect. I only ordered a cup because I needed to hit the road to make a big discovery for my 9 o'clock chapter.

No wonder Joanie got a blue ribbon for her chili recipe! It was thick, not too beanie and had a great flavor. Just as I finished scraping the cup to get out every last speck of the most awesome chili this side of heaven, a guy walked in and said to my great dismay "It's starting to come down." Crap! I thought, and bolted to the door. It was raining alright. Crap!

I ran back to the bar and asked for a plastic bag. Joanie shot back to the kitchen and returned with a restaurant size garbage bag which I used to cover my seat on the bike. I looked skyward and it didn't look good so I walked back in wet and disappointed. It was now 3 o'clock.

Trying to make the best of the situation, I ordered another Straub, decided to wait-out the rain and asked about the town. It was time for another story from Mr. Kephart. He told me that Osceola Mills had its hay-day back in the early part of the 20th century. Her glory days are only seen now by beautiful Victorian homes that rise up gracefully above the streets. Like many PA towns, Osceola Mills lived and breathed (literally) that black petrified form of ancient organic matter – Coal.

As the name implies, this town not only mined the coal but mills processed and shipped it out by rail. Most likely the coal traveled only a short distance to Johnstown or Pittsburgh were the giant Bessemer converter used it to produce steel – the structural backbone of the world. I also found out Mr. Crain worked for the railroad that transported it from 1946 to 1986. His trade was as a diesel mechanic for the Juniata Shop. I never did find out what Mr. Kephart did back then, but I'm sure it was something that honed his wit and bantering skills.

He went on to say how back in the day the town had four or five hotels and even more bars (go figure). The railroad kept a flow of goods rolling in and out, and the town thrived as it enjoyed the victories of a war with more than two fronts. The first two were the victories in Europe and then the Pacific Theater. The others were the Great Depression, and the sorrows and life struggles it caused.

After WWII though, both men and women were enjoying a reprieve and the valiant and victorious brotherhood of soldiers could finally have a well deserved drink! VFW Post 5020 was formed by two friends and comrades on February 26, 1946 and the two of them along with only a handful of other charter members still enjoy a cold beer together to this very day! It's like the good ol' days have never ended. But with all things, even the most loved have an ending.

When Mr. Kephart got up to hit the "head," Susan leaned over the bar and told me a heart melting story about him. She told me he lost his beloved wife 15 years prior. Now every morning after he takes care of things around the house, he gets dressed and heads to the cemetery. There he visits with his wife. After that he leaves to pick up a dozen doughnuts and bring them to the gang at the VFW. Then before he retires for the night he returns once again to visit with his beloved. Everyday the same routine, everyday two visits with his wife and everyday for fifteen years.

As I was writing this I did a quick calculation and Mr. Kephart has visited his sweet bride nearly 11,000 times since her death in 1991. Mr. Kephart, I salute you sir. You endured a horrific war, returned home to help provide a haven of brotherhood and camaraderie to other Vets and, you have deeply loved and committed yourself completely to your wife. Way to go sir may your sweet wife rest in peace.

Do you need a moment? I did when Susan shared that with me. And now I was beginning to understand what was happening to me here in this little rural town.

Mr. Kephart returned to the bar and said "follow me." I then got the grand tour of the place. I followed him into the adjacent restaurant area called the Golden Cantina. Simple in style and décor, it provides a basic place to sit with friends and family and enjoy Joanie's homemade offerings. Here is where you and I can come anytime and as often as we like. There is no need to be a member of the club and all ages are welcome. Lunches and dinners are served here just like any other ordinary restaurant.

He then walked me through to a recently renovated back room that was designated as non-smoking (nice). Clearly this part was done with some thought and attention to atmosphere. The walls were painted with the soft warm colors of earth and framed artwork adorned the walls. Tables were set with colorful placemats and tablecloths. A backdoor led you out onto a high deck to enjoy your food or beverage in the afternoon or evening sunshine. "This was an expensive project" he said, but they really wanted to provide it in hopes that more people would come to enjoy the place (hint hint). He was very enthusiastic as he showed me around as if he owned it himself, which in a way he did.

Next he told me about a renovated basement for private parties and as a place for the ladies to get away and have a place of their own (like all VFW's, they have a very active Ladies Auxiliary – this is so old school – I love it!). He was about to take me downstairs to show me, when a young woman appeared and said that a baby shower was going on. Well, Mr. Kephart let something fly that totally cracked me up and I remember thinking he could be a standup comic. And, if he were to partner with his straight man and sidekick Mr. Crain, the two of them would sweep the comedy club circuit.

As we walked back to our barstools, I noticed how it was a bit tough for Mr. Kephart to get around. He was so proud though of his club, home, what they had built and how it serves the community that he never slowed down a bit. I walked over to the door, opened it and peeked out and it was still raining. I just smiled this time and returned to my mug of Straub and new friends. I thumbed my nose to the weather outside, put my map away and settled in for awhile. It's early I thought, and if the rain stops later, I'll take off and journey westward anyway. Little did I realize that what had been happening was to continue and become a blessing that few ever experience.

Oh, by the way, the whole time I had been there at the VFW on this serendipitous day, I kept seeing a sign taped to the walls that read:

DANCE!
March 10th
9pm to ? Music by DJ Retroactive

Hmm, it's the 10th today I thought, but I wouldn't be there that late even though I was totally enthralled with this place and was definitely including it in my book at this point. However, I still wanted to see what was down the road and I just didn't want to stay that long.

By this time I think the old boys as well as the rest of the bar were really starting to wonder about this "youngster" and all his questions and scribbles he was writing in a big sketchbook – I just had to tell them. Everybody was delighted about my project but I'm not sure if it was because I was including them in my book or that I wasn't really from the Liquor Control Board.

Everybody gathered around as I told them about my book and showed them my map and where I had been so far. I explained the concept of the book and how passionate I was about encouraging people to support local restaurants, pubs and cafés. I also said that we need to support them now before they all fall to the corporate giants, and to embrace places like their VFW where community lives, and gives life back to the community.

I could hear the sighs of agreement throughout the bar, and almost felt the pride they were feeling as they realized they were apart of something so rich and important. I looked up at the clock on the wall and it was now 3:30 and the place was beginning to clear out. Even the boys were calling it a day and I said goodbye to them as they walked out into the falling rain. There goes history and the future all in one I thought. History is where they've been and what they've done, the future in the example they set and legacy they continue to live out for us youngsters to emulate.

Apart from my dad and mom, these two men along with some others I know are at the top of a short list of people I admire the most. However, as they were leaving I could have sworn I heard Mr. Crain murmur... "I still say he's with the PLCB!"

Scene III

The place now empty, except for Susan and the kitchen help, I once more checked outside to see the rain still falling. I unzipped my pack and pulled out my laptop and moved to a cozy booth to try and make the most of my time for now. As I was typing away at my insane speed of 8 words a minute, a young woman walked up and asked "are you the writer?" (Well I guess the word was out and I must admit it felt pretty good – especially considering my "writing" so far had been just stories written in an art sketchbook).

She was nice and told me she had been journaling for 17 years and wanted to turn those writings into some sort of book. However, she was struggling because as she transcribed her original words, she felt a renewed pain from a childhood of sorrows. In my humble attempt to give her advice, I simply told her to try and channel that emotion back into the writing and turn it into a story rather than just a recounting of events. She held out her hand and told me her name was Maggie and thanked me. I wished her well in her writing and sat back and pecked away a little more humbled.

By now people were beginning to shuffle in and sit at the booths around me. They were ordering dinner and I laughed to myself that only old people eat at 4 o'clock, but it was now 5:30 and the rain was still falling so I just continued to work (You know, its normal in Boalsburg or State College to sit around a place of business, especially a restaurant, and work on a laptop. But here, it seems to be quite the oddity. I kept feeling liked I was being watched, which in fact I was. Every once in awhile I would look up to see someone smile and then look away. I didn't mind, because I knew they were just curious). At this point I decided to order dinner too and just head for home after the rain stopped.

After I finished my dinner, a middle aged guy with slicked back hair bolted by and plopped down at a booth in front of me that was only occupied by a jacket slung over the back. He was with his mom who had just sat down a second earlier. He said something to her like "I guess you're my date for awhile" I looked over to see her with an annoyed look on her face. I was already feeling uncomfortable about taking up a four person booth, so I said to the guy "Excuse me, if you two need more room you can always sit here, I don't bite." Now granted, the "I don't bite" part wasn't necessary but the look I got from the guy wasn't necessary either. He just stared at me. No smile, but with a look like – Back off junior, this is my turf! I directed my eye's back to my laptop.

About a minute later his mom came over and very politely asked if she could sit down at my table. With the age of chivalry kicking me in the butt, I jumped up and said "Sure, please do." It was awkward at first but then she leaned over the table and said "That man came and sat down just as I was sitting down. He said that was his booth and he was saving it." She went on to say she had only thought the jacket was a random one that someone just put there as lots of people do. I knew now she wasn't his mom. I looked back to the booth and the guy had already returned to the bar and left "his" table empty while he schmoozed with the ladies.

"Dorothy's my name" she said as she held out a small tender hand. Her lovely smile beamed from a face that had seen twice my life's experiences and still looked good. Her white hair was fixed nice and she was dressed for a dance! She told me that she belonged to the Ladies Auxiliary and that her and her husband had been coming there for years. Sadly he passed away many years ago but their long time and mutual friend Norman kept up their friendship and he was to be joining her for a "drink" or two.

She kept clutching her purse with a vise-like grip as she looked backwards to see if Norman had walked in (I think she was a bit suspicious of me but you wouldn't have known by her friendliness). We chatted awhile and pretty soon a very tall and fit looking older gentleman appeared. "Norm!" Dorothy said and he spun around not expecting her to be sitting with a "young" guy sporting a laptop. Dorothy said "this is Norm but I call him Cowboy!" I didn't ask.

Note: What you're about to read next, is not meant to be disrespectful to these two wonderful characters involved. However, it's so funny and I cannot in good conscience leave it out.

Norm looked down at me and said "I'm Cowboy, niceshh to meet ya young feller!" I guess he had decided that dentures were just not needed at the dance, besides he certainly didn't figure I would be there sitting with his "friend" Dorothy. He then proceeded to explain his tardiness to Dorothy and me. Why he involved me in that I'll never know, but I'm sure glad I was there to hear it.

Without breaking stride he said "I would have been here earlier but I got the diarrhee (not "I got diarrhea" mind you – but "the diarrhee") and you know how that is, it just knocks the crap outta ya. I had to wait awhile before I even had the energy to get out of the house." Luckily I had just swallowed a drink of water or it would have been all over Dorothy and Cowboy! He laughed with a wheezing sound that almost threw me into convolutions, which made the two of them laugh even more, which made me laugh…you get the picture.

Well, whether Cowboy intended it to be or not, that was by far the best ice breaker I've ever heard. After that, I closed my laptop and the three of us proceeded to have the best time as we waited for Retroactive to start spinning the tunes.

That's right, I was staying for the dance! I wasn't about to go anywhere now even if the sky was clear. I was deep in an experience that was a true blessing. But, being the great one he is, God had still not revealed his entire hand.

Scene IV

By now the place was packed and DJ Retroactive was laying it down. Young and old alike were out on the dance floor shaking their collective bootys! Even this really old dude, and I mean old! was out on the floor groovin' like he was eighteen. I kinda wanted to dance too but Dorothy, Cowboy and I were having too much fun watching.

Remember the song "I touch myself" by the Divinyls? Well, while Cowboy was up getting "drinks" (straight cranberry juice, mind you) for he and Dorothy, that song came on loud and clear. Not more than a few seconds into it Dorothy says "I like this song, its pretty." I acted like I didn't hear her (if only she knew). Then about halfway into it she said again "Do you know what that's about? It's about touching yourself" (Did I tell you that Dorothy is like 80 and the quintessential grandma type?). Now she's telling me about a song about touching yourself! Again, I acted like I hadn't heard her.

She then said "look, there's a girl doing it now." She pointed to the dance floor where a young woman was taking her hands down across her sides and over her hips to her thighs. "See, she's touching herself" Dorothy said. I think I said something like "oh, yeah, that's nice." Just then Cowboy returned and I quickly changed the subject to his potent choice of beverages.

When the clock turned to 10:15 pm, Norman was ready to go. I was just behind him and getting my jacket when he said "Are you ridin' that motor-cicle out there?" Dorothy beat me to it and said "He rode in here today from down near State College. He's been here staying out of the rain since noon!" Then Norm said "Oh, I backed into a cicle when I parked. I almost ran up over it but only knocked it down. Was that yours?!" He wheezed out a laugh and thought he was pretty funny – which he was.

He then got really serious and said that on his way there he could hardly see because of the fog. "It was all I could do to see the road" he said, "I wouldn't ride that cicle over no mountain tonight." He then said goodbye and the two of us walked him to the door. He was right, it was like pea soup now and getting really cold (late night, wet roads, fog and dropping temp-eratures – not a good combination for riding forty miles home). It looked like I was staying the night, but where?

Dorothy stayed behind too because she wanted to hear the Karaoke part of the evening and asked me to stay on as well. I said sure and then walk up to the bar to order a glass of wine. I wasn't even sure if they had wine, but when I asked the bar lady she responded "red or white." No wine list, no sommelier's recommendation, only "red or white." For some reason I hadn't remembered my 90 cent beer from lunch so as I was contemplating this decision I had a flashback.

I remembered that chichi place in State College where they freaked out when I tried to park my motorcycle on the sidewalk. I had gone there one evening for dinner and ordered a glass of their house Pinot Noir. When I got it I swear there was only 3 to 4 oz. in the glass. It was good but I had to nurse it for all it was worth just to make it last through my entrée. When I got the bill, that weenie "glass" of wine cost me $9.00 and when I asked my server about it he replied "Sir it's not about quantity, it's about quality." I'm not kidding, he actually said that. I may not be a "sommelier," but I'm not an idiot either. Jerk!

So when I ordered a glass of "red" at the VFW, and the lady sat a 12 oz. beer glass on the bar, I got a little nervous. She poured that beer glass just about to the brim with a nice California Cabernet Sauvignon and I sheepishly asked how much I owed. "One dollar and fifty cents" was her reply. It took me a second or two but when I regained my senses

I said "excuse me?", thinking Retroactive's subwoofer had caused me to have a hearing problem. She said again ***"One Dollar and Fifty Cents"*** like I really was deaf. I just smiled, handed her $5 and walked away. I figured that same size glass at the chichi place would have been $27.00 and this wine tasted just about as good. I sat back down with Dorothy, Retroactive pulled out the karaoke stuff and talent night at the Golden Cantina was on!

A lot of people participated and they were all good – some were just having fun, but others were into it. There was one guy there who was singing his heart out and doing a great job. When he finished everyone shouted and clapped, I rubbed my chin and smiled thinking how supportive this town is to their own and how welcoming they have been to me, a stranger. Only I was becoming less of a stranger now and more like "The Thing That Wouldn't Leave."

Dorothy stayed till almost midnight so she could watch and listen to the whole karaoke session (I have friends one third her age that poop out by 9!). After they were done she got up and said she was going to go home. I stood up with here and what do you think she did? She gave me a big hug and a kiss on the cheek, and said how much fun she had with me and how kind I was to have shared my table with her and Norm. I said it had been my pleasure and she headed out into the foggy night all by herself. What a great lady I thought and that Cowboy, what a guy! I hoped I would see both of them again someday soon.

As Dorothy was walking out she pointed to a guy out to me and said "see that man? He's the Commander here." She went on to tell me he was the big cheese at the post. "Cool" I said, and as I looked at him I could tell he was a man of education and high standing. He just had that look about him that was respectable. I went back to watching the dance and a little while later he was standing in front of me and said "I hear you're writing a book" (and you thought information travels fast over the internet). I said yes and he put out his hand to introduce himself and asked if he could join me for a few minutes. I felt honored.

He told me all about Osceola Mills and about the great library they have in town and practically made me promise to come back to visit it. He also said he was a meteorologist and had graduated from good ol' Penn State. He was really interested in my book project and said he would like to be of help in any way. I thanked him as he got up to go back and be with his wife to enjoy the rest of the night. Man! I thought, everybody in this town is so nice and so welcoming!

Scene V

Well, my "date" had gone but the music kept going and the feet kept dancing! I was having a ball, but something was still hanging out in space – where was I going to spend the night? I walked to the bar to see what was going on and there was Susan having a drink with a guy. She had seen me before she quit for the day but I think she was surprised to see that I was still there so late. It was after 1 in the morning now and I had been there for over 12 hours straight.

She introduced me to Rob, her boyfriend who was a local guy. He was really nice and made me feel like a friend from the start. He was a gentle type of guy but his build would indicate that you wouldn't want to mess with his girl or him. He asked me about my book and said to be sure to mention that he owned Philipsburg Plumping and Heating just down the road. Susan punched him on the arm and said "He's not here to write about plumbing or advertise your business!"

While the three of us were laughing, Rob asked "You're not going home tonight are you?" I said I didn't think so and that I might be sleeping there on the pool table if the Post didn't mind. Without hesitation he said "Hey, I've got an old cabin down the road that I'd be happy to let you stay in for the night. I keep the door unlocked and there's a great bed upstairs with lots of blankets. It doesn't have heat so you'll have to build a fire in the woodstove if you get cold."

That was a great offer, but honestly, I wasn't sure. I didn't know this guy or this area. An old cabin... down the road... what did that mean! Was it a rat infested shanty? Did it have holes in the roof? Or worse, was there a guy living next door with six fingers, playing a banjo and wearing Ned Beatty's underwear? Well if there was, hopefully he would be asleep by now with his sister.

So far I was having the time of my life. Everyone from Mr. Kephart and Mr. Crain, to Dorothy and Cowboy, to Susan and now her boyfriend Rob (who owns Philipsburg Plumbing and Heating) were treating me with such genuine kindness and down home friendliness. Something here was special, something here was honest and something here was safe and good. I felt a peace with Rob's offer and I accepted.

He took a coaster from the bar, turned it upside down and drew a tiny map on it to show me the way (I still have it). I memorized it, stuck it in my pocket, got all my gear together and slung my pack over my shoulder. I returned to the bar and must have thanked Rob twenty times. I told him how much I appreciated his hospitality and generosity. He said "It's a little rough but you'll like it. There's plenty of wood, stay warm and have a good sleep."

Retroactive was still pumping out the tunes when I said goodbye to my new friends. It had been fun but a long day and I was beat. As I was leaving, Rob yelled out "Be back here by 10am because I make breakfast every Sunday for anyone who shows up!" I yelled back "Thanks Rob I'll try!"

The Mighty Steed was soaked to the bone but the plastic did its job and the seat was dry. When I turned the key and hit the switch the dead silence of night was split asunder as the powerful V-Twin exploded into action. I tried to quietly putt out of town but even at this hour and in this place a pin drop could be heard. I clicked up to the highest gear and rolled out as stealthy as I could.

Just before I left downtown, I pulled over to check my "coaster map." Under the foggy glow of an overhead streetlight I made sure the route was locked in to my GPS-like brain. I looked back towards the bank clock and the temperature flashed 34 and the time was 1:23am. It was late, cold and I set out into the deep dark of a country night.

Since the roads were still wet, and I didn't want to spray myself, I rode the 5 miles through the countryside at about 10mph. Even at that speed after 2 miles or so, my fingers were beginning to freeze despite my good cold weather gloves. I made the various landmark points Rob told me about and I was within reach now of the last crossroads.

There is was! I made a right and down a tiny road. According to Rob I would see a big white farmhouse at the end of this road and the cabin would be just to the right down a short dirt road. Well thank goodness it was short! Between the all day rain, remaining snow, ice and the pitch dark of a moon-less night, this was the wildest 100 yard ride of my life. The Steed wiggled and wobbled and I fought with everything I had to keep him from sliding right out from under me. With both feet dragging, I tried to make as many points of contact I could in this quagmire of snow, ice and six inch deep mud. Torn between looking directly in front of me to navigate and seeing where I needed to go, I had to try and do both.

At one point I looked up and the headlight had cut a sharp beam ahead and the dark wood of a cabin came into view. Now I could see the little electric candles glowing through the old sash windows and the place was way bigger than I imagined. I parked the bike out front and feared that the kickstand would sink right into the water saturated ground. It didn't as the ground was now starting to freeze.

Fingers near frozen now, I struggled to undo my bungee's holding my back-pack on and then unpack my saddlebags. I fished out my mini flashlight from the pack and got my first look at my accommodations from the outside. Wow, it was huge and the logs used for the walls were massive – way bigger than the ones forming the walls of my cabin.

As I approached the red front door, I was praying that Rob wasn't playing a cruel joke and the door would actually be locked. I flipped up the old style latch and pushed on the door. Crap! It was locked! Kidding! The door gave way to my push and what I saw before me almost made me cry. Lit only by the eight or so candles in the windows and the beam of my flashlight, this place was absolutely beautiful! It was as though I had again gone back in time. But this trip was back to the 1700's and before me was like a scene from Little House on the Prairie.

The space was sparsely furnished with old wooden antiques, braided rugs on the floor, quilts hanging over the backs of chair and a huge woodstove in the corner. Seriously, I thought this place must have been a backdrop for the latest Country Living magazine photo shoot. Since there was electricity, I switched on a few floor lamps and the place came alive.

With flashlight in hand, I climbed the wooden steps to the second floor. There in the corner was a grand wooden framed bed with a headboard that must have been five feet high and beautifully carved. Big heavy quilts covered the mattress and when I pushed my hand into it, it gave way with the only material that would react as it did – down feathers. This was so great because it was freezing! I think it was actually colder inside than outside.

I walked back downstairs to build a fire and before long a roaring blaze was going. The old stove popped and cracked as the frozen metal expanded from the intense heat. I stuffed it full of wood and made a beeline to the featherbed. I knew it would be hours before any heat would warm things up so I kept my polypro layers on just in case.

It was now 2:30 in the morning but it was also the first year of the early Daylight Savings Time change. I forwarded my watch and 3:30 am was staring me in my sleepy face. Even though I was dead tiered I couldn't help but go to my knees in thanks for this amazing day. As I slipped in under the deep sea of quilts, I recounted the day's events and fell asleep with a smile on my face.

I woke up five and a half hours later to beams of sunshine blasting through the second floor windows. I looked out the window next to my bed and the scene outside was magical. A snow covered meadow with horses playing in the warm morning sunlight. It was obviously still cold as puffs of steam shot from the nostrils of the steeds as they bucked and bolted through the snow.

My little belly was reminding me of Rob's offer for a home cooked breakfast at 10 so I geared up and said goodbye to the sweetest impromptu accommodations I could have ever imagined. I took a short video of the place right before I left and every time I watch it, I can't believe Rob's trust and generosity!

I turned the key to my Steed and he burst forth with his own puffs of steam as his engine bucked and shivered from the cold night out. We rode off leaving this beautiful cabin behind. With the sun warming my black leather, I retraced my steps backwards towards Osceola Mills.

The main road back was bathed in sunlight and the surface had dried, but when I turned onto the smaller road for the last 3 miles it was in total shade. The morning chill bit my face and something felt funny. My bike, which is normally steady as a rock seemed to be slightly unstable. Sometimes I ride back roads a little aggressively, but something kept me from throttling up and hitting the curves hard this morning.

I put a foot down to feel the road surface and it was black ice! Both feet went down as I eased off the gas. Underfoot felt as though I was in flip-flops on a skating rink. For the first time in my 36 years of motorcycle riding I was really scared. I knew if the Steed would go down out here in the middle of nowhere, as cold as it was, on a Sunday morning, I'd be walking the rest of the way, if I could even walk at all. *I prayed.*

Scene VI

I walked through the door of the Osceola Mills VFW and felt as though I had been there before. Ha ha. The smell of bacon and fresh brewed coffee caressed me like a morning lover (give me a break I was hungry.) Passing through the kitchen door I saw Rob with an apron on and standing over a skillet of the most beautiful sizzling bacon I had ever seen. Next to it was another skillet full of sliced potatoes also sizzling in a pool of bubbling bacon fat (mmm, bacon fat).

Rob smiled and said "Good Moring! How'd ya sleep?" I told him how much I loved my accommodations and thanked him over and over. As I stood starring at the bacon and potatoes, he whipped up some dippy eggs and golden brown toast. He then called out to Rita the janitorial engineer and said "git yer butt in here for some breakfast! Rita said something I cannot include here, but let me just say it was "colorful." She came in and it was just us. It seemed everyone else was feeling a little "off" from the night before. The three of us enjoyed a hot delicious breakfast and strong coffee, courtesy of Rob (and Philipsburg Plumbing and Heating).

When we were about done Susan came in. Rob asked her to join us and she just made a groaning sound and walked away to take care of the till from the night before. Rita went right back to work and Rob and I cleaned up. When we were finished I collected my things and suited up for the ride home. We all talked awhile and recapped my near 24 epic odyssey.

We laughed and laughed about Mr. Kephart and Mr. Kline, about Cowboy's "diarrhee" story and Dorothy's "song." They told me how sweet all those folks were and how much a part of the town they were and how everyone loved them. I told them about my night at the cabin and how appreciative I was to them as well as practically the whole town for treating me so well and welcoming me into their community.

I threw back my last gulp of coffee and bid my new friends goodbye. I told them I would return again with my book and we all could celebrate. They all waved and said goodbye as I walked out of Post 5020 and The Golden Cantina into the bright light of day. I fired up The Mighty Steed and pointed him east towards home.

As I approached the bank sign it had just flashed 12:15, so I stopped and waited till it changed to exactly 12:16 and I rode out of town. My 24 hours were complete and my eyes began to water as they sometimes do on rides below 50°. However, when I looked back towards the town I thought was dead, the bank sign flashed 58°. Those weren't tears from the cold after all – God's hand was now revealed. It turns out he had been holding a royal flush for me the whole time and I didn't even know it. I sure do now.

The End

10 O'CLOCK
CHAPTER 10

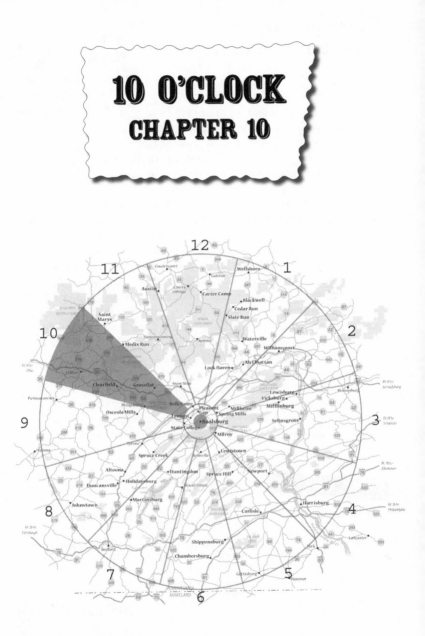

Cooney's Tavern
GRASSFLAT, CLEARFIELD COUNTY

One day while traveling the back roads north of Black Moshannon State Park, I found myself in unfamiliar territory. With hunger pangs calling to my attention and not a restaurant in sight, I was sure I was going to go without lunch that day (or at least have a very late one).

Not too many people were around as I rolled through a small rural town late that morning, but as I came up to the local post office building, I saw a guy walking out with his mail. I rode over to him and asked if he was from around the area. He seemed kinda apprehensive at first but he had a gentle spirit about him and said he was a recent transplant. I said that I was looking for a good place for lunch that was unique and where locals go. His face lit up as he told me about a little tavern up the road towards the town around the town of Grassflat.

He raved about the food there, but it was just one word that he used in his description of it that sealed the deal for me, he said it was "superb." Not too often in such a remote place does one use

JUST A TASTE

Name of establishment:
Cooney's Tavern

Contact info:
4199 Kylertown-Drifting Hwy. Rt 53N
Morrisdale, PS 16858
814-345-5191
cargo@pennswoods.net

Owned by:
The Yontosh Family

Hours:
11am to ?

Price range:
Very inexpensive

Cuisine / specialty:
Sandwhiches, Salads, Wraps and Wings

Offers vegetarian, heart healthy or organic selections:
Yes

Support local farmers:
Yes

Locally owned accommodations:
Whispering Sisters B & B

that adjective when describing the food at a local
haunt, but when he did, I knew I had to check it
out, and my stomach agreed.

I hung a right off the road I was on and laid a course
up Rt. 53 north. Just a few miles up the road, was a
little tavern called Cooney's. Not an amazing façade
by any means, but not seedy either. It was built like
a combination gingerbread house and old time roadhouse saloon. The glowing neon sign for beer let me
know they were open and I walked in. Immediately I
knew I was going to like this place!

It was clean, had great décor, and a really good
vibe! A young woman greeted me from behind the bar
and said I could sit in the bar area or the new
dining room. Right from the start I could tell she
was not your average barkeep. She worked the place
like a seasoned pro and greeted each incoming patron
by their first name. There was no wasted movement as
she mixed drinks, poured beers, took orders for
lunch and shuttled all the above out to her hungry
and thirsty guests. Her enthusiasm for the menu items
was amazing and I had her pegged as a newbie right
away. I took a seat at a high table near the bar and
thought about something to "wet" my appetite.

I noticed Straub as a draught selection on the way
in so when she came over to drop off a menu I ordered
one. Looking over the menu, I was impressed with all
the selection and there were too many to list so I
just made note of the categories. Starters, French
Fries (lots of varieties), Great Juicy Burgers, Sides,
Donny's Wings, Cheesesteaks – Hoagies – Grinders,
Sandwiches, Our Fish "Story," That's A Wrap, Fresh
Made Salads, Extra's and Beverages. They even offer
fixed price "Yummy" desserts (Man, I'm getting hungry).

Opened in 1953 Cooney's was named after the owner
who had retired as a high steel worker. Many steel
workers would simply walk from beam to beam even at
shear heights. Those with less nerve or more sense,

whatever the case, would crawl gripping the beams like a raccoon. Apparently this old guy was a crawler and garnished the nickname Cooney. Now after four changes of ownership it's still going strong and it's totally a family affair!

The young woman I thought was a newbie because of her hard work and enthusiasm turned out to be one of the family. Actually she and her brother were the true owners but mom and dad were the ones who co-signed the loan so they could buy the place. Now Jan works the bar, her brother Donnie runs the kitchen, mom Carol is the sous chef and food buyer and dad "big D" (Don Sr.) runs errands, tends bar, is resident ambassador and a heck of a nice guy.

The Yontosh family is very passionate and committed to what they're doing. Their goal is to keep Cooney's a viable and reliable stop for the working man, local and traveler. In fact Carol told me that their place was for the working man. "It's a workin' man's place" she said. "We serve good food and lots of it. We want our customers to leave here full and happy so they'll want to return." I like that philosophy.

Jan told me as I enjoyed my Straub, that they take real pride in their food. It's fresh, never frozen, the meats are all butchered and bought locally, all produce is local when in season and they even use their own grown and neighbor grown produce. They stress consistency in their offerings and always strive to give their customers their very best.

I asked Jan what the best thing on the menu was and I had to stop her because my head was spinning and my mouth was watering so I ordered the Grilled Chicken Cesar Salad wanting to go for something healthy. When it arrived I was glad I was hungry because it was huge! It was also delicious! The lettuce was fresh Romaine, the chicken grilled to perfection and Carol's homemade dressing was mmm, mmm, good!

As mentioned earlier the décor here is great, very clean and comfortable. Even in the bar area they put out little vases with fresh flowers at each table (nothing against the Yontosh men but, you just can't beat a woman's touch). The whole family takes pride in the place and it shows. These folks are as down to earth as they come and it's all about family, community and damn good eats!

So whether you ride, drive, walk, run or "crawl" to Cooney's just go! You'll be impressed by the down home elegance, fresh and well prepared foods and a family ownership and staff that care about you and want you to always be full, happy and coming back again and again. I know I will!

Enjoy!

Denny's Beer Barrel Pub
CLEARFIELD, CLEARFIELD COUNTY

Here's a place that was featured on The Food Network. Not because of its haute cuisine or its internationally known chef, but for the size of its burgers! They say (who's they?) that size doesn't matter, at Denny's Beer Barrel Pub it sure does. And it's not just the size of the burgers but the menu itself. It's seven pages front and back and there's got to be at least 100 items on it and that's not counting the many varieties. There are 33 styles of wings, 11 salads, 20 different wraps and 30 types of burgers.

But what put Denny's on the gastronomic map so to speak is something that few places offer, let alone could even conceive of - "The Challenge Burgers." There's even a special section in the menu devoted to this and their cult following of big burger enthusiasts come from all over to step up to the plate, and a big plate it is.

Imagine if you will what it would take to consume one of these behemoths. The Pub Challenger: 2 lbs., The Pub Super Challenger: 3lbs., Ye Olde 96er: 6 lbs.,

JUST A TASTE

Name of establishment:
Denny's Beer Barrel Pub Inc.

Contact Info:
1452 Woodland Road
Clearfield,PA 16830
814-765-7190
dennypub@pennswoods.net
www.dennysbeerbarrelpub.com

Owned by:
Dennis & Jean Liegey

Hours:
Mon–Thurs: 10 AM - midnight
Fri & Sat: 9:30 - 1 AM
Sun: 11AM - 11PM

Price range:
$5.00 TO $15.00

Cuisine / Specialty:
All types

Offers vegetarian, heart healthy or organic selections:
Yes

Support local farmers:
Yes

Locally owned accommodations:
Christopher Kratzer House
Bruce & Ginny Baggett
101 E Cherry St
Clearfield, PA 16830
814-765-5024, 888-252-2632

Local attractions:
State Parks
Parker Dam and Elliot State Park
Curwnsville Dam
Grice Gun Shop
Antique Car Museum

Beer Barrel Belly Buster: 15 lbs., Beer Barrel Belly Bruiser: 50 lbs. and The Beer Barrel Main Event Burger: a whopping 100 lbs. Those last two are not included in the Challenge but the first three are. The "Challenge" is, if you can eat all of the burger including fixins' within a time limit, you get 50 to 100% of the price taken off your bill. The Belly Bruiser is more for large groups and the Main Event is for charity fundraisers. I have made moderation a point in this book but once in awhile you just gotta let your hair down and go for it, or at least for the fun of it!

Saturday September 1st 2007, I went to Denny's for their 30 year anniversary celebration. The place was packed and the vibe was pure unadulterated fun! The only seat available was at the bar and even that was tough to get. I hovered around for 15 minutes or so just to get that seat.

Everyone was in a great mood and they were offering a 99 cent burger deal to commemorate the occasion. As much as my brain wanted a 2 pounder my common sense went with the special. As I sat at the bar I heard nothing but fun conversation and laughter. You might be thinking "Well, it was a special occasion." No, this is the norm at Denny's because I've been there many times and it's always the same.

This, my friends, is what sets the "corner pub" apart from the chain or chichi places. Don't get me wrong, it's hard to beat a fine dining experience especially when you're with your sweetie. However, it's harder to beat a place where everyone is having fun and you're right in the middle of it! Here's an example of the fun that was going on around me at the bar.

Gene, a local guy next to me was leaning over the bar telling the owner's son a bit of wisdom. When I asked him to share this ancient Chinese proverb with me he said "Man who loses key to woman's room, gets no new key." Get it, Nookie? I busted up and so did he. My burger special arrived and all was right in the world.

I ordered up a Tröegs Tröegenator and to my surprise it was on the house! A very nice young woman named Christy paid for a "chip" for me. Chip? That's what I said. What she did was paid the barkeep ahead of time for me to have a beer on her sometime in the future, and the future was then. Turns out, Christy is one of Altoona's finest and had the weekend off and was feeling generous. I thanked her for the chip (beer) and asked that if she ever pulled me over in Altoona would she remember she bought me a beer?!

As I was enjoying my burger, Curious Jones, a local band started playing and if I thought the previous couple hours was a blast, things just got better! These guys were great but what I thought was funny was their keyboard player. I was told he was an ER Doc which may account for this - All the band members were really into it except for him. He was good, no doubt, but so serious. I swear he was thinking to himself "Maybe I should have closed that laceration today with sutures rather than staples... humm."

After a song, the band leader made an announcement. He informed all of us that four guys were there that night who had driven 24 hours from Louisiana just to take the burger challenge! A 24 hour road trip to Clearfield PA just to eat a giant burger! Not only that, but I think they ordered just about everything on the menu because when I walked by they were surrounded by a plethora of pub grub. If those boys aren't a sign of fame for Denny's and their crazy menu offering, I don't know what is.

The burgers and pub grub are an attraction at DBBP for sure, but they are also one of a few rural bars that have such an extensive beer selection which is a bigger attraction for me. The last time I checked they had 17 taps, two of which were Tröegs and one for Guinness! And, I think this is really cool, if you go to their web site and click on the Beers tab you will see exactly what they have and each tap handle shown is a hot link to the brewery's site!

So if you click on the Tröegs tap (which I hope you do) you go right to the Tröegs web site. I sure wish they'd put Straub's on - it's just up the road - you can't get much fresher than that!

All in all Denny's is a very fun place with an outstanding menu which includes traditional Irish, Italian and Mexican food. They even offer seafood and steaks as well as some nice heart healthy choices. The beers are good and the newly renovated building is really nice. So whether you go because of the big burgers, big menu, big exposure on the Food Network, big tap selection or big fun, just go! The folks there are super nice and try very hard to provide you with a wonderful pub experience and quality food and drink.

Denny Leigey and family opened their place in 1977. Denny Jr. and daughter Stephanie are the hard working second generation who, I have no doubt, will take Denny's Beer Barrel Pub on to 2037 and hopefully beyond!

Enjoy!

11 O'CLOCK
CHAPTER 11

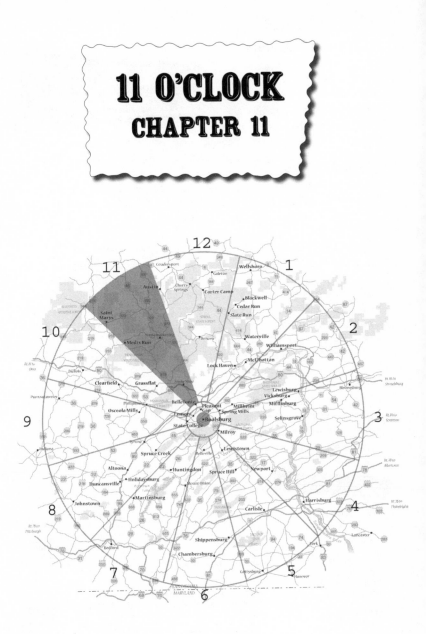

Medix Hotel
MEDIX RUN, ELK COUNTY

When I arrived in Medix
Run after a long chilly
ride, I was pleased to
see the warm light of a
tavern as I crossed the bridge over the Bennett
branch of Sinnemahoning Creek. I pulled up to the
building, parked the bike and walked in. I talk
a lot about how every head turns and looks my way
when I walk into a place like this. Well, today
my "usual greeting" was ignored.

This time nobody paid much attention to me at all
because all attention was on a kid's birthday party.
I gladly proceeded through the party to the only
table that was open - a table for four under a giant
buffalo head at the back of the room. This was
great! It was not only a great cover for my clandestine note taking, but afforded me a good vantage
point to watch how they do birthdays up yonder.

First off the parents were having as good or better
time as the kiddos! They were throwing back the
drinks and yakking and laughing so much I wish I
could have been included. The kids were playing
games and kinda running amuck of the place but no

JUST A TASTE

Name of establishment:
Medix Hotel

Contact Info:
23155 Quehanna Highway
Weedville, PA 15868
814-787-5920
medixinninc@alltel.net
medixhotel.com

Owned by:
Peggy G. DeCarli

Hours:
Wednesday, Thursday, Friday,
5 PM – Close (Bar/Restaurant)
Sat & Sun 1 PM – Close
Hotel – 7 days a week

Price range:
Food: $2.00 – $20.00

Cuisine / Specialty:
American Cuisine
Specialty: Wings, elk burgers &
elk steak

**Offers vegetarian, heart healthy
or organic selections:**
No

Support local farmers:
Yes

Locally owned accommodations:
Medix Hotel

Local attractions:
Elk herd, wildlife, hiking, biking,
snowmobilers, ATV riding,
horseback riding, scenic drives,
RMEF (Rocky Mt. Elk Foundation)
Visitors Facility

one seemed to mind. If this were at a chain or chichi place, I'm afraid both kid and parent would have been "cautioned" at least. Here at the Medix Hotel, it's all good, its kid friendly and fun.

The kids were getting increasingly restless though as the anticipated climax of the celebration was nearing. You could almost cut the tension when the lights were dimmed and the entire pub started in on a very eclectic a cappella rendering of Happy Birthday. From the kitchen came that traditional birthday treat, the cake. I watched with equal anticipation as the server ceremoniously carried it out to where I could finally see it. To my surprise, the traditional birthday cake was no cake at all. When the kids got a look they went crazy (parents too), and the party shifted into high gear!

What came out of the kitchen and set before 12 kids and partying parents was the biggest bucket of chicken wings I've ever seen. Seriously. Apparently the birthday boy or girl wanted wings and by gosh they got 'em. What happened next was a feeding fest that could only be equaled by Penn State students at a tailgate where it was All Wings, All Day, ALL FREE!

I set back with my glass of Straubs under the giant moose head and just enjoyed the moment. It was actually fun and everyone seemed to be having a good ol' down home time of it! I was writing furiously in my sketchbook so as not to miss a single detail when a group of four walked in. They were caught off guard as I was but even more, they were caught without a table because the place was still packed.

A table of two was just leaving and I was sitting at a table for four. I wanted so much to sit under the moose but my conscience was telling me to give it up for this group. After losing the argument with myself, I stood up and asked if they wanted my spot. They were very appreciative and took my offer. I sat down at a little table and continued to write.

The party went on, but by now the natives were full and calm was setting in. The two couples under the buffalo where enjoying a few cold ones and some food when one of the women asked me what I was doing (lost my buffalo cover). As I've said before, it's not unusual to write in a journal or type at a laptop here in "the big city," but up there, deep in the wilds, you'll be sure to get some looks if not even the stink-eye once in awhile.

This gal was super nice though and after we talked a bit, the group asked me to join them. They even bought me a beer and made me feel like an old friend. I could kick myself because I lost the paper they gave me with their names. All I remember is that one of the guys was a DuBois police officer and one of the women knew someone I did. I know that's so vague but what's clear is how they treated me - a stranger - like a friend! Thank you guys!

Before they left they offered to buy me another beer but since I had my limit of two they bought me a coffee. The problem was they ordered me an Irish coffee which contains Bailey's. Not really a problem, but I had to stick around a bit longer. This gave me a chance however to meet and talk with the owner Peggy DeCarli.

She was very nice and told me of some crazy ghost stories from the hotel that made those little hairs on the back of my neck stand up. They were spooky and very convincing even for me. I then told her of my project and she said she was excited and she offered to help in any way she could.

I left Medix Hotel that day a little scared but very happy! I made a few more friends and came away with the assurance that a bucket of wings not only beats the icing on the cake, it beats the cake itself!

Enjoy!

Straub Brewery
SAINT MARYS, ELK COUNTY

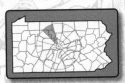

When a family has been
making something for 135
years, you've got to assume
that they must know what
they're doing. If what that
family's been doing is brewing
good beer, and that beer is sugar
free, salt free, preservative free and carries the
motto "Honestly Fresh," there's just no assuming.
And if they have something to my knowledge no other
brewery in the world has, you've got to know about it.

Like my friends at Tröegs, Straub Brewery is not a
restaurant, pub or café. However, that "something"
they have that no other has allows you and me to
taste the goodness of their beer, fresh from the
source, any-time we want whenever they're open and
totally comp-limentary. This something is the famous
Eternal Tap.

Ah, The Eternal Tap...

JUST A TASTE

Name of establishment:
Straub Brewery, Inc.

Contact Info:
303 Sorg Street
St. Marys, PA 15857
www.straubbeer.com
straub@straubbeer.com
814-834-2875

Owned by:
80 Straub family members

Hours:
Mon – Fri: 8:30 AM – 4:30 PM
Sat: 8:30 AM – 1:00 PM

Cuisine / Specialty:
Beer: regular, light, and dark

**Offers vegetarian, heart healthy
or organic selections:**
Yes

Support local farmers:
Yes

Locally owned accommodations:
Old Charm Bed & Breakfast
444 Brusselles Street
St. Marys, PA 15857
814-834-9429

Local attractions:
The Brewery

My first recollection of this bottomless well of fermented goodness flows from the stuff of urban legend
and lore swirling in the imagination of a teenaged
boy. As a youth growing up in central PA, I would
imagine a brewery where they had a beer tap sticking
out through the wall of the building and old dudes
would hang out there all day drinking for free. It
never ran out and was always on - 24 hours a day,
seven days a week.

I would imagine endless summer days, with chairs and
tables placed in groups around the tap. The dudes
would play cards or chess, drinking glass after glass
under the shade of a grand oak and everyone having
a good ol' time and no one ever getting drunk.

Unfortunately, my dreams were shattered one Sunday
afternoon when my riding buddies and I rolled up to
Straub Brewery and not a soul was to be found. No
gathering of gentlemen playing chess under a canopy
of green, no laughter and spinning of tales and most
sadly, no spigot sticking out of the wall with a
continuous flow of beer. My friends watched as I
stood silent in the parking lot.

Shoulders slumped - I walked back to The Mighty
Steed, mounted up and signaled to the boys that we
were moving on. I vowed that one day I would return
- I would come back to Saint Mary's and find this
enigma called The Eternal Tap. Sensing my disappointment, the boys corralled me as we rode beyond
town. When they rolled
back on their collective
throttles, and we shot
like bullets up the
mountain pass, I felt
a little smile
return to my face.

Now years later, after
having scouted out pub
after pub where they

proudly serve Straub, I felt it was time for a reckoning. Yet one more event was needed to set this in motion, and what stranger place than a PSU football game tailgate?

While doing a pre-promo of my book near Beaver Stadium, I happened to look across the sea of humanity to see towering above it all a giant inflatable bottle of Straub. Like something out of a science fiction film, I walked glassy-eyed and mesmerized across parking lots to finally arrive at a motor home which was the base for the giant bottle. There, I saw many folks gathered around drinking Straub beer and they all seemed like they were having a great time. I made my way into the crowd and asked for the "keeper of the bottle."

Peter Straub was a very nice guy who was a forth generation descendent of the family. He didn't work for the brewery but was a shareholder and ambassador. He offered me a beer and gave me a name of someone to contact at the brewery - a guy named Dan. We enjoyed a cold bottle of Straub together and I returned to my promo table much happier and one step closer to The Eternal Tap.

I made a call up to Saint Mary's and arranged a meeting with the guy named Dan. When I arrived on a chilly morning in September aboard The Steed, steam was rising from the brewery, men and trucks were moving about and the distinct smell of fermenting mash was in the air. This time they were open. This time The Eternal Tap, if it even existed, would be mine.

When I walked into the small office I was greeted by Dan - Dan Straub, President, who is one of 80 some Straub family members who still claim their beer making heritage with pride. Dan is one of only a few involved in the brewery, and I had a very privileged opportunity to sit down with him and chat about what makes Straub beer so fresh and so good.

The freshness comes from a belief that their beer should be enjoyed before a ninety day length of time. As stated before, they use no salt, no sugar, but most of all, no preservatives. They do pasteurize the bottled beer but that's it - the keg beer isn't even pasteurized (because it's required to say cold).

Dan had a great freshness analogy. "Unlike wine, which is meant to age, beer should be enjoyed as fresh as possible. I like to compare beer to bread - beer is like liquid bread in a way - it's made with yeast and a lot of similar ingredients. Bread fresh out of the oven is the best. You can maybe keep it for a week but that's it. If you refrigerate it, it lasts a little longer and if you freeze it, you can keep it even longer. But, it's never as good as bread straight from the oven."

Something else that makes the moniker "Honestly Fresh" so appropriate is that they do not ship any of their beer farther than would allow it to be enjoyed within the three month time window. Straub only ships to within a day to day and a half distance of the brewery. It's a local beer and it will most likely stay local. This practice and philosophy if you will, stems from a comment Dan made in his early years to his dad - "We could sell a lot more of this beer if we would just expand." He went on to say "My dad almost kicked me in the rear-end." His dad's response to his young protégé was "Big breweries big headaches, little breweries little headaches."

So, how do you know it's fresh and within the window of enjoyment? Dan informed me that Straub was one of the first breweries to date-stamp so that the public could know when the beer was bottled. He said that actually breweries have been dating bottles for a long time, but it was in the form of a code that only distributors, dealers and the breweries themselves could decipher. He told me that Straub beat both Anheuser-Busch and Pepsi with date-stamping by years.

Freshness, purity and date-stamping aside, one other thing stood out to me as a result of my talk with Dan Straub, and that was pride. I'm not sure about anyone else other than my dad that is so proud of what they do. Dan loves his brewing heritage, he loves his community that supports him and he is proud of that fact that his small family brewery has lasted so long. "It's an amazing success story when you see how few breweries are left that has stood the test of time." At that, Dan asked if I wanted to try his beer. I think he wanted me to taste the pride, to taste how fresh and how good his beer really is. And he invited me to taste it at its source – the enigmatic and haloed Eternal Tap.

Finally! After all these years, all the daydreams and disappointment, I was finally going to partake. Not only that, but I would partake with the president of the company – the great, great grandson of the founder.

I was tingling with excitement and anticipation as we walked out of his office, down a short hallway of memorabilia and into the keg room. There, sticking out of the wall was not one, but two (regular and light) plainly appointed, but absolutely beautiful tap heads (I swear there was a glow around them). Dan walked up, picked up a glass and pulled back on the regular handle. Sweet beer flowed out into the glass, forming a snow white head over a golden body. Dan handed it to me and drew one for himself. He raised his glass and made a humble toast to life and beer.

I then drank in 135 years of hard work, pride, the success of a small mountain brewery and the goodness of a locally made beer. And let me tell you, urban legend, lore and my imagination did not equal this moment or the taste that flowed so smoothly over my tongue. Straub beer is good, damn good and Honestly Fresh!

Enjoy!

12 O'CLOCK
CHAPTER 12

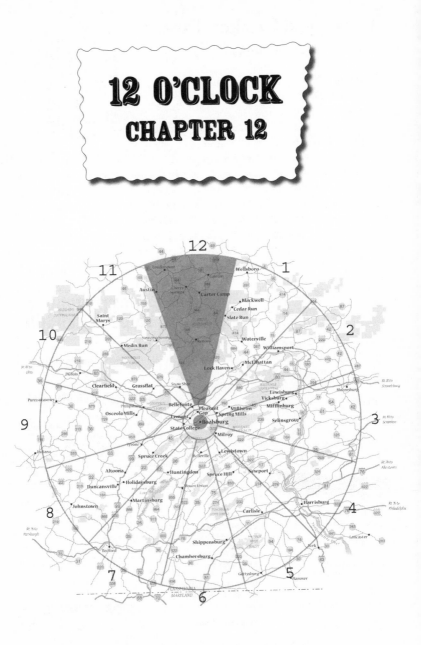

Cock-eyed Cricket Tavern
AUSTIN, POTTER COUNTY

I love when this happens - when serendipity is waiting for me.

I was cruising through the north country along Rt. 607 and off my planned route (my planned route was Rt. 6) to see what was beyond the next curve, when I came upon the remote Potter County town of Austin. Unlike its Texas counterpart, this Austin has no River Walk and no big music scene. But two things this Austin has that the Texas one doesn't, is a very interesting National Historic Landmark dedicated to a town being flooded and a very cool tavern called the Cock-eyed Cricket.

Yes, like Johnstown PA, Austin had a devastating flood. Back on September 30, 1911 the whole town was wiped out and you can sill see the remains of the dam to this day. Check out this newspaper clipping from October 2nd...

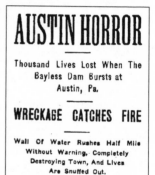

AUSTIN HORROR

Thousand Lives Lost When The Bayless Dam Bursts at Austin, Pa.

WRECKAGE CATCHES FIRE

Wall Of Water Rushes Half Mile Without Warning, Completely Destroying Town, And Lives Are Snuffed Out.

JUST A TASTE

Name of establishment:
Cock-Eyed Cricket,Inc.

Contact Info:
P.O. Box 42 51 Main St.
Austin, PA 16720
cricket1pa@zitomedia.net

Owned by:
Dave and Cindy Crumrine

Hours:
Monday: closed
Tuesday – Saturday: Noon to 2:00
Sunday: 1:00 to 9:00

Price range:
Standard prices for short orders and pizza $2.00 to 20.00

Cuisine / Specialty:
Short Order and Pizza

Offers vegetarian, heart healthy or organic selections:
Yes

Support local farmers:
Yes

Locally owned accommodations:
The First Fork Lodge
1104 Costello Rd.
Austin, PA 16720
814-647-8644

Local attractions:
Damn Site
Museum
Great Fall Scenery
Friendly People

This site is amazing because you can walk right up to where the massive concrete dam failed. Huge towers of concrete remain like giant monoliths standing silent and reminding me of something between Stonehenge, modern art and the day after 9/11 at ground zero. The disaster is a compelling story and can be read about at **GenDisasters.com** (cool links). I doubt the Cock-eyed Cricket was there when it happened but I hope the folks that survived had a place to go for a beer when the clean-up was done.

Now in the 21st century, an old time building along Rt. 607 and is a "lifesaver" so to speak for the back mountain traveler who is in need of nourishment and a cold drink - I was one such traveler.

As mentioned, I was more or less "lost by design" when I rolled into Austin. How convenient was it then, that my hunger and parched throat just happened to coincide at this place along the way. I just about missed the Cricket, but thank goodness for neon! seeing a sign hanging in the window with the words Cock-eyed Cricket Tavern, a little voice inside me said "You gotta check this place out." I love my little voice!

Coming in from the bright sun to the dimly lit pub, I stumbled through the door like the town drunk. Again as always, every head in the place turned towards me. The thing is, there were only two heads and one was the bartender. I saddled up to the bar

SINNEMAHONING PATH
An Indian path ran up the valley of the Sinnemahoning Creek to Canoe Place, now Emporium Junction, and on to the Seneca villages at the Big Bend of the Allegheny. Early settlers in Clinton, McKean, Cameron, and Potter Counties used this path.

with my pack in tow. The barmaid asked if she could help me while the other woman sitting at a stool next to me smiled with a layer of curiosity. No wonder, if carrying a daypack stuffed with a laptop, sketch-book, maps, snacks and a myriad of other accoutrements doesn't scream "outta towner" I don't know what does.

Since my hand was pretty much already revealed I broke protocol and told them what I was doing. I said that I was searching for cool places to eat and drink and caught this place unexpectedly. The woman behind the bar introduced herself as Cindy Crumrine, the owner, and then turned around and walked away. I thought that was kinda quick but maybe she was just busy.

The woman sitting next to me introduced herself as Angela and said "I think I know what Cindy's doing, she'll be back." Just as Angela finished saying that, Cindy came and plopped some things down on the bar in front of me. Both women had smiles on their faces and seemed to be anticipating something. When I looked to see what Cindy put before me, I didn't just smile I started laughing!

There in front of me was a giant orange ink pen and a hermetically sealed condom. Both were "promotio-nal" items and what was written on the condom packa-ge was so funny that I thought I was going to fall off my bar stool! Cindy and Angela got a big kick out of my reaction and after we all settled down, Cindy gave me the "chirp" on the Cricket.

"The food here is the best" she said. "It's just short-order and pizzas but folks say it's the best!" She said they don't do dinners but they offer great pizza and sandwiches. "In this little burg we do about 100 to 125 pizza's a week and about that in sandwiches, that's a lot for a town of only 600 people." Angela jumped in and said it was the por-tions that really bring people in. "And the Cheddar Melt, oh, it's so delicious" she said.

They both raved about the food but also about their little town. "Everybody knows everybody here and everybody's down to earth. We have a lot of history too and even a new museum across the street" said Cindy. She asked me if I had heard about the dam disaster and at that stage I hadn't. She said at the turn of the 20th century Austin had the largest tannery in the world.

Since then, hunting, fishing and camping were the main draws to Austin. But, because of being off the main drag and that "the hunting isn't what it used to be," Cindy said that now people come just to get away from it all. "It's safe, quiet and no cell phone service. People are going 7 days a week at 90 miles per hour, they need a place to come and relax."

As I sat there enjoying my Cheddar Melt (Angela was right by the way), sipping a Straub and listening to Cindy and Angela talk about the town, their neighbors, the history and the great food and fun times at the Cricket, I realized that once again when I go off the main route and a little out of my way, serendipity is usually there waiting for me. She welcomes me in, gives me a big hug and when she happens to be in Austin at the Cock-eyed Cricket, she hands me a condom too. What a gal!

Enjoy!

Carter Camp Café

CARTER CAMP, POTTER COUNTY

A tale of intrigue, heavenly bodies and a hot breakfast.

It was a brilliant sunny day and the heat of August carried over a few days into September. I was supposed to have rendezvoused with my friends Matt and Lisa Meyers in a part of Potter County I was not too familiar with. I mean, I've been up north many times aboard my bike but their cabin was off the beaten path and near a place called the Quehanna Research Facility which is just about as remote as you can get.

I had heard of Quehanna by way of my high school principal who was a former member of The Manhattan Project – that clandestine group of physicists who developed the atomic bomb – Yikes! Well Charlie Boyd was one such scientist on the project and he and I used to hang out during my study halls and talk about everything from music to physics. One day while we were building a mini pyramid to test a theory that organic objects don't decay when placed directly under the structures apex, Charlie told me a fantastic tale of this place called Quehanna up north.

He said that one day he took a road trip to check out a rumor that some secret testing was going on in an area that covered many square miles. He said that somewhere away from the facility he found a dirt road that led him miles into the forest, only to end up at a huge locked gate baring No Trespassing signs. Charlie got out of his old beatup Volvo and started to walk east along a jeep trail that ran parallel to the near 8 ft. high security fence that went out in both directions.

Within minutes after beginning his trek he heard the whining sound of four wheel drives. He looked back towards where he had parked and saw an olive drab vehicle approaching quickly. Spinning around, he saw a second one now coming at him the direction he was going. In an instant, two men dressed in camo emerged from each vehicle and approached Charlie. Fir-earms in hand, they immediately asked him for identification and fortunately (but I have no idea why) Charlie still carried his Pentagon ID which he handed over to one of the men.

Scrutinizing the ID, the man said "Dr. Boyd, what is your purpose here?" Charlie said that he was "just out for a hike." The man responded "This is a restricted area Dr. Boyd and despite your clearances you are not permitted here sir." Charlie then asked what was on the other side of the fence and GI Joe said firmly "Sir I have to ask you to return to your vehicle immediately and leave this area." Charlie being the true scientist tried again to ply the camouflaged Spartan with questions only to be told that if he did not leave the area on his own and at that moment, he would be removed by force. Well Charlie, in his 60s' was no match for four military dudes packing heat. He returned to the Volvo, turned around and headed back, all the while keeping one eye on the mirror to see them standing firm until he was out of sight.

Charlie went on to tell me that while he was working at the Groom Lake Testing Facility in New Mexico (you know it as Area 51), he saw those same vehicles but they were painted a light tan to match the surrounding desert. At the boarders of Groom Lake, highly sensitive motion detectors were planted under the sand as well as listening devices placed in artificial vegetation. The entire boarder surrounding the dry lake bed was under constant surveillance. If anyone came within a few hundred feet of these detectors, an intercepting party would immediately be dispatched from hidden buckers stationed within minutes of each other. He could only image that what was behind that fencing at Quehanna was of such great secrecy and worthy of such intense security that it would warrant the same protocol as Area 51.

For a teenage boy this was better than the Holy Grail. He asked me if I would like to go there with him that coming summer "for a closer look." I had no idea what exactly he meant, but I said "Yes" before he even finished the sentence. Sadly though, Charlie Boyd passed away before we could realize this adventure together and I've never forgotten that tale or him to this day.

Now nearly 30 years later as I was cruising north to meet up with my friends, I saw a sign indicating that I was in the Quehanna area. I had finally made it and all those memories came streaming in. As I slowed down and passed by the facility, an eerie chill raced up my spine as I thought about Charlie's tale and what might be going on there. I thought for a moment and considered trying to find that dirt road that Charlie spoke of, but my friends were waiting and so was Lisa's home cooking. I rolled back on the throttle, felt the G-force of The Steed as he hit the top of his power curve and my eerie chill turned to an adrenaline rush as we laid into the curves ahead.

Oh, one more thing. Quehanna does not appear on any maps to this very day. (Twilight Zone music)

As I finally reached Matt's family lodge, I noticed no cars parked outside, no usual sign of life and no scent of home cooking from Chez Lisa. I parked the bike, walked up on the porch and tried the door – locked – Crap! I peered in the windows and... nothing. I thought if I hang out they would return soon but they didn't. I was starving and my dreams of Lisa's cooking quickly faded away (I found out the next day, I had the wrong weekend).

This folks is where packing a snack comes in handy. My riding buddies constantly tease me about my snack packing, but isn't it funny how eager they are to partake when we're stopped out on a ride and miles from a place to eat. Anyway, I had packed my homemade trail mix and a couple Reese Cups which were now just a molten blend of chocolate and peanut butter goo. I cut a corner off the square wrapper with my trusty Swiss Army Knife and squeezed the molten mess into my mouth. That and my trail mix paired well with my bottled water and I had a pretty nice little snack. But, a real diner was needed soon.

Before I hopped back on the bike I consulted my Gazetteer pages which I had torn out before I left home (whenever I ride, I always take a PA road map and the Delorme Gazetteer pages for as much of the state I might cover). According to it, if I continued northeast on the dirt road, I would intersect a main road that would be the conduit for a return trip home without retracing my earlier route. However, I didn't pay attention to the scale of miles and the road was long, dusty and the pace was slow. If that wasn't bad enough, I got behind some dudes in a pickup and they completely coated me with dust before they realized I was behind them.

I hit the main road just as planned, turned right, opened it up and blew that dust right off me. But my throat was not as lucky and only a cold glass of fermented barley, wheat, water and hops could help. I throttled up, The Steed knew his mission, and the two of us made haste for the nearest town. The problem was, the nearest town wasn't a town at all, and I was to find this phenomenon all too common on this adventure.

It was now getting dark when I cruised into Cherry Springs and my belly was growling and my throat parched. I looked around and the only light was my bike's headlight. No homes, no restaurants, no pubs, no little stores, no nothin'. There were plenty of buildings all around but they were either empty or had no walls at all. This was just a state park, a nice state park, but still just a state park. Ugh!

At this point, I needed to accept that I was not getting dinner, and with no ranger in sight I wasn't getting a campsite either. I remembered that I had heard of this place being something called a "Dark Sky Park", and that amateur astronomers came here to gaze into the night sky. But apart from that I knew of nothing else and after reading the information sign, my only option for a place to bed down was an "Astro Field" across the road.

I cut the engine and pushed all 583 lbs. of The Steed along a dirt road, around a closed gate (oops) and into this huge open area for astronomers. As my eyes adjusted to the darkness I could see eerie dome shapes in the field. When I got close enough I realized they were little observatories. Cool! I pushed the bike up beside one and decided that was were I was spending the night. Eyes now completely adjusted, I looked skyward. What I saw took my breath away.

Note: Folks, if you have never been outside a town, out at sea, in a desert or at a Dark Sky Park and have looked up into the night sky, you are missing one of the most awesome sights in all of nature. You will be humbled if not brought to tears at what's above your head at night.

 This was a moonless night and I was gazing out into a sea of stars like I have never seen before. The Milky Way, an arm of our own home galaxy, hung over me like twinkling blanket of light. Vegas, Time Square, Tokyo and even my beloved Eiffel Tower can never equal the Milky Way on a moonless night in a place like this. I laid out my sleeping bag, crawled in, grabbed my remaining trail mix and had dinner with billions of shining friends. I kept my eyes fixed heavenward

as I said my prayers and gave thanks for this moment. Yeah, I didn't get a real dinner but it didn't matter, I was filled with awe.

The next thing I knew, it was daylight as the sun pierced my sleepy eyes. I rolled up my bag, wiped the dew from the seat of my bike, fired him up and set out to find a hot breakfast. I knew of a place called Carter Camp at the junction of Rt. 44 and 144 about 15 miles away and hoped they had something there. When we hit the paved road outside the Astro Field, I cracked the throttle and broke the silence of a serene September morning and we were on our way.

Like Cherry Springs, Carter Camp looked like a town on the map but when I got to the cross roads where it actually was, again there was no town – only a little store and main house beside it. But that's cool, who needs the town anyway, I just needed breakfast. I walked into the little store which was open, but there was no shopkeeper around. I wandered about calling out the classic "hellooo, hellooo" but no one appeared so I walked over to the house next door. As I did, I saw a sign that read Carter Camp Café and B&B. Four Harleys were parked out front and I caught a whiff of that inter-nationally known smell of breakfast – Bacon! All was right in the world.

When I walked up onto the porch of the main house two older biker dudes were sitting in Adirondack chairs having coffee. I asked if the café was open and the one said "Yep and the food's damn good." I smiled and nodded my head because he had no idea what those two words meant to me. I opened the screen door and…

Do you remember the first time you met your sweetie? How you felt a rush of excitement and at the same time tried to act as though you weren't inter-ested? Well, I was never much for hiding my feelings and this was no exception. I tried to act all coy but I'm sure the look on my face gave me away. It wasn't because I was overwhelmed by the elegance or felt out of place, it was because I was starved and thought I had walked in to my gramma's house.

As I looked around I saw a woodstove, simple tables and chairs, a sofa and cushy chairs around a coffee table, a small counter with a cooking area behind it. There were two other guys dressed like weekend bikers at a table finishing up their breakfast and a young girl busily shuffling about. Behind the counter was a woman and behind the grill was guy who looked as though he was a little kid playing in mud. Do you even remember those days? Remember how the dirtier you got the happier you were? Or have you grown out of those days? Well this guy didn't.

I went to a table that I thought was vacant, but when I looked at the chair I was about to sit on there was a huge fluffy cat already there and sleeping away. Well, I think one of the Ten Commandments is Thou Shall Not Disturb a Sleeping Cat, so I sat down at the other chair. I was greeted by the woman behind the counter and told that Abby (short for abi-normal) was no threat unless I ordered anything involving dairy. The cook said "You can move her, because it'll take a half hour for her to even realize she's been moved anyway." We all laughed as the young girl walked over with a menu.

It was simple and complete. I ordered eggs, bacon (of course), home fries, toast, pancakes, juice and coffee (hey, I hadn't eaten a real meal since lunch the day before). When my food arrived it was hot and oh so delicious! I admit I was famished but it really was delicious.

I found out that the woman and guy were married and the owners. John and Barbara Andrews came to Carter Camp from Easton to escape the jungle and made it there home and life. It was a good idea! I don't know how they survived "the jungle" because here in the mountains of PA, they seemed to be in their element. They were so nice, hospitable and funny. John told me that he and Barbara are Carter Camp – "one of us is the Mayor and the other, the village idiot. We take turns."

What a find! After a wonderful night's sleep under the Milky Way this was just the thing to start a new day of adventures, or perhaps end a book of them. Either way, Carter Camp Café is what happens when folks like you and me who have a dream and passion to open a little eating place do it, and do it well. I can't help but love these little mom and pop places. As I rode out of Carter Camp that morning with a full belly, I looked at the big welcome sign standing at the crossroads. At the top it reads:

Carter Camp : Population 2

I laughed and pointed The Mighty Steed south. What a great day! What a great adventure!

Enjoy!

CONCLUSION

A lot of these stories are accumulated over years of loyal patronage, but some are new finds. Whether a place you go to is an "old friend" or new find, make it a point to go back, and keep going back. In doing so, you will help support them, find your favorites and surely have great stories of your own to tell.

I've eaten a lot of great food on this journey, had incredible adventures and have been kissed by serendipity over and over again. I've taken the back roads and stopped in the littlest towns where the life may not be Big Time and flashy, but life is there and just as beautiful. I've done what parents preach to kids not to do - I've talked to strangers. In doing so I've been directed to some of the best places in the state for food and drink and have met some of the most interesting and wonderful people ever. All in all I believe the best part was, that I saw, touched, tasted, experienced and ultimately understood the real concept and blessings of *going LOCAL!*

Now it's your turn...

INDEX

Boalsburg Introduction   14

Boxers Café   202

Brewers Café   24

Bullfrog Brewery   132

Café on the Park   77

Carter Camp Café   286

Cedar Run Inn & General Store   104

Cinque Terre of Pennsylvania   89

Cock-Eyed Cricket   282

Conclusion   297

Cooney's Tavern   262

Denny's Beer Barrel Pub   266

Duffy's Tavern   17

East-West Crossing   46

Eddie Agostinelli's Market & Deli   21

Elizabeth's American Bistro   144

Elk Creek Café & Ale Works   128

Espresso Yourself   166

Happy Valley Introduction   36

Heavenly Grounds Coffeehouse   195

Herwig's Austrian Bistro   50

Herwig's Austrian Cuisine (Lewisburg)   148

Honey Creek Inn   162

Hotel Manor   99

Johnstown Brewing Co.   231

Kelly's Steak & Seafood   30

La Bella Trattoria   73

Mamie's Café   205

Market Cross Pub & Brewery   187

Marzoni's Brick Oven & Brewing Co.   228

McGrath's Tavern   170
Medix Hotel   272
Meyer Dairy   42
Mt. Nittany Vineyard & Winery   38
Otto's Pub & Brewery   62
Pump Station Café   27
Red Horse Tavern   69
Restless Oaks Restaurant   85
Saint Drogo Coffee Bar   221
Scarlet D Tavern & Mifflinburg Hotel   138
Selin's Grove Brewing Co.   154
Spruce Creek Tavern   212
Spruce Hill Lunch   182
Straub Brewery   275
The Blackwell Hotel   110
The Cheese Shoppe   55
The Cottage Pub & Restaurant   197
The Daily Grind   141
The Knickerbocker Tavern   216
The Lewisburg Hotel   151
The Niche   192
The Old Corner   82
The Water Street Grill   124
The Waterville Hotel Mountain Cookery & Saloon   95
Tröegs Brewing Co.   172
U.S. Hotel Restaurant & Tavern   225
VFW Post 5020 & The Golden Cantina   238
Waterfront Tavern   176
Webster's Bookstore & Café   58
Wellsboro Diner   114

NOTES

NOTES